Praise for Jim Highsmith's
Agile Project Management

"Jim Highsmith is one of a few modern writers who are helping us understand the new nature of work in the knowledge economy. A transition—from industrial-age thinking to management more suited to reliable innovation—is well underway. But few people yet understand the implications of this shift. *Agile Project Management* explains what's going on with startling clarity. Perhaps more importantly, it provides the vital management structure and practical advice that will support ongoing innovation in your company."

—*Rob Austin, Assistant Professor, Harvard Business School*

"There is a lot of attention these days being given to whether organizations are harvesting the maximum benefits from their IT investments. This book is totally in alignment with that theme and should be a must-read for all project participants who are passionate about their projects delivering 'value for money.'

"The one constant in the vast majority of large projects I see in my role as Project Management Practice Manager for Fujitsu Consulting is change. Yet, true to the observations that Jim has made in this book, the majority of these projects have been executed as if change is not the norm and as if the project initiators were 'seers' who could foretell the future with a high degree of certainty. These projects were run on the basis of traditional project management practices, where, simplistically speaking, the project plan was 'king,' and performance was measured and couched in terms of 'delivery to plan.'

"In the past 12–18 months, Fujitu Consulting has seen the potential benefits of adopting more 'Agile' approaches in the way we deliver and manage some of our projects and have encouraged our clients to embrace an 'adaptive' project culture."

—*Karen Chivers, Senior Consulting Director and Project Management*
Practice Manager, Fujitsu Consulting (Asia Pacific)

"There is a common set of values that all the Agile methods share, and, in this book, Jim Highsmith uses those values plus his knowledge of the Agile methods to present a common framework for Agile project management. Jim shows us what an Agile approach to project management is about—the essential insights and experiences—plus he expertly combines tools and techniques with proven project management value, those of his own and those from other methods, into this framework."

—*Jeff De Luca, Project Director, Nebulon Pty. Ltd. (Australia)*

"Jim's book, Agile Project Management, addresses one of the key questions asked when adopting an Agile software development methodology, 'How do you manage the project?' He spends a lot of time on the values and principles needed to be successful in a less bureaucratic development environment. It requires individual discipline and a substantial mindset shift by all parties. He has done an excellent job of documenting the behaviors that will create a winning team, no matter what process is being used. I applaud Jim for creating a book that will help take the Agile movement to a new level."

—*Christine Davis, Visiting Scientist, Carnegie Melon University/*
former Executive Vice President and General Manager, Raytheon

"Welcome to the second generation of Agile methodologies! *Agile Project Management* is an Agile methodology thoughtfully built on the key ideas and experiences of other AMs. The result is a coherent whole, from principles to practices. If your job is to deliver serious software, keep this book at hand on your library, since in the next ten years you will use it too many times!"

—*Michele Marchesi, Professor of Software Engineering,*
University of Cagliari, Italy

"The world of product development is becoming more dynamic and uncertain. Many managers cope by reinforcing processes, adding documentation, or further honing costs. This isn't working. Highsmith brilliantly guides us into an alternative that fits the times."

—*Preston G. Smith, Founder and Principal of New Product Dynamics/*
Coauthor, Developing Products in Half the Time

"Finally a book that reconciles the passion of the Agile software movement with the needed disciplines of project management. Jim's book has provided a service to all of us.

"Agile software development is largely a grass-roots movement that focuses on reliably delivering software products in a dynamic world. To date, much of the Agile literature has focused on the engineering practices that support an Agile philosophy, and thus the coverage of project management has been limited. In this book, Jim Highsmith addresses project management in the Agile environment. He doesn't limit this coverage to simply making a case for a new style of project management. Rather, Jim also offers a practical framework and supporting practices that project managers can use to help software development teams be more productive and reliably deliver products that add business value."

—*Neville R(oy) Singham, CEO, ThoughtWorks, Inc.*

"Software development is a human activity, although we sometimes try to deny that fact by wrapping high ceremony processes and tools around our teams which, if unleashed, can produce some truly amazing things. Jim knows this all too well from his broad experience in working with a variety of projects, and that experience shines through in this very pragmatic and much needed take on Agile project management."

—*Grady Booch, IBM Fellow*

"Agile methods, whether for software development, project management, or general product development, are the ideal approach for building things where change is a risk factor. Everywhere? Highsmith clearly shows how iterative development methods can be successfully applied to project management generally. It is truly groundbreaking when methods refined in the software space can actually inform other disciplines."

—*Charles Stack, Founder and CEO, Flashline, Inc.*

"This is the project management book we've all been waiting for—the book that effectively combines Agile methods and rigorous project management. Not only does this book help us make sense of project management in this current world of iterative, incremental Agile methods, but it's an all-around good read!

"Many IT organizations have made a mess of Agile methods and component development. Organizations that abandoned waterfall methods for undisciplined software hacking have given Agile methods a bad reputation in some businesses. A cure for these woes can be found in Jim Highsmith's new book. You really can combine the benefits of Agile methods with project management disciplines. Jim shows us the way."

—*Lynne Ellyn, Senior VP & CIO, DTE Energy*

"Jim Highsmith's *Agile Project Management* is a refreshing change in the flow of project management books being published today. The book combines project management theory and practice cast in common-sense terms in a manner valuable to both the student and user. The author's recasting and renaming of the phases of a project life cycle adds an approach likely to be emulated in the future literature in this discipline.

"His treatment of the general principles to be followed in the Agile Revolution for new product development provides a model of behavior valuable to the enlightened scholar and practitioner of the project management process."

—*Dr. David I. Cleland, Professor Emeritus, Industrial Engineering Department, School of Engineering, University of Pittsburgh*

"Product development in the 21st century must move from the world of structure and compliance to one of agility and rapid learning. As a result, project management must change from the administration of tasks to the flexible balancing of possibilities against constraints—'managing on the edge of chaos,' as the author puts it. This book explains the process of doing just that and should be the foundation for change—readable, full of logic, and a sound process."

—*Michael Kennedy, President, Product Development Solutions/ Author,* Product Development for the Lean Enterprise

"This is a wonderful and highly practical book. Within hours of putting it down I was putting some of its advice into practice. It's a highly thought-provoking book that argues, for instance, that agility is more attitude than process and more environment than methodology. Because of the complexity of today's software projects, one new product development project can rarely be viewed as a repeat of a prior project. This makes Highsmith's advice to favor a reliable process over a repeatable one particularly timely and important."

—*Mike Cohn, President, Mountain Goat Software/*
Author, User Stories Applied: For Agile Software Development

"Jim's book removes the mystery around Agile project management and its associated techniques while providing a framework of discipline that can be easily applied to any high-tech development and is not limited to software development."

—*Ken Delcol, Director, Product Development, MDS SCIEX*

"Iterations are clearly the best way to create the innovative products that customers want to buy. *Agile Project Management* contains a wealth of ideas and insights about how to make a flexible product development process work."

—*Michael A. Cusumano, Professor, MIT Sloan School of*
Management/Author, The Business of Software

"Practical and provocative advice allows the reader to examine Agile project management in unusual depth, which is what sets this book apart. Jim opens the gateway to the clockworks of Agile project management and does it using a great storyline that takes you all the way through the journey. A must-have for any leadership collection."

—*Wes Balakian, PMP, Chairman and Executive Advisor,*
PMI eBusiness SIG/President TSI

"*Agile Project Management* is the first book to successfully bring together the theory of complex adaptive systems and the practice of project management in a usable, 'how-to' format. The book offers a range of concrete suggestions including, my favorite, how to develop a product vision statement by creating a prototype of the final package. Agile project management also helps the project manager with issues of scalability through offering specific suggestions on tailoring the APM approach and by devoting an entire chapter to managing the large team. If you're looking for practical suggestions on how to deliver the best product you can given the normal constraints of time and budget, then APM is one book you absolutely want to have on your book shelf."

—Donna Fitzgerald, Partner, Knowth Consulting/former Project Director for Project Management Software, Oracle

"In this landmark book, Jim Highsmith catapults project management into the 21st century. The book's a goldmine of the essential principles and practices you need to succeed in delivering innovation and business value on any new product venture."

—Doug DeCarlo, Principal, The Doug DeCarlo Group

"Jim Highsmith has done a great service in this book by providing an easy-to-read and valuable reference for project managers who want to foster greater agility through a common-sense set of practices."

—Kevin Tate, Chief Product Architect, Alias

Agile Project Management

The Agile Software Development Series

Alistair Cockburn and Jim Highsmith, Series Editors

Agile software development centers on four values identified in the Agile Alliance's Manifesto:

- Individuals and interactions over processes and tools

- Working software over comprehensive documentation

- Customer collaboration over contract negotiation

- Responding to change over following a plan

The development of Agile software requires innovation and responsiveness, based on generating and sharing knowledge within a development team and with the customer. Agile software developers draw on the strengths of customers, users, and developers, finding just enough process to balance quality and agility.

The books in The Agile Software Development Series focus on sharing the experiences of such Agile developers. Individual books address individual techniques (such as Use Cases), group techniques (such as collaborative decision making), and proven solutions to different problems from a variety of organizational cultures. The result is a core of Agile best practices that will enrich your experience and improve your work.

Titles in the Series:

Alistair Cockburn, *Surviving Object-Oriented Projects,* ISBN 0-201-49834-0

Alistair Cockburn, *Writing Effective Use Cases,* ISBN 0-201-70225-8

Lars Mathiassen, Jan Pries-Heje, and Ojelanki Ngwenyama, *Improving Software Organizations: From Principles to Practice,* ISBN 0-201-75820-2

Alistair Cockburn, *Agile Software Development,* ISBN 0-201-69969-9

Jim Highsmith, *Agile Software Development Ecosystems,* ISBN 0-201-76043-6

Steve Adolph, Paul Bramble, Alistair Cockburn, and Andy Pols, *Patterns for Effective Use Cases,* ISBN 0-201-72184-8

Anne Mette Jonassen Hass, *Configuration Management Principles and Practice,* ISBN 0-321-11766-2

DSDM Consortium and Jennifer Stapleton, *DSDM, Second Edition: Business Focused Development,* ISBN 0-321-11224-5

Mary Poppendieck and Tom Poppendieck, *Lean Software Development: An Agile Toolkit,* ISBN 0-321-15078-3

Craig Larman, *Agile and Iterative Development: A Manager's Guide,* ISBN 0-131-11155-8

Jim Highsmith, *Agile Project Management: Creating Innovative Products,* ISBN 0-321-21977-5

For more information visit www.awprofessional.com/series/agile

Agile Project Management

Creating Innovative Products

Jim Highsmith

✦✦ Addison-Wesley

Boston • San Francisco • New York • Toronto
Montreal • London • Munich • Paris • Madrid
Capetown • Sydney • Tokyo • Singapore • Mexico City

Many of the designations used by manufacturers and sellers to distinguish their products are claimed as trademarks. Where those designations appear in this book, and Addison-Wesley was aware of a trademark claim, the designations have been printed with initial capital letters or in all capitals.

The author and publisher have taken care in the preparation of this book, but make no expressed or implied warranty of any kind and assume no responsibility for errors or omissions. No liability is assumed for incidental or consequential damages in connection with or arising out of the use of the information or programs contained herein.

The publisher offers discounts on this book when ordered in quantity for special sales. For more information, please contact:

U.S. Corporate and Government Sales
(800) 382-3419
corpsales@pearsontechgroup.com

For sales outside of the United States, please contact:

International Sales
(317 581-3793)
international@pearsontechgroup.com

Visit Addison-Wesley on the Web: www.awprofessional.com

Library of Congress Cataloging-in-Publication Data
Highsmith, James A.
  Agile project management : creating innovative products / Jim Highsmith.
    p. cm.
  Includes bibliographical references and index.
  ISBN 0-321-21977-5
  1. Software engineering. 2. Computer software—Development—Management.   I. Title.

  QA76.75.H54 2004
  005.1'2—dc22   2004041144

Cover photos at far left, far right, and center courtesy of Alias.

ISBN 0-321-21977-5
Text printed on recycled paper
Third printing, January 2006

To Wendie, Debbie, and Nikki

Contents

Preface

When the *Manifesto for Agile Software Development* (www.agilealliance.org) was written in spring 2001, it launched a movement—a movement that has raced through the software development community; generated controversy and debate; connected with related movements in manufacturing, construction, and aerospace; and been extended into project management.

The essence of this movement, whether in new product development, new service offerings, software applications, or project management, rests on two foundational goals: delivering innovative products to customers (particularly in highly uncertain situations) and creating working environments in which people look forward to coming to work each day.

Innovation continues to drive economic success for countries, industries, and individual companies. While the rates of innovation in information technology in the last decade may have declined from prodigious to merely lofty, innovation in areas such as biotechnology and nanotechnology is picking up any slack.

New technologies such as combinatorial chemistry and sophisticated computer simulation are fundamentally altering the innovation process itself. When these technologies are applied to the innovation process, the cost of iteration can be driven down dramatically, enabling exploratory and experimental processes to be both more effective and less costly than serial, specification-based processes. When it takes a pharmaceutical company months to develop a chemical compound and test it, errors are costly and careful laboratory design becomes the norm. When combinatorial chemistry can create hundreds, if not thousands, of compounds in a day and sophisticated instruments can test them in a few more days, careful specification and design can be less effective and more costly than careful experimentation. This same dynamic is at work in the automotive, integrated circuit, software, and pharmaceutical industries. It will soon be at work in your industry.

But taking advantage of these new innovation technologies has proved tricky. When exploration processes replace prescriptive processes, people have to change. For the chemist who now manages the experimental compounding process rather than designing compounds himself, and the manager who has to deal with hundreds of experiments rather than a detailed, prescriptive plan, new project management and organizational processes are required. Even when these technologies and processes are lower cost and higher performance than their predecessors, the transformation often proves difficult.

Experimentation matters, as the title of Harvard Business School professor Stefan Thomke's recent book exclaims (Thomke 2003), but many project managers are still mired in a prescriptive, conformance-to-plan mentality that eschews that very experimentation.

Project management, at least that sector of project management dealing with new product development, needs to be transformed, but to what? It needs to be transformed to move faster, be more flexible, and be aggressively customer responsive. Agile Project Management (APM) and agile product development answer this transformational need. APM brings together a set of principles and practices that enables project managers to catch up with the realities of modern product development.

The target audience for this book is project managers, those hearty individuals who shepherd teams through the exciting but often messy process of turning visions into products—be they cell phones or medical electronic instruments. APM rejects the view of project managers as functionaries who merely comply with the bureaucratic demands of schedules and budgets and replaces it with one in which they are intimately involved in helping teams deliver products. Agile project managers focus on products and people, not paperwork.

There are four broad topics covered in *Agile Project Management*: opportunity, principles, framework, and practices. The opportunity lies in creating innovative products and services—things that are new, different, and creative. These are products that can't be defined completely in the beginning but evolve over time through experimentation, exploration, and adaptation.

The principles of APM revolve around creating both adaptive products that are easy and less expensive to change and adaptive project teams that can respond rapidly to changes in their project's ecosystem. The framework is a set of high-level processes, or phases—Envision, Speculate, Explore, Adapt, and Close—that support exploration and experimentation and deliver results reliably, even in the face of constant change, uncertainty, and ambiguity. Finally, the practices—from developing a product vision box to getting the right people—provide actionable ways in which project teams can deliver results.

At its core, APM focuses on customers, products, and people—delivering value to customers, building adaptable products, and engaging talented people in collaborative work.

Jim Highsmith
January 2004
Flagstaff, Arizona

Introduction

Agile Project Management contains four focal points: the agile revolution and its impact on new product development; the values and principles that drive agile project management; a process framework; and the specific practices that embody the principles and deliver results.

Chapter 1, The Agile Revolution, introduces changes that are occurring in product development—from cell phones to software—and how these changes are driving down the cost of experimentation and fundamentally altering how new product development should be managed. The chapter outlines the business objectives of APM and how organizations need to adapt to operating in a chaotic world.

Chapters 2 and 3 describe the values and principles that actuate APM. The values were first articulated in the *Manifesto for Agile Software Development*, and the principles are derived from the Manifesto, but they are adapted from a development to a project management perspective. Chapter 2 covers the principles related to customers and products, while Chapter 3 covers principles related to leadership and management. Chapter 2 will also introduce you to Herman and Maya, project managers from different companies and different cultures, who will explore through a series of chapter opening dialogues some of the principles and practices of APM.

Chapters 4–8 cover the APM process framework and individual practices. Chapter 4 describes the phases in the process framework—Envision, Speculate, Explore, Adapt, and Close—and Chapters 5–8 identify and describe practices in each of the phases.

Chapter 9, Building Large Adaptive Teams, examines how agile principles are used, together with additional practices, to scale APM to larger projects and larger teams.

Chapter 10, Reliable Innovation, underscores how APM helps address the changing nature of new product development, summarizes the role of the agile project manager, and reflects on the need for conviction and courage in implementing agile project management and development.

Acknowledgments

All books are collaborative efforts, and this one is no exception. Many people have contributed ideas, reviews, comments, and inspiration that have helped me turn my ideas about agile project management into the reality of this book.

Although I take full responsibility for the content of the book, I had a wonderful group of reviewers who contributed significant time and effort to turning my drafts into a final product. I owe a tremendous thanks to Ken Delcol, Kevin Tate, Donna Fitzgerald, Luke Hohmann, Wes Balakian, Mike Cohn, and Lynne Nix.

Many people contributed to the material in this book. They include Jeff DeLuca, Martyn Jones, Anne Mullaney, Michele Marchesi, Norm Kerth, Scott Ambler, Doug DeCarlo, Ed Yourdon, Tim Lister, Glen Alleman, Rob Austin, Ken Orr, Don Olson, Tom DeMarco, Sam Bayer, Alistair Cockburn, Ken Schwaber, Pollyanna Pixton, Ken Collier, Sanjiv Augustine, Ole Jepsen, Greg Reiser, Roy Singham, Robin Gibson, Lynda Belhoucine, Bob Charette, and Ian Savage.

My special thanks goes to Karen Coburn, president of the Cutter Consortium, for her support of agile project management and permission to include material I wrote for various Cutter publications in this book.

And last, but (to use the cliché) not least, my thanks to Paul Petralia at Addison-Wesley for his support and encouragement and to Karen Pasley for her superb editing.

The Agile Software Development Series

Among the people concerned with agility in software development over the last decade, Alistair Cockburn and I found so much in common that we joined efforts to bring to press an Agile Software Development Series based around relatively light, effective, human-powered software development techniques. We base the series on these two core ideas:

1. Different projects need different processes or methodologies.
2. Focusing on skills, communication, and community allows the project to be more effective and more agile than focusing on processes.

The series has the following main tracks:

- *Techniques to improve the effectiveness of a person who is doing a particular sort of job.* This might be a person who is designing a user interface, gathering requirements, planning a project, designing, or testing. Whoever is performing such a job will want to know how the best people in the world do their jobs. *Writing Effective Use Cases* (Cockburn 2001) and *Patterns for Effective Use Cases* (Adolph et al. 2003) are individual technique books.
- *Techniques to improve the effectiveness of a group of people.* These might include techniques for team building, project retrospectives, collaboration, decision making, and the like. *Improving Software Organizations* (Mathiassen et al. 2002) and *Surviving Object-Oriented Projects* (Cockburn 1998) are group technique books.
- *Examples of particular, successful agile methodologies.* Whoever is selecting a base methodology to tailor will want to find one that has already been used successfully in a similar situation. Modifying an existing methodology is easier than creating a new one and is more effective than using one that was designed for a different situation. *Agile and Iterative Development: A Manager's Guide* (Larman 2004), *DSDM: Business Focused Development* (DSDM Consortium 2003), and *Lean Software Development: An Agile Toolkit* (Poppendieck and Poppendieck 2003) are examples of methodology books.

Three books anchor the Agile Software Development Series:

1. This book, *Agile Project Management*, goes beyond software development to describe how a variety of projects can be better managed by applying agile principles and practices. It covers the business justification, principles, and practices of APM.

2. *Agile Software Development Ecosystems* (Highsmith 2002) identifies the unique problems in today's software development environment, describes the common principles behind agile development as expressed in the Agile Manifesto, and reviews each of the six major agile approaches.

3. Alistair's book, *Agile Software Development* (Cockburn 2002), expresses his thoughts about agile development using several themes: software development as a cooperative game, methodologies as conventions about coordination, and families of methodologies.

You can find more about Crystal, Adaptive, and other agile methodologies on these Web sites:

- http://alistair.cockburn.us/
- www.jimhighsmith.com
- www.agilealliance.org
- www.agileprojectmgt.com

Chapter 1

The Agile Revolution

Innovative Product Development

Product development teams are facing a quiet revolution in which both engineers and managers are struggling to adjust. In industry after industry—pharmaceuticals, software, automobiles, integrated circuits—customer demands for continuous innovation and the plunging cost of experimentation are signaling a massive switch from anticipatory to adaptive styles of development. This switch plays havoc with engineers, project managers, and executives who are still operating with anticipatory, prescriptive mindsets and processes geared to a rapidly disappearing era.

Symyx creates and operates highly integrated, complete workflows that enable scientists to explore their ideas to discover and optimize new materials hundreds to thousands times faster than traditional research methods. These workflows consist of robotics that synthesize arrays of materials on a miniaturized scale, creating hundreds to thousands of tiny experiments on one silicon chip. These materials are then rapidly screened in parallel for desired physical and functional properties, including chemical, thermal, optical, electronic, or mechanical attributes. The results are captured in database systems for mining large sets of data to help scientists make well-informed decisions on the next steps of the discovery process.[1]

---

1. Quote courtesy of Symyx Technologies, Inc., www.symyx.com.

Symyx boasts 100 times the speed at 1% of the cost of traditional research. Drug companies used to *design* compounds for specific purposes by having scientists pore over how to make just the right one. Today they generate tens of thousands of compounds and then test them quickly using ultra-sophisticated, ultra-speedy tools such as mass spectrometers. *There are new product development economics at work here.*

In mid-2002, when Alias Systems of Toronto, Canada, started developing Alias Sketchbook Pro, a software package to be announced concurrently with Microsoft's launch of its Tablet PC operating system, the product management and software development team didn't begin with a lengthy product planning effort. The team's marketing and product strategy work evolved over several months, but its product development effort began early, and in parallel, with the strategy process. The team had a vision—an easy-to-use consumer-focused sketching product worthy of a professional graphics artist—and a deadline, the November Microsoft launch date. The product evolved in two-week iterations. For each iteration, a short planning session identified features to be developed. Then, within the "platform" architecture constraints of the operating system and Tablet PC computers, the product evolved—iteration by iteration. In the end, the product was delivered on time, met high quality standards, and has been a success in the marketplace. The product wasn't planned and built, it was envisioned and evolved. Alias didn't start with anticipated architectures, plans, and detailed specifications—it began with a vision followed shortly by the first iteration of the product. The product, the architecture, the plans, and the specifications evolved as the team adapted to the ever-unfolding reality of the market and the technology.

With Alias Sketchbook Pro, the team literally didn't know past the next iteration which features would be included in subsequent development iterations. Team members did have a clear product vision and a business plan. They did have a general idea about what features were needed in the product. They did have active involvement from product marketing. They did have an absolute time deadline and resource expenditure constraints. They did have an overall product platform architecture. Within this vision, business and technical constraints, and overall product release plan, they delivered tested features every two weeks and then adapted their plans to the reality of actual product testing. The team's process was one of evolution and adaptation, not planning and optimization.

In the automobile industry, Toyota employs set-based design in its design process—maintaining multiple design options on components until late in the development process. Similarly, BMW uses simulations to improve car crashworthiness. During one design effort, it ran 91 simulations and two real crashes. The results were a 30% improvement in design and 2.5 days per simulated crash versus 3.8 months (for simple tests)—and the 91 simulations cost less than the two real crashes (Thomke 2003).

All of these approaches to product development point to a very critical issue. When we reduce the cost of experimentation enough, the entire economics of how we do product development changes—it switches from a process based on anticipation (define, design, and build) to one based on adaptation (envision, explore, and adapt). When the cost of generating alternatives plunges and the cost of integrating them into a product is low, then great products aren't built, they evolve—just like biological evolution, only much, much faster than in nature. Biological evolution begins with experimentation (mutation and recombination), exploration (survival of the fittest), and refinement (producing more of the survivors). Increasingly, product development processes are being built using this analogy.

Time is also a driving factor in new product development (NPD). In the short and intense decade of the 1990s, the average new product time to market in the US dropped from 35.5 to 11 months (Wujec and Muscat 2002). "Corporations everywhere are engaged in a new products war," says NPD expert and author Robert Cooper. "From soup to nuts, from can openers to automobiles, companies are at a competitive war with each other—and the advance troops are product development teams. On this new product battlefield, the ability to mount lightning attacks—well-planned but swift strikes—is increasingly key to success…. And mobility or speed enables lightning strikes designed to seize windows of opportunity or to catch an enemy off guard" (Cooper 2001).

But uncertainty, shrinking time schedules, and the need for iterative exploration are not restricted to new product development. New business practice implementations, such as those fostered by customer relationship management (CRM) installations, are often fraught with uncertainty of a different kind. The high rate of failures reported in CRM implementations can, in part, be attributed to anticipatory (plan-driven) project management approaches that failed to "explore" into the uncertainty caused by major business process changes. Companies tried to plan and do when they needed to envision and explore. As authors Preston Smith and Guy Merritt (2002) write, "Innovative product development depends on exploring the uncertain to add product value and maintain competitive advantage."

But innovation and faster development aren't good enough. Companies have to deliver better products geared to what customers want at the time of shipment, which may or may not resemble what the team guessed they wanted when the project was initiated. Ultimate customer value is delivered at the point-of-sale, not the point-of-plan. Companies that have the ability to quickly and inexpensively evolve a product closest to the end of the development lifecycle will have a tremendous competitive advantage.

So why isn't every company doing this? Because for most companies there is a great gap between needing and delivering new products. NPD is a multifaceted and extremely difficult challenge. The Product Development and Management Association (PDMA) estimates newly launched product failure rates of around 59%, which has changed little from the early 1990s. Also, cancelled or failed (in the market) products consumed an estimated 46% of product development resources (Cooper 2001). Yet some companies are consistently more successful than others, and a growing number of these successful companies are practicing agile development and project management methods.

The product development efforts targeted by agile methods include new products[2] and enhancements to products in the domains of:

- Software products (examples are PC applications, operating systems, middleware products, enterprise resource planning)
- Industrial products with embedded software (from electronics equipment to autos)
- Internally developed IT products that fit the speed, mobility, and exploration factor criteria

The key point is that opportunity, uncertainty, and risk reside in the proposed product—not in the approach to project management. Our

---

2. In Robert Cooper's (2001) definition, new product development applies to products that have been on the market five years or less.

approach to project management needs to fit with the characteristics of the product in order to improve our chances of capitalizing on the opportunity by systematically reducing the uncertainty and mitigating the risks over the life of the project.

Companies need results from their high-pressure product development efforts, but they shouldn't come at the expense of quality. John Wooden, the legendary basketball coach of UCLA whose teams won 10 national championships, used a saying with his teams that applies to product development: "Be quick, but don't hurry." In other words, do the right things, but learn how to do them quickly. Strip away the overhead, the non-value-adding activities. Create quality products *and* do it quickly. Agile development focuses on speed, mobility, *and* quality. To accomplish this, individuals and teams must be highly disciplined—but with self-discipline rather than imposed discipline. Anyone who practices ad hoc development under the guise of agile methods is an imposter.

There is no reason to think the changes in the next ten years will be of less magnitude than those of the previous ten, although the emphasis will likely change from pure information technology to the integration of information and biotechnology. The underlying codes of information technology are zeros and ones. The underlying codes of biotechnology are A, T, C, and G (the components of DNA). When biological codes can be reduced to computer codes, as in the Human Genome Project, and then be manipulated by computer programs (as is happening), the potential impact on product development of many types is staggering. "New materials, programmed molecular factories, and self-organizing fabrication processes could change the cost and performance characteristics of everything from drugs to dragsters, paint to plastics, china to chairs" (Meyer and Davis 2003). Scientific and technological advances in the coming decade and beyond will continue to irrevocably alter product development processes, and those changes, in turn, will cause us to rethink the management of those processes.

Linear thinking, prescriptive processes, and standardized, unvarying practices are no match for today's volatile product development environment. So as product development processes swing from anticipatory to adaptive, project management must change also. It must be geared to mobility, experimentation, and speed. But first of all, it must be geared to business objectives.

Reliable Innovation[3]

There are five key business objectives for a good exploration process such as Agile Project Management (APM):

1. Continuous innovation—to deliver on current customer requirements
2. Product adaptability—to deliver on future customer requirements
3. Reduced delivery schedules—to meet market windows and improve return on investment (ROI)
4. People and process adaptability—to respond rapidly to product and business change
5. Reliable results—to support business growth and profitability

Continuous Innovation

As I discussed in the opening section, developing new products and new services in today's complex business and technology world requires a mind-set that fosters innovation. Striving to deliver customer value, to create a product that meets today's customer requirements, drives this continuous innovation process. Innovative ideas aren't generated in structured, authoritarian environments but in an adaptive culture based on the principles of self-organization and self-discipline.

Product Adaptability

No matter how prescient a person, a team, or a company, the future will always surprise us. For some products, changes in the market, technology, or specific requirements happen weekly. For other products, the timeframe for incorporating changes varies from months to years. But for every product, the timeframes are shrinking, and the only way to survive is to strive for

---

3. Colleague and Harvard Business School professor Rob Austin introduced me to the concept and term "reliable innovation."

product adaptability—a critical design criterion for a development process. In fact, in an agile project, technical excellence is measured by both delivering customer value today *and* creating an adaptable product for tomorrow. Agile technical practices focus on lowering the cost of change (adaptation) as an integral part of the development process. In an agile project, developers strive for technical excellence, and project managers champion it.

Reduced Delivery Schedules

As the statistics for rapidly shrinking product development times indicate, reducing delivery schedules to meet market windows continues to be a high-priority business goal for managers and executives. The iterative, feature-based nature of APM contributes to reducing delivery schedules in three key ways: focus, streamlining, and skill development.

First, the constant attention to product features and their prioritization in short, iterative timeboxes forces teams (customers and developers) to carefully consider both the number of features to include in the product and the depth of those features. Constant attention reduces the overall workload by eliminating marginally beneficial features. Second, APM—like its lean development counterparts—streamlines the development process, concentrating on value-adding activities and eliminating overhead and compliance activities. Third, APM focuses on selecting and developing individuals with the right skills for the project.

People and Process Adaptability

Just as products need to adapt to marketplace reality over time, so do people and processes. In fact, if we want adaptable products, we must first build adaptable teams—teams whose members are comfortable with change, who view change not as an obstacle to resist but as part and parcel of thriving in a dynamic business environment. The APM guiding principles and framework encourage learning and adapting as an integral part of delivering value to customers.

Reliable Results

Production processes are designed to be repeatable, to deliver the same result time after time after time. Good production processes deliver the anticipated result (a known result), for a standard cost, within a given time—they are predictable, if you will. Exploration processes are different. Because of the uncertainty surrounding requirements and new technology, exploration projects can't deliver a known, completely pre-specified result, but they can deliver a valuable result—one that meets customer and business requirements as they become known. Good exploration processes can deliver innovation reliably—time after time. But while performance measures for production processes can be based on actual scope, cost, and schedule versus their predicted values, exploration processes need to be measured somewhat differently.

Rather than scope, cost, and schedule, exploration projects should be measured on vision, cost, and schedule. Did the project deliver a valuable product (implemented vision) to the customer? Did the project deliver the product within the cost and time constraints placed on the project? These subtle but extremely important differences between repeatability and reliability will be revisited in Chapter 3. The bottom line: APM reliably delivers innovative results to customers within cost and schedule constraints.

Core Agile Values

Agility is more attitude than process, more environment than methodology. In 1994 authors Jim Collins and Jerry Porras (1994) wrote *Built to Last,* a book based on their research that set out to answer the question, "What makes the truly exceptional companies different from the other companies?" One of their core findings was that exceptional companies created a foundation that didn't change and strategies and practices that did: "Visionary companies distinguish their timeless core values and enduring purpose, which should never change, from their operating practices and business strategies (which should be changing constantly in response to a changing world)."

I think one reason that agile software development has grown in recognition and use during the last few years is that the founders of the movement stated explicitly what we believed in the *Manifesto for Agile Software Development.* We stated our core values and enduring purpose. Why teams exist, what we intend to build, whom we build it for, and how we work together also form the core principles of APM. If we want to build great products, we need great people. If we want to attract and keep great people, we need a great organization. The core value of an egalitarian meritocracy runs deep in the agile movement. It is surely not the only core value that can produce products, but it is a core value that defines how the majority of agilists view themselves.

We live in an age in which the volume of available information stupefies us. On any relatively interesting subject we can find thousands of Web pages, tens—if not hundreds—of books, and article after article. How do we filter all this information? How do we process all this information? Core ideology and principles provide one mechanism for processing and filtering information. They steer us in the direction of what is more, or less, important. They help us make product decisions and evaluate development practices.

Principles, or "rules" in complexity theory terminology, affect how tools and practices are implemented. Practices are how principles are acted out. Grand principles that generate no action are mere vapor. Conversely, specific practices in the absence of guiding principles are often inappropriately used. While the use of practices may vary from project team to project team, the principles are constant. Principles are the simple rules, the generative rules, of complex human adaptive systems.

The *Manifesto for Agile Software Development*[4] established a set of four core values, which, with a single word change, form the core values of APM:

We are uncovering better ways of developing [products] by doing it and helping others do it. Through this work we have come to value:

---

4. ©2001 by Kent Beck, Mike Beedle, Arie van Bennekum, Alistair Cockburn, Ward Cunningham, Martin Fowler, James Grenning, Jim Highsmith, Andrew Hunt, Ron Jeffries, Jon Kern, Brian Marick, Robert C. Martin, Steve Mellor, Ken Schwaber, Jeff Sutherland, and Dave Thomas.

Individuals and interactions over processes and tools
Working [products]⁵ over comprehensive documentation
Customer collaboration over contract negotiation
Responding to change over following a plan.

That is, while there is value in the items on the right, we value the items on the left more.⁶

"This should not be construed as indicating that tools, process, documents, contracts, or plans are *unimportant*. There is a tremendous difference between one thing being more or less important than another and being *un*important" (Highsmith 2000). Tools are critical to speeding development and reducing costs. Contracts are vital to initiating developer-customer relationships. Documentation aids communication. However, the items on the left are the most critical. Without skilled individuals, working products, close interactions with customers, and responsiveness to change, product delivery will be nearly impossible.

While these core value statements were originally written for agile software development, they apply directly—with a bit of interpretation, and some reordering—to APM.

Responding to Change

Responding to change over following a plan. This statement reflects the agile viewpoint characterized further by:

- Envision-Explore versus Plan-Do
- Exploration versus production
- Adapting versus anticipating

Every project has knowns and unknowns, certainties and uncertainties, and therefore every project has to balance planning and changing. However, balancing is required because projects also run the gamut from production-

---

5. The Manifesto's wording is "software." I use the word "products" here as a more general term.
6. For an in-depth explanation of the Agile Manifesto, see (Fowler and Highsmith 2001).

style ones in which uncertainty is low, to exploration-style ones in which uncertainty is high. Exploration-style projects are characterized by a process that emphasizes envisioning and then exploring into that vision rather than detailed planning and relatively strict execution of tasks. It's not that one is right and the other wrong, but that each style is more or less applicable to a particular project type.

Another factor that impacts project management style is the cost of an iteration; that is, the cost of experimenting. Even if the need for innovation is great, high iteration costs may dictate a process with greater anticipatory work. Low-cost iterations, like those mentioned earlier, enable an adaptive style of development in which plans, architectures, and designs evolve concurrently with the actual product.

Companies trying to thrive in our turbulent economy must alter both their processes and their perspectives with respect to change. We are no longer talking about 15% to 20% scope creep on projects; we are talking about everything changing—scope, features, technology, architecture (but not vision)—within the span of a few months. I'm continually surprised by the magnitude of change products and projects undergo. The common project management aim of "conforming to plan" fails dramatically in these situations.

In *Artful Making*, Harvard Business School professor and colleague Rob Austin and his coauthor Lee Devin (2003) discuss a $125 million IT project disaster in which the company refused to improvise and change from the detailed plan set down prior to the project's start. " 'Plan the work and work the plan' was their implicit mantra," they write. "And it led them directly to a costly and destructive course of action…. We'd all like to believe that this kind of problem is rare in business. It's not."

Working Products

Working products over comprehensive documentation. Innovation drives companies. The core ideology at 3M has always emphasized innovation. Motorola recently launched a new cell phone innovation initiative. In early 2003, General Electric changed its motto to "Explore Imagination at Work." Jeffrey Immelt, chairman and CEO of GE, has placed a high priority on innovation and new business. "The companies that know how to develop things are ultimately going to create the most shareholder value. It's as simple as that," says Immelt (Budeir 2003). Many companies have innovation initiatives; fewer are willing to create processes and practices that directly support those initiatives. Switching from delivering documentation artifacts—characteristic of a serial development style—to delivering iterative versions of the real product is one of those mind and practice shifts that supports innovation.

Large, front-loaded projects that spend months, and even years, gathering requirements, proposing architectures, and designing products are prone to massive failures. Why? Because teams proceed in a linear fashion with little reliable feedback—they have good ideas, but they don't test them in the cauldron of reality. Documents don't work. Products do.

Agile development and project management stress delivery of versions of the actual product, or in the case of high-cost materials, effective simulations or models of the actual product. Finishing a requirements document verifies that a team has successfully gathered a set of requirements. Completing and demonstrating a set of working product features verifies that the development team can actually deliver something tangible to the customer. Working features provide dependable feedback into the development process in ways that documentation cannot.

Again, working products don't preclude the need for documentation. Documents support communication and collaboration, enhance knowledge transfer, preserve historical information, assist ongoing product enhancement, and fulfill regulatory and legal requirements. They are not unimportant, just less important than working versions of the product.

However, there is a fundamental flaw in many people's understanding of documentation—*documentation is not a substitute for interaction.* When a customer and a developer interact to jointly develop specifications and produce some form of permanent record (documents, notes, sketches, feature cards, drawings), the documentation is a by-product of the interaction. When the customer sits down with a product manager and they write a requirements document that gets *sent* to a development group, then the document has become a substitute for interaction. In the first scenario, the documentation may be valuable to the development team. In the second, it has become a barricade to progress. Little knowledge is either gained or transferred. Furthermore, as interaction decreases, the volume of documentation often increases in a fruitless attempt to compensate.

Customer Collaboration

Customer collaboration over contract negotiation. Customers and product managers drive agile development. The customer team (depending on the product type, the participants may be actual customers, product managers, product champions, or other customer proxies) and the development team form a partnership in which each has specific roles, responsibilities, and accountabilities. In highly volatile, ambiguous, and uncertain new product development efforts, the customer-developer relationship must be collaborative, not marked by adversarial contract disputes.

The goal of a project team is to deliver value to customers. While there are, in big organizations, a variety of stakeholders, the customer should reign supreme. Furthermore, the definition of customer can be reduced to a simple statement—the *customer* is the individual or group who uses the created product to generate business value or, in the case of retail products, the person who uses the product. Customers define value. Other stakeholders define constraints. When we confuse customers and stakeholders, our projects become muddled.

Customers define requirements (features) that provide value and the business objectives (schedule, cost) that assist in quantifying that value. Today, value arises from implementing features that meet this set of requirements and constraints as they evolve over the life of a project. Once a product has been delivered initially, tomorrow's benefits are a function of how quickly and cost effectively the product can be adapted to requirements and constraints that arise in the future. The formula for success is simple: deliver today, adapt tomorrow.

Individuals and Interactions

Individuals and interactions over processes and tools. Ultimately, unique, talented, and skilled individuals—individually and collectively—build products and services. Processes provide guidance and support, and tools improve efficiency, but without the right people who have the right technical and behavioral skills, all the processes and tools in the world won't produce results. Processes (in moderation) and tools are useful, but when critical decisions must be made, we rely on the knowledge and capabilities of individuals and the team.

Companies often issue flowery statements about how important their people are and then tie them down with unyielding procedures and forms. In the 1990s business went through a period of infatuation with process—much of it under the banner of business process reengineering (BPR). Process literally became more important than people. BPR proponents thought that structured processes would somehow make up for mediocre individual capabilities, but no process can overcome the lack of good engineers, product managers, customers, suppliers, and executives. Good processes should support the team rather than dictate its actions. Processes are adapted to the team rather than the other way around.

APM supports creators, not stewards. Colleague Rob Austin defines the differences between these two types of individuals:

> *The problem the creators have is that they want to go for the big prize, to realize their visions in pure form; anything short of that they see as less than successful. The stewards, on the other hand, can't get excited about an innovation until ... they understand how the economic value (profit) will be created (Austin 2003).*

Stewards are critical to business success—they manage the numbers and invest prudently. Businesses without stewards often fail in their fiduciary responsibilities to employees, customers, and investors. However, without creators, the stewards have nothing to steward. Without innovation—new product development, new processes and practices, new ways of creating business value—the stewards are left maintaining an empty husk. Without the stable foundation provided by stewards, creators may spin out of control.

The agile movement supports individuals and their interactions through dedication to the concepts of self-organization, self-discipline, egalitarianism, respect for individuals, and competency. "Agile" is a social movement driven by both the desire to create a particular work environment and the belief that this "adaptive" environment is critical to the goal of delivering innovative products to customers.

Agile Project Management

The central question for project managers, project team members, and executives is, "How does project management add value to a project?" Unfortunately, many development engineers consider project management to be a roadblock—a hindrance, not a help. Project managers are viewed as administrators who put together detailed task schedules, create colorful resource profiles, bug team members about micro-task completions, and write reams of status reports for upper management, not as direct contributors to delivering value to customers. Teams often view project management as overhead. As Michael Kennedy (2003), author of *Product Development for the Lean Enterprise* (about Toyota) says, "Our product development philosophy is based more upon administration excellence than technical excellence, and it's getting worse."

"Buy pizza and stay out of the way" expresses too many product engineering teams' view of "good" project management. Rather than overhead, project management should be seen as offering inspirational leadership focused on delivering customer value. We have missed this point because many project management practices and project managers are focused on compliance activities, not delivering value. They are project administrators, not project managers. Customers pay for value; everything else is overhead—necessary overhead in some respects, but overhead nonetheless. Team activities or deliverables that help comply with government regulations are necessary, but they rarely add customer value. Documentation that conforms to legal requirements may be necessary, but it may not add value—at least not directly. Status reports assist managers in meeting their fiduciary responsibilities, but they don't add value. Endless milestone approvals may delude management into thinking they are in control, but they don't add value.

But how do we measure customer value and project management's contribution to that value? Motorola's ill-fated, multibillion-dollar Iridium project was a spectacular failure in the market. Meanwhile, the movie *Titanic*, which was severely over budget and time—and viewed by early pundits as a $200 million flop awaiting release—was the first movie to generate over $1 billion in worldwide revenue. By common compliance-based project management practices of budget, scope, and schedule performance,

Titanic was a failure. Within some circles, Iridium was considered a success because it fulfilled the original specifications.

All products face similar demands—customer needs, profit, development speed, constant change, high quality—that require high levels of competency in multiple domains of expertise. These often contradictory constraints and demands on product development—speed *and* quality, great functionality *and* low cost, uncertainty *and* predictability, mobility *and* stability—have created the need for project managers and project management practices that focus on delivering value.

APM is a set of values, principles, and practices that assist project teams in coming to grips with this challenging environment. The core values of APM address both the need to build agile, adaptable products and the need to create agile, adaptable development teams.

Agility Defined

There is no *Agility for Dummies.* Agility isn't a silver bullet. You don't achieve it in five easy steps. So what is it? For myself, I've characterized agility in two statements:

> *Agility is the ability to both create and respond to change in order to profit in a turbulent business environment.*
>
> *Agility is the ability to balance flexibility and stability (Highsmith 2002).*

In an uncertain and turbulent world, success belongs to companies that have the capacity to create change, and maybe even chaos, for their competitors. Creating change disrupts competitors (and the entire market ecosystem); responding to change guards against competitive thrusts. Creating change requires innovation: developing new products, creating new sales channels, reducing product development time, customizing products for increasingly smaller market segments. In addition, your company must be able to respond quickly to both anticipated and unanticipated changes created by your competitors and customers.

An example of a product development effort in which all the aspects of agility come into play is that of small, portable DNA analyzers. These instruments, which are still five or more years away from commercial deployment, could be used for analyzing suspected bioterror agents (e.g., anthrax), making a quick medical diagnosis, or performing environmental bacterial analysis. These instruments must be accurate, easy to use, and reliable under wide-ranging conditions, and their development depends on breakthroughs in nanotechnology, genome research, and microfluidics. A half-dozen companies are racing to build versions of a DNA analyzer, often with grants from agencies such as the US National Institutes of Health (Gardner 2003). Developing these leading-edge products requires blending flexibility and structure, exploring into various new technologies, and creating change for competitors by reducing delivery time. These are not projects that can be managed by traditional, prescriptive project management methodologies.

Some people mistakenly assume that agility connotes a lack of structure, but the absence of structure, or stability, generates chaos. Conversely, too much structure generates rigidity. Complexity theory tells us that innovation—creating something new in ways that we can't fully anticipate, an emergent result—occurs most readily at the balance point between chaos and order, between flexibility and stability. Scientists believe that emergence, the creation of novelty from agent interaction, happens most readily at this "edge of chaos." The idea of enough structure, but not too much, drives agile managers to continually ask the question, "How little structure can I get away with?" Too much structure stifles creativity. Too little structure breeds inefficiency.

This need to balance at the edge of chaos to foster innovation is one reason process-centric methodologies often fail. They push organizations into over-optimization at the expense of innovation. Agile organizations don't get lost in some gray middle ground; they understand which factors require stabilization and which ones encourage exploration. For example, in a high-change product development environment, rigorous configuration management stabilizes and facilitates flexibility just as a focus on technical excellence stabilizes the development effort. The concepts and practices described in this book are designed to help project teams understand this balancing between flexibility and stability. They help answer the question of what to keep stable and what to let vary.

Agility means being responsive or flexible within a framework or context. As I've said elsewhere, "The problem with many traditional software development and project management approaches is that they have too narrowly defined the context; that is, they've planned projects to a great level of task detail, leaving very little room for agility to actually happen" (Highsmith 2002).

Balancing at the edge of chaos between flexibility and stability requires people who are good improvisers—who have the ability to deal effectively with the ambiguity, and the paradox, of pursuing two seemingly dissimilar goals at once. Organizations that support these improvisers have three key traits:

- An adaptive culture that embraces change
- Minimal rules that encourage self-organization, combined with the self-discipline to closely adhere to those rules
- Intense collaboration and interaction among the project community

Each of these traits will be further described in the chapters on the guiding principles of APM.

The APM Framework

Project management processes and performance measures are different for exploration- and experimentation-based approaches than they are for production- and specification-based ones. Production-oriented project management processes and practices emphasize complete early planning and requirements specification with minimal ongoing change. Exploration-based processes emphasize nominal early planning, good enough requirements, and experimental design with significant ongoing learning and change. Each approach has its place, but the lifecycle framework for the latter has a very different flavor from the former. The APM framework consists of five phases, each with supporting practices. They are Envision, Speculate, Explore, Adapt, and Close.

These phases resemble a scientific investigative process more than a production management process. The Envision phase results in a well-articulated business or product vision—enough to keep the next phases bounded. In the Speculate phase, the team hypothesizes about the specifications of the product, knowing that as the project continues both technology and customer specifications will evolve as new knowledge is gained. The Explore phase then becomes a parallel and iterative operation in which the preliminary specifications and design are implemented. Components labeled "uncertain" are subject to more experimentation than others whose specifications or design are more certain. In the Adapt phase, the results of these experiments are subjected to technical, customer, and business case review, and adaptive actions are incorporated into the next iteration.

One of the most common questions about APM is, "What about the planning, architecture, and requirements phases?" The simple answer is that these things are activities and not phases. An agile approach can easily include as much time for these activities as in a conventional serial phase approach, *but* the activities are spread across multiple iterations.

A second area of concern is the risk of rework in agile development if the initial architecture work (the discussion in this section could refer to architecture, plans, or requirements) misses a critical item. But there is an equal if not greater risk in serial development that often goes unnamed—that of getting the up-front architecture wrong. In a serial process, the validation of the early architecture decisions comes late in the project lifecycle, when the actual building occurs. By that time, a tremendous amount of time and money has been spent. Changing the architecture then becomes a major, and costly, decision—if it is possible at all.

Within this general APM framework, the successful completion of each phase depends upon a series of key practices that actually guide the work effort. Some of these practices are simple and straightforward, like the product vision box and project data sheet, which I'll discuss in Chapter 5. Others such as customer focus groups and iterative planning are based directly on the core values of agile organizations, while such practices as workload self-management and participatory decision making focus on building an agile, adaptive culture. Values and guiding principles describe the *why* of APM, and practices describe the *how*.

Thriving in a Chaordic World

Former Visa International CEO Dee Hock (1999) coined the word "chaordic" to describe both the world around us and his approach to managing a far-flung enterprise—balanced on the precipice between chaos and order. Our sense of the world dictates management style. If the world is perceived as static, then production-style management practices will dominate. If the world is perceived as dynamic, however, then exploration-style management practices will come to the fore. Of course, it's not that simple—there is always a blend of static and dynamic, which means that managers must always perform a delicate balancing act.

In the last decade, a vanguard of scientists and managers have articulated a profound shift in their view about how organisms and organizations evolve, respond to change, and manage their growth. Scientists' findings about the tipping points of chemical reactions and the "swarm" behavior of ants have given organizational researchers insights into what makes successful companies and successful managers. Practitioners have studied how innovative groups work most effectively.

As quantum physics changed our notions of predictability and Darwin changed our perspective on evolution, complex adaptive systems (CAS) theory has reshaped scientific and management thinking. In an era of rapid change, we need better ways of making sense of the world around us. Just as biologists now study ecosystems as well as species, executives and managers need to understand the global economic and political ecosystems in which their companies compete.

A complex adaptive system, be it biologic or economic, is an ensemble of independent agents:

- Who interact to create an ecosystem
- Whose interaction is defined by the exchange of information
- Whose individual actions are based on some system of internal rules
- Who self-organize in nonlinear ways to produce emergent results
- Who exhibit characteristics of both order and chaos
- Who evolve over time (Highsmith 2000)

For an agile project, the *ensemble* includes core team members, customers, suppliers, executives, and other participants who interact with each other in various ways. It is these interactions, and the tacit and explicit information exchanges that occur within them, that project management practices need to facilitate.

The individual agent's actions are driven by a set of internal rules—the core ideology and principles of APM, for example. Both scientific and management researchers have shown that a simple set of rules can generate complex behaviors and outcomes, whether in ant colonies or project teams. Complex rules, on the other hand, often become bureaucratic. How these rules are formulated has a significant impact on how the complex system operates.

Newtonian approaches predict results. CAS approaches create emergent results. "Emergence is a property of complex adaptive systems that creates some greater property of the whole (system behavior) from the interaction of the parts (self-organizing agent behavior). This emergent system behavior cannot be fully explained from measured behaviors of the agents. Emergent results cannot be predicted in the normal sense of cause and effect relationships, but they can be anticipated by creating patterns that have previously produced similar results" (Highsmith 2000). Creativity and innovation are the emergent results of well-functioning agile teams.

Another pair of words that indicate this perspective difference are optimization and adaptation. Optimization processes focus on efficiency and cost reduction. They are documented, measured, refined, and repeated. Adaptation processes focus on innovation, exploration, speed, and constantly reacting to meet external changes. Optimizing processes thrive in low-change, predictable environments, whereas adaptive processes thrive in high-change, uncertain ones.

An adaptive development process has a different character from an optimizing one. Optimizing reflects a basic prescriptive Plan-Design-Build lifecycle. Adapting reflects an organic, evolutionary Envision-Explore-Adapt lifecycle. An adaptive approach begins not with a single solution, but with multiple potential solutions (experiments). It explores and selects the best by applying a series of fitness tests (actual product features or simulations subjected to acceptance tests) and then adapting to feedback. When uncertainty is low, adaptive approaches run the risk of higher costs. When uncertainty is high, optimizing approaches run the risk of settling too early on a particular solution and stifling innovation. The salient point is that these two fundamental approaches to development are very different, and they require different processes, different management approaches, and different measurements of success.

Newtonian versus quantum, predictability versus flexibility, optimization versus adaptation, efficiency versus innovation—all these dichotomies reflect a fundamentally different way of making sense of the world and how to manage effectively within it. Because of high iteration costs, the traditional perspective was predictive and change averse, and deterministic processes arose to support this traditional viewpoint. But our viewpoint needs to change. Executives, project managers, and development teams must embrace a different view of the new product development world, one that not only recognizes change in the business world, but also understands the power of driving down iteration costs to enable experimentation and emergent processes. Understanding these differences and how they affect product development is key to understanding APM.

Our Journey

The objective of this book is to outline the values, principles, and practices of Agile Project Management—to describe what I believe constitutes a better approach to project management *within a specific context,* which I will also endeavor to describe. If this context does not fit your organization, then APM may not be for you. However, if the context does fit, you may find that the concepts and practices of APM will help you achieve your goals of delivering innovative products to customers and improving your work environment.

Many, if not most, of the practices of APM are not new. Iterative lifecycle development, for example, has been around since the 1950s (Larman 2004). Good practices for building a project community have developed steadily over the years. Fundamental project management practices have evolved, and many are useful in fast-moving, rapidly changing projects.

There are fewer than 20 practices described in this book. Why, then, are there 1,500-page project management books with dozens, if not hundreds, of practices? Is something missing here? One of the key concepts of agile project management and development is that the practices, when driven by guiding principles, are generative, not prescriptive. Prescriptive methodologies attempt to describe every activity a project team should do. The problem with prescriptive approaches is that people get lost. They have much to choose from and so little guidance as to applicability that they have trouble eliminating extraneous practices from their projects.

A set of generative practices is a minimal set that works well together as a system. It doesn't prescribe everything a team needs to do, but it identifies those practices that are of extremely high value and should be used on nearly every project. By employing these practices, project teams will "generate" other necessary supporting practices as part of their tailoring and adapting the set to fit their unique needs. Starting with a minimal set of practices and judiciously adding others as needed has proven to be more effective than starting with comprehensive prescriptive practices and attempting to streamline them down to something usable (Boehm and Turner 2003).

So is APM new? Well, yes and no. Complexity theory tells us that biological agents evolve by recombining existing building blocks until a different organism emerges. APM involves carefully selecting existing building blocks—practices that have proven useful to project teams in the past—and linking these practices to core values, a set of guiding principles, and a conceptual framework that draws on CAS theory as its foundation. The "combination" of all these building blocks—practices, values, principles, and conceptual framework—results in Agile Project Management. APM draws on a rich project management legacy, but it is very selective about which parts of that legacy it incorporates. APM also draws on a rich legacy of management, manufacturing, and software development literature and practice that incorporates a worldview and ideological foundation better suited to mobility and speed.

APM isn't for everyone or every project; it is *not* a universal best practice. APM works well for certain problem types, in certain types of organizations, with people who have a particular cultural perspective, and for managers who have a certain worldview. It thrives in innovative cultures and on projects in which speed, mobility, and quality are all key to success, such as in product development. APM is not defined by a small set of practices and techniques. It defines a strategic capability to create and respond to change, to balance flexibility and structure, to draw creativity and innovation out of a development team, and to lead organizations through turbulence and uncertainty.

Chapter 2

Guiding Principles: Customers and Products

Herman and Maya

Maya, a little tired from her late-night arrival, ducked into the room just as the speaker was getting started. Sliding into a chair beside a slightly dorky-looking guy—in a suit and tie no less—she reflected briefly on why she was attending the conference.

A month ago, her boss, Alan, had stopped by. "Maya, your last project went so well, I'd like you to manage Jupiter. It's big, complex, and thorny. Just the kind of project you want, right?" Alan grinned.

"Right." Maya smiled back. Herding a bunch of sharp, opinionated geophysicists, chemical engineers, and software developers would keep her busy, but she loved the challenge. Also, the Jupiter project was producing a new line of test equipment for the oil and gas industry that would be pushing the state of the art.

"Anyway, just so I don't get accused of setting you up for failure, I brought you something," Alan said as he tossed a brochure for the Project

Universe conference on her desk. "You can get away from our hot Austin weather for a few days. The sessions on complex projects and agile development especially caught my eye. Interested?"

"Sure, sounds like fun," said Maya.

Maya's reverie was broken when the speaker called for a short break, and the man sitting next to her slammed his notebook closed.

"What?" Maya responded, looking over in his direction.

"Oh, sorry," he responded sheepishly. "Do you think any of this agile stuff really works?"

Maya looked at his name tag. "Yes, Herman, it works. We use a similar approach at Geo-Tech. I'm here trying to figure out how to scale it to a larger project."

"I guess I'm a little lost. The presentation rambled a bit," said Herman.

"Well, maybe I can help. From my experience, let's see...," Maya flipped through the presentation until she found the slide. "Remember this slide? There's a product vision created with the customer. It's a quick start method that gets the project underway in days or weeks, and it's iterative. It focuses on individual capability and knowledge. It uses feature-based delivery with frequent feedback. And lots of collaboration and self-discipline within the team."

"Sorry, Maya, it's just fancy words. In the real world, my projects are late, ugly, and generally on the verge of heading south every minute... You know the world where Murphy is in charge?"

"Sounds like you've had some tough projects. But this approach works, for us at least. Don't get me wrong—you have to get some things right, but if you do, the rest just sort of falls into place."

"I guess we need to get out of here," said Herman. "The next session is starting. Could we grab a cup of coffee? I've just been asked to head up a new Web development project, and my development team keeps telling me to lighten up and have more confidence in them. I don't see how I can. They're mostly kids right out of college, but I've got to get this project done on time. I'm skeptical, but I'm willing to listen."

"Sure," said Maya. She realized that talking to Herman would make her articulate her own ideas more clearly. Also, with a larger project looming, she didn't want to pass up an opportunity to learn something that might help.

The Guiding Principles
of Agile Project Management

Individual knowledge, the interactions of knowledgeable team members, and the team's ability to learn and apply new knowledge drive success. Success in an agile context is about people and their interactions, not structure and process. And since people are guided by their value systems, creating agility depends on aligning the environment with their value systems—which is why implementing APM will be nearly impossible for some teams and organizations. APM is value driven because people are value driven. A team can employ agile practices, but it won't achieve the potential benefit of agile development without embracing agile values and principles.

According to Carl Larson and Frank LaFasto (1989), whose research is source material for a long list of teamwork books, principled leadership is one of the most critical of the eight characteristics of effective teams. In high-performance teams, "the leaders managed the principles, and the principles managed the team."

Six principles, derived from the core values of the Agile Manifesto, guide APM (see Figure 2.1). Without these guiding principles, even seemingly agile practices—iterative delivery, for example—are often used in the wrong way, or even worse, used such that teams consider themselves agile when they aren't. These guiding principles can help teams determine what practices are appropriate, generate new practices when they are necessary, evaluate new practices that arise, and implement practices in an agile manner. The six principles are divided into two categories, one product and customer related and the other management related:

Customer Value through Innovative Products
- Deliver Customer Value
- Employ Iterative, Feature-Based Delivery
- Champion Technical Excellence

Leadership-Collaboration Management Style
- Encourage Exploration
- Build Adaptive (Self-Organizing, Self-Disciplined) Teams
- Simplify

Figure 2.1
APM Guiding
Principles

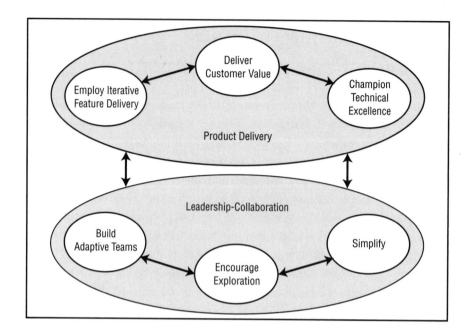

These six principles form a system-of-principles—they work together effectively. While separately each principle may be helpful, the six together create an environment that encourages emergent results. For example, delivering customer value and encouraging exploration are both linked to building self-organizing teams. The linkage reminds us that the product is built by the interactions of competent individuals who are constantly self-organizing. Similarly, championing technical excellence and encouraging exploration are linked in that one key goal of design should be to reduce the cost of change.

This chapter will address the customer- and product-oriented guiding principles, and Chapter 3 will cover the management principles.

Deliver Customer Value

While this may appear to be a simple principle, one nearly too simple to articulate, it is one that must be emphasized over and over lest project team members forget. When organizations get bigger and administrivia increases, when compliance activities take a larger and larger portion of a team's time, when the communications gap between customers and project team members widens, and when project management plans focus on interminable intermediate artifacts, delivering something useful to the customer gets lost.[1]

In defining customer value, one question always comes to the fore, "Who are the customers? Are they users of the product, or managers, or other stakeholders?" A direct answer is that the *customer* is the individual or group that uses the created product to generate business value. This definition separates customers from other stakeholders, so in this book the word "stakeholders" will represent these other individuals associated with the project.

If we want products that deliver outstanding customer value, then we must have a customer-developer partnership, one with responsibilities and accountability on both sides (and similar relationships with key suppliers). Agile teams constantly seek customer involvement and are always asking the question, "Is what we are doing useful to you in meeting your business goals?"

While delivering something useful to the customer remains paramount, keeping all the participants informed and involved is critical to success. Senior management may have different project objectives than the project sponsors. For IT projects, the project sponsor may be a marketing executive who focuses on features and business value, while IT management may constrain the project with architectural requirements.

The success of any product involves meeting expectations—those of the ultimate customer, those of management stakeholders, and those of the project team itself. There is a big difference between requirements and expectations: requirements are tangible; expectations are intangible. Yet ultimately, it is the intangible expectations against which actual results will be measured. Cultivating committed customers and stakeholders means involving them in dialogue about both requirements and expectations. As colleague Ken Delcol comments, "This also includes the Kenny Rogers

---

1. In this book, the term "customer" represents a wide range of entities—commercial business-to-business customers, retail consumers, and customers internal to an organization. The people included in each of these instances vary, from those who actually use a product, to executives who approve purchase, to product managers who coordinate customer interactions with development organizations. I will use the terms "customer team" and "product manager" to represent all of the potential combinations of customers.

school of managing the communications with customers and stakeholders—know when to hold, when to fold, when to walk away, and when to run. Project managers must have the business savvy to understand this."

There are two particularly important issues involved in delivering customer value in a new product development (NPD) environment: focusing on innovation and adaptability rather than efficiency and optimization and concentrating on delivery rather than compliance activities.

Innovation and Adaptability

"We live in a time where creativity, innovation, and imagination drive the world," write Tom Wujec and Sandra Muscat (2002). Creating new products and services differs from making minor enhancements to existing ones. The first must focus on innovation and adaptability, while the second usually focuses on efficiency and optimization. Efficiency delivers products and services that we can think of. Innovation delivers products that we can barely imagine. Efficiency and optimization are appropriate drivers for a production project, while innovation and creativity should drive an exploration-type project. A production mindset can restrict our vision to what appears doable. An exploration mindset helps us explore what seems impossible.

Optimization implies that we already know how to do something but that we now need to improve it. Innovation implies that we don't know how to do something, and searching for that knowledge is paramount. No project, no product development effort is all one way or all the other, but project managers (team members, customers, and executives) should understand this fundamental difference when deciding how to plan and manage their projects.

The customer value goal of APM has two equally critical components: creating innovative products that deliver outstanding customer value today *and* tomorrow. The *and tomorrow* phrase speaks to the need for adaptability, which in turn speaks to the importance of technical excellence. Products that meet today's customer requirements but cannot adapt easily to future needs are doomed to short life spans.

APM's core purpose of creating innovative new products and services means dealing with constant technological and competitive change, generating novel ideas, and continually reducing product development schedules. The core purpose is not reducing cost, although that may happen, or gaining efficiency, although that may happen also. However, there are times when even the most innovative team needs to bring a bit of efficiency to their project—all part of the balancing act that makes project management interesting, and difficult.

Planning and Control to Execution

When project managers focus on delivery, they add value to projects. When they focus on planning and control, they tend to add overhead.[2]

A quick review of the general management literature uncovers hundreds of books on leadership and strategy, but interestingly enough, very few on how to actually execute. Ram Charan, a distinguished author and consultant to CEOs, echoes this observation. "As I facilitated meetings at the CEO and division levels, I watched and studied, and I saw that leaders placed too much emphasis on what some call high-level strategy, on intellectualizing and philosophizing, and not enough on implementation" (Bossidy and Charan 2002).

With respect to project management, Greg Howell and Lauri Koskela (2001) argue that traditional project management practices focus too much on management-as-planning and a thermostat model for control, and not enough on what the major project management focus should be—execution.

According to Howell and Koskela, the common project management approach is composed of three processes that exchange information—planning, controlling, and executing. In construction projects, they see several troubling aspects of traditional planning. First, the motivation for planning often comes from outside the project; that is, plans are developed to satisfy legal, regulatory, or management requirements rather than being based on the work that needs to be accomplished. Second, the motivation to plan often relates more to the desire for control than the needs of actual work execution, perhaps because the people planning the work are not involved in the doing of the work. This happens constantly in software development, where the task-based planning that project managers use for control has little relationship to how software engineers really work. Third, planning and

---

2. Ken Delcol observes, "The reality in NPD is that you need both, and the trick is balance, which changes through the development lifecycle. Most people don't get this."

control become the focal points; execution is considered of minor importance, and legitimizing the project takes precedence over producing results.

Control has historically centered on correction rather than learning, because plans were viewed as reasonably correct, and translating the plan into action was considered a simple process. Witness the conventional "wisdom" that construction itself (carpentry, electrical, plumbing, etc.) is merely manual, mechanical work without much decision making or creativity (just follow the plans) or that software programming is just coding what's specified. If plans are viewed as correct, then control focuses on fixing mistakes and explaining discrepancies, not learning something new that might legitimately alter the plans. Other problems with this historical view of control include inappropriate manipulation of work in order to meet the plan, reduced possibilities for collaboration, incorrect interpretation of performance, and reluctance to revise plans.

APM is an execution-biased model, not a planning-and-control-biased model. In APM, the project manager's primary role is to facilitate creation of a product vision and guide the team toward making that vision a reality, not to develop plans and schedules and control progress such that the "plan" is implemented. However, we need to interpret the forgoing ideas carefully— APM is *not* an anti-planning model. Planning (and control) is an integral part of APM; it is just not the focal point. As with many aspects of agile development, there is a wide gap between one thing being *less* important than something else and being *un*important.

Once project teams focus on execution, a next critical step is then to concentrate on value-adding activities, those that assist the team in delivering results, rather than those that merely ensure compliance.

Delivery versus Compliance

APM is first and foremost about delivery—delivering results and delivering value to customers. Too many project managers, too many project office members, too many organizations have drifted toward compliance as their primary, if often implicit, focus. Compliance activities, at their best, attempt to mitigate the risk of mistakes, fraud, poor performance, and financial overruns. Managers want reports. Accountants want numbers. Auditors want sign-offs. Governmental agencies want documents. Standards groups

(ISO, SEI, and others) want proof of compliance. Legal departments want everything. Failure to differentiate between delivery and compliance results in ever-increasing compliance work—producing documents for regulators, lawyers, or management—while delivering products falls to secondary priority.

In one of my favorite books, *Systemantics: How Systems Work and Especially How They Fail*, John Gall (1977) warns against the rising tide of "systemism"—"the state of mindless belief in systems; the belief that systems can be made to function to achieve desired goals." Gall's point is that "the fundamental problem does not lie in any particular system but rather in *systems as such*." These systems become the goal rather than the means to a goal.

Adherents of these "systemisms" would argue that implementing these programs *should not* result in losing track of the primary goal (results rather than process). But Gall points out how this subversion becomes inevitable through two of his axioms: 1) "Systems Tend to Expand to Fill the Known Universe" and 2) "Systems Tend to Oppose Their Own Proper Functions, Especially in Connection with the Phenomenon of 'Administrative Encirclement' "(Gall 1977).

Consider, for example, the rounds of procedures and mounds of documentation that are required to gain ISO or CMM certification. I worked with a company that had workaround after workaround to circumvent its ISO processes. Changing the standard processes was so burdensome that everyone used workarounds. However, they did have one solution for the volumes of process documents—a sophisticated automation system in which just the list of processes went on for page after page after page. I examined an auditor's report (ISO certification requires periodic audits) of some 10 pages that were filled with compliance issues such as failures to sign or date a form or the absence of some document. There was not a single substantive delivery issue mentioned in the report! Managers had to spend time analyzing this audit report and then writing another report about how they would keep these terrible things from happening again, when of course their only concern was to placate the auditors, not to make meaningful improvements in the system.

Clearly, this company's ISO "system" had run amok. However, the system had become so ingrained in the company—and maintaining certification such a mantra—that getting out from under the burden was proving exceedingly difficult. This illustrates Gall's first axiom, which says systems tend to expand to fill the known universe. Once underway, systems become very difficult to change, and compliance, not delivery, becomes the goal. At the point where employees are trying to deliver results, these systems are almost universally hated because they impede progress. The systems, as Gall says, inevitably tend to oppose their own proper functioning.

Project managers need to relieve the project team from as much compliance work as possible, even if that means taking on the tasks themselves. Several years ago, when talking to a project manager of a very successful CMM Level 5–certified software development organization, I asked him about all the documentation, metrics, and reporting work that went into certification. "Oh," he said, "I take care of most of that myself. The development team needs to concentrate on the real work."

Building process frameworks that don't succumb to Gall's axioms is difficult. Agile frameworks do need minimal documentation and a mechanism to convey knowledge about project success and failure to others in the organization. The answer isn't eliminating either documentation or process, but approaching both from a simplified, lean, barely sufficient, just-enough perspective. Streamlining processes, targeting a level of bare sufficiency, and recognizing the difference between compliance and delivery activities (although some activities have aspects of both that aren't always easy to separate) will pay big dividends in delivering value to customers faster and at a lower cost.

Lean Thinking

Many of the ideas of the agile movement first arose within lean manufacturing, which began in the automotive industry in Japan in the 1980s. One of the fundamental tenets of lean manufacturing is the systematic elimination of waste; that is, any activity that doesn't deliver value to the customer. One way to streamline projects (doing fewer things, doing the right things, eliminating bottlenecks) involves differentiating between delivery activities and compliance activities and applying appropriate strategies to each.[3]

While lean manufacturing ideas have been used in the United States for a while, lean product development ideas, especially those of Toyota, have

---

3. For background information in this area, although the authors don't refer to compliance or delivery activities, see (Womack and Jones 1996).

gained less recognition. The Toyota development system offers huge potential productivity gains by eliminating non-value-adding compliance activities—many organizations stand to increase their productivity *three to four times!* Allen Ward is the man responsible for bringing many of the ideas from Toyota's lean product development system to the US. When Ward asks Toyota's American engineers and managers how much time they spend adding value (i.e., actually doing engineering work), their response averages 80%. The same question asked of engineers and managers at American automobile companies averages 20%. How can you compete with companies that are getting four times as much value-adding work from their development engineers? (Kennedy 2003)

Try this survey in your organization, but be prepared for a shock. Ask your entire staff or your project team, including managers, how much time they spend doing engineering or development activities—how much time do they spend adding value to the customer? How many of your "improvement" initiatives (CMM, ISO, Six Sigma, TQM, BPR) have just added layer after layer of forms, procedures, meetings, and approvals to teams trying desperately to produce something useful? Too much structure not only kills initiative and innovation, it consumes enormous chunks of time. The fundamental issue is not that these initiatives are valueless, because they are not, but that they fundamentally value structure over individual knowledge and capability. And that's why they are so difficult to implement—people feel devalued.

The issues surrounding delivery versus compliance activities have special significance for project managers. First, project managers need to analyze project activities to maximize time spent on delivery. Second, project managers must analyze their own activities to determine whether they are contributing to delivery or compliance. For example, when a project manager creates a status report for management, she is "complying" with a management dictum. However, when she is coordinating the activities between two feature teams or assisting a team in reaching a critical design decision, she is contributing to delivery—she adds value to the delivery process.

Lean thinking provides one way to separate delivery from compliance activities, which in turn enables companies to optimize delivery activities (Womack et al. 1990; Womack and Jones 1996). The four tenets of lean thinking are:

1. Specify value
2. Identify the value stream

3. Flow
4. Pull

Value can only be defined by the ultimate customer, and it is expressed in product terms—customer needs, price, time, and quality. The customer in this analysis is always the end consumer, one out in the marketplace. Identifying the wrong customer (e.g., internal management) can lead to misinterpretation of marketplace value.

A value stream consists of the activities required to bring a product to customers: product development, order processing through delivery, product manufacturing. Each of the specific activities is then analyzed to determine where it adds value and where it doesn't.

Flow thinking encourages everyone—managers and staff—to abandon the traditional batch-and-queue mode of thinking for that of small-lot flow. In other words, whatever the step, keep activities flowing from one to the next without delays for approvals or waiting for the next department. For example, a drug development team using rapid experimentation techniques would not be exhibiting flow if it constantly had to wait for lab testing results.

Finally, pull thinking means waiting for customers to ask for products, rather than building a large inventory and then "pushing" product to customers. Dell Computers operates a pull system, waiting until a customer's order "pulls" the product through the system.[4]

Necessary Compliance

It is important to note that there are good reasons for *some* compliance activities—we just need to keep them from impeding progress. Project managers can add value to a project by handling compliance issues well.

Every organization, every company, every project team has legitimate compliance issues. For example, in the automotive industry, an enormous volume of documentation must be retained for potential product liability lawsuits and government crash investigations. In the pharmaceutical industry, companies may decry US Food and Drug Administration (FDA) inefficiencies, but few consumers would want to buy drugs unfettered by federal

---

4. For more on Lean Development, see (Poppendieck and Poppendieck 2003).

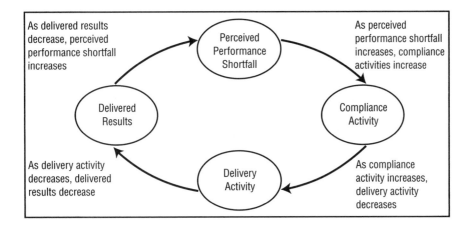

As delivered results decrease, perceived performance shortfall increases

As perceived performance shortfall increases, compliance activities increase

As delivery activity decreases, delivered results decrease

As compliance activity increases, delivery activity decreases

Perceived Performance Shortfall

Delivered Results

Compliance Activity

Delivery Activity

Figure 2.2
The Compliance Loop

regulation. Executives have a responsibility to shareholders, employees, and customers to exercise oversight, which may take the form of audits, project status reports, purchasing policies, or certifications.

The activities surrounding these compliance efforts don't deliver customer value (except in a convoluted, roundabout way), but they are necessary activities nonetheless. In short, compliance is a cost of doing business. But compliance work can also strangle innovation, raise costs dramatically, and lengthen product development cycles.

As Figure 2.2 shows, compliance activities can spiral out of control as performance shortfalls are "fixed" by additional compliance activities ("We'll never make that mistake again!"), which in turn negatively impact delivery results. Large companies tend to put heavy processes in place to prevent low-probability mistakes, burdening the delivery process with paperwork and controls.

There are actually two kinds of compliance activities—internal and external. External compliance can't be avoided and shouldn't be. Government regulations were established for a reason, but when the reasons expire, the regulations rarely follow. The strategy for most external compliance activities is to do just enough, but no more than is absolutely required. Internal compliance activities grow with the size of an organization. Clearly a 50,000-person organization will have more compliance activities than a 100-person one. But the objectives of APM are the same—reduce the burden of compliance work as much as possible and don't let it interfere any more than necessary with delivery activities.

For necessary compliance activities, the strategy should be to minimize them and get them off *the critical path and the critical people.* Compliance activities should be examined from a risk management perspective: What do we have to accomplish in order to balance the cost of compliance with potential risks? This is an extremely important point. Compliance activities do not, nor should they be expected to, produce customer value. We should think of all compliance activities as overhead and oversight cost, necessary to some degree but subject to minimization based on the risk involved.

Delivering Value

Another salient point is that too many people (especially managers and process designers) think compliance activities—reviews, checkpoints, formal documentation, and elaborate and detailed plans—add value. One of the other tenets of lean thinking (and agile development) is to trust the people actually doing the work and to push decision making and collaboration down to the working level. A very simple but infrequently used method of distinguishing delivery from compliance activities is to ask those doing the work, "Does this activity help you deliver customer value, or is it overhead?" Unfortunately, many managers and process designers don't like the answers they receive.

A colleague recently recounted a story that illustrates the trouble (along with confusion about "empowerment") that this confusion between delivery and compliance can cause. In a company he previously worked for, senior managers decided to "empower" employees, so they pushed all the project management activities down to the engineers. Now, rather than designing products, engineers spent much of their time on budgeting, status reporting, and other administrivia that project managers had previously handled. The engineers didn't feel empowered, they felt burdened. They were spending valuable engineering design time feeding the company's paper mill.

While compliance activities can be costly, an even more serious problem is their impact on development time. For example, if we view formal documentation (e.g., a design document) as helping deliver value, we would assign the task to developers. However, if we view that design document as a compliance artifact, we would try to offload it from developers so they could concentrate on value-adding activities.

Let's postulate that during a design session, a team constructs a series of design diagrams on a whiteboard. From a product delivery perspective, taking digital photos of the diagrams and storing them in a project folder may be sufficient. However, from a compliance perspective (say, to maintain ISO certification), the diagrams need to be formalized and documented in a standard format. Once the design diagrams are complete on the whiteboards, support staff—not the engineers—should be available to transfer the low-ceremony diagrams into formal documentation. Support staff free the engineering staff to continue delivery activities with minimal schedule impact, plus their salary costs are lower. When we fail to differentiate delivery and compliance activities, we mistakenly regard cleaning up and formalizing documentation as helping developers build better products. By offloading, we force ourselves to confront the true cost of compliance, and we keep compliance activities from wrecking development schedules.

Employ Iterative, Feature-Based Delivery

If you want to innovate, you have to iterate!

The serial, or waterfall, development lifecycle has been under attack for years, but it still has its defenders. For example, Donald Reinertsen (1997) writes, "The vast majority of academic literature on product development is skewed towards the sequential approach. This is in striking contrast to the enormous shift that has taken place in managerial practice towards a more concurrent approach."

In the software development field, the attack on waterfall approaches goes back decades, as thoroughly documented by Craig Larman (2004). As Larman recalls, a 1970 paper by Winston Royce was credited with starting the "waterfall" trend. In fact, Royce was an advocate of iterative development for anything more than simple projects. In 1985 the US Department of Defense adopted a waterfall-based standard (DOD-STD-2167), which it largely abandoned for iterative methods after experiencing high failure rates.

But even though serial approaches have been attacked as too simplistic, not only do they continue to be widely used, they continue to influence contracting procedures and executive perspectives. So in order to respond to the widespread misinformation about serial development, teams that practice APM need to understand why iterative, feature-based delivery is useful, and in fact critical, to innovative product development.

Creating a Better Product

Iterative, feature-based development can be defined by four key words: iterative, feature-based, timeboxed, and incremental. Iterative development means that we build a partial version of a product and then expand that version through successive short time periods of development followed by reviews and adaptations. Feature-based delivery means that the engineering team builds features of the final product or, particularly with industrial products, at least a close representation of the final product (such as a simulation model).

Iterations are constrained to produce a result within a certain period of time—a timebox. Timeboxes force closure; they force us to make something concrete, often before we are quite ready. Incremental development means that we build these partial products such that they will be deployed at the end of one or more of the iterations. Partial products can be delivered in hardware to allow for earlier testing of key performance attributes. For software companies, iterative development and incremental delivery have become a competitive advantage.

Short, timeboxed iterations are a fixture of APM. However, iterations are only half the story—features, rather than tasks, are the other. Customers don't understand, nor do they care about, the engineering tasks required to build a DVD player or an automobile. They do, however, understand the features of each of those products.

If we are to build products that deliver customer value each and every iteration, then the highest-level control on the process must be features about which the customer can say, "Yes, that feature does what I expected it to do, and it is valuable." Saying to the customer at the end of milestone 1, "Yes, we finished the relational database schema" or "We got the CAD drawings of the fluid transfer valve done" just doesn't work. This information isn't something the customer can relate to, much less make a priority decision about.

The feature delivery approach helps define a workable interface between customers and product developers. Customers get to schedule and prioritize features; product engineers figure out what tasks will be necessary to deliver those feature and what it will take in terms of time and cost. Showing a customer a task plan can be dangerous, as they'll often ask, "What's this four weeks at the end for testing? Can't we cut that down?" This feature-based approach applies to everyone else, too. Senior management is restricted to feature management, rather than task management; they can cut features but not tasks.

For projects and products in which the requirements can evolve over time, it is critical that the results reviewed by customers during the development process be as close to versions of the actual product as possible. Customers have a very difficult time visualizing from documents how a product will function, which is why in industry after industry, companies have embraced modeling, simulations, and prototyping to improve the feedback loop from customers to the development teams. One of the four core values of agile project management speaks to "working products over comprehensive documentation," indicating that customers respond to real versions of products they can actually use.

Shoe developers build versions of shoes during the development process. Airplane designers use extensive simulations (that are heavily visual) to make sure systems will integrate well before spending hundreds of millions of dollars building the first version of a plane. Automobile designers build both full-scale and reduced-scale models of new cars. In each of these cases, the developers have support documentation—but the proof is in the actual product. Whether the feature is implemented in a prototype, model, or simulation has to do with the cost. Software features can be demonstrated fairly inexpensively and then be easily changed. Building versions of an airplane would be much more expensive, hence the industry's heavy reliance on simulations.

Michael Schrage (2000) describes the differences between models, simulations, and prototypes in his book *Serious Play*. He then goes on to say, "In effect, models, simulations, and prototypes have become 'flavors' of the same thing—the effort to use technology to re-create some aspect of a reality that matters." And what matters is that the project team and the customer team have common ground, a shared space, in which to discuss, debate, and decide on critical product feature issues. Features are closer to reality than other intermediate artifacts. They indicate real, not artificial, progress. Once we are faced with real progress, project teams, customers, and stakeholders are forced to confront the difficult tradeoff decisions around cost, schedule, and scope. Customers, product managers, and other stakeholders can no longer be indifferent bystanders in the development process.

Iterative development, when accompanied with reasonable end-of-iteration reviews—product, technical, process, team—is also self-correcting. For example, architecture is considered, in the serial development world at least, as complete near the beginning of a project. However, several types of feedback can indicate poor architectural decisions. Finding extensive integration problems at an iteration or milestone can point to poor coordination between subteams, poor component or module subdivision or interface designs, or a combination of both. Iterative development teams expect to confront problems like these and either evolve the architecture or put additional coordination mechanisms in place.

Probably the most important aspect of self-correction is customer feedback on the product as it evolves. As these evolutionary changes get incorporated in later iterations, the customer's confidence in the product grows, or conversely, it becomes clear that the product isn't working and should be abandoned—early.

Producing Earlier Benefits

Driving exploration is critical, but knowing when to stop is also critical. Product development is exploring with a purpose, usually within a set of constraints. Frequent, timeboxed iterations compel the development and customer teams and executives to make difficult tradeoff decisions early and often during the project. Feature delivery contributes to realistic evaluations because the product managers can look at tangible, verifiable results.

In my early years of iterative development, I thought timeboxes were actually about time—making sure things were accomplished within the specified timeframe. What I came to realize is that timeboxes are actually about forcing tough decisions. If a team plans to deliver 14 features in an iteration and it can only produce 10, then the development team, customer team, and possibly the executive sponsor must face the shortfall and decide what actions to take. Many factors will influence the decision making— whether this iteration is early in the project or late, whether the shortfall will impact the delivery date or product viability (every product has a set of features that constitutes the minimum viable set)—but the salient point is that these decisions are addressed frequently in an agile project.

All too often, sequentially developed products reach the final stages, only to discover major problems when the options available are limited. By forcing difficult decisions early and often, timeboxed feature delivery gives the team more options for solving problems. Iterations allow you to manage risk sooner—you do not have to build the whole product to find out if you can meet a particular specification.

Another benefit of continuous feature delivery is that for some products, software being a good example, incremental releases can provide early benefits. Rather than wait 12 or 18 months for new software features, incremental delivery can provide quarterly or even more frequent ones. Incremental releases can favorably alter ROI calculations because they allow product managers to address opportunities that would be lost in 18 months. However, even though some products can be developed iteratively using simulations or prototypes, they are very difficult to release incrementally. As the battle over Web browsers showed in the late 1990s, customers often can't assimilate new product releases every three to four months.

Progressive Risk Reduction

Product development is risky business. As Tom DeMarco and Tim Lister (2003) so pithily state, "If a project has no risks, don't do it." "Risk is an essential characteristic of product innovation," says Preston Smith. "Product development involves innovation…there are always pieces of information that we need now that will not be known until we are further downstream" (Smith and Merritt 2002).

Risk covers a wide range of topics, from technical (can we build it?) to marketing (can we sell it?) to financial (can we sell it at a profit?). In many organizations risk management is a "bolt-on" to project management activities: "Well, we'll do some risk management if we have time." Iterative, feature-based development integrates the consideration of major risk issues directly into the process. At each stage of planning and development, the customer and engineering teams discuss both business value and risk: "What features are highest priority from a business value perspective?" and "What features will have the greatest impact on risk reduction?" Sometimes the answers to these questions are the same features, sometimes not, but in certain respects the two questions are just different perspectives on the same issue—delivering value.

For example, in a planning exercise for a product, there may be a combination of technical risk (a new technology architecture for us) and feature risk (we're not sure what the features should look like). In prioritizing features for iteration planning, the team will need to balance a strategy of broad feature implementation early (to reduce feature risk) or in-depth technical development (to reduce technology risk). Sometimes the highest "value" will be to reduce the technical risk first.

Champion Technical Excellence

Agile developers are dedicated to technical excellence, not because of aesthetics (although that may be a rationale for some), but because a dedication to technical excellence delivers customer value. Project managers must be champions of technical excellence; they must support and advocate technical excellence while maintaining a watchful eye on other project objectives.

Championing technical excellence is critical both to creating the product customers want today within the established constraints of time and cost and to reducing the cost of change so the product remains responsive to future customer needs. If APM's core purpose is to create innovative products, and if competent individuals are a key part of delivering those products, then it's impossible to support a principle that advocates technical mediocrity—either explicitly or, as is usually the case, implicitly.

Few products today, particularly industrial products, are one-shot wonders. Products evolve over time, improving constantly. For example, the Boeing 747 passenger jet has been in existence for over 30 years, but the 747–400 planes rolling off the assembly line today are much different than the 100 series planes first put into service in January 1970. Technical excellence is key to product evolution.

In discussing the Toyota lean product development system, Michael Kennedy (2003) laments that in too many organizations project management has become focused on administrative excellence rather than technical excellence. He goes on to state that one of the four pillars of the Toyota system is an "Expert Engineering Workforce," which encourages both technical excellence and individual responsibility.

Some critics consider agile methods to be ad hoc, undisciplined, and, ultimately, technically inferior. They are wrong. First, for traditionalists, who thrive on process, procedure, and documentation, the informality of agile methods is interpreted as undisciplined. Nothing could be further from reality. Discipline is doing what you said you would do. Using this definition, many organizations with elaborate processes fail—they have volumes of processes, procedures, forms, and documents that are systematically ignored. Agile organizations have less-elaborate process structures, but they tend to follow the ones they have.

Second, the difference of opinion isn't over *whether* technical quality is important but over *how* technical quality can be achieved. Critics say, "Agile development ignores design." What they are really objecting to is the lack of extensive up-front design, believing that it is the only valid design process. Agile developers believe that iterative, emergent design and frequent feedback yield superior designs. So again, it's not a question of design versus ad hoc development, but a disagreement over design approach.

As a software development consultant, I've never encountered a successful software company (although my sample size is limited) in which the team leaders and project managers were not technically savvy. Whether a company is building electronic instrumentation, jet engines, or pure software products, project managers need specific technical expertise to adequately manage projects. Championing technical excellence requires that the project manager, and team members in general, understand what technical excellence means—in the product, the technology, and in the skills of the people doing the work. They must understand, within the context of their specific product, the difference between excellence and perfection. No company can afford to produce a *perfect* product, but building a product that delivers customer value and maintains its technical integrity is essential to commercial success and the technical team's satisfaction.

Some practitioners operate on the premise that project management practices are generic and can be applied across any project. They may argue that someone with good project management skills doesn't need deep domain expertise. While this premise may be true in some domains, in general it doesn't apply to product development where technical, scientific, or engineering skills are paramount. "Project managers who don't understand the technology they are managing can lose the confidence of their teams, particularly teams that are proud of their technical ability," says author Eric Verzuh (1999).

Some project managers, in particular those isolated in project management offices, also bandy about the notion that product development and project management can be separated—again, believing that the project managers can somehow glide along above the work of product development, monitoring and controlling without getting their hands dirty. While generating an iterative feature plan and gathering the requirements for a product feature are different kinds of activities, they are each so dependent on the particular type of product that separating them is a sure path to failure. The fallacy that project management and product development can be separated may have roots in the widespread use of serial lifecycles—Plan, Design, Build, Test. From this perspective, planning, designing, building, and testing an electronic instrument may not seem very different from doing the same for a motorcycle. However, employing a feature-based approach rapidly points out the need for an integrated approach to the two activities.

One of the reasons project managers (in their role as decision makers or influencers) need a technical background is that while technical excellence is a laudable goal, there may be considerably different approaches to achieving that excellence. Should the software team focus on refactoring, automated testing, and simple design? Extensive front-end modeling? Or some balance of the two? Project managers need to be involved with the team in debating and deciding on the technical approach to development, as well as keeping the team aware of the business objectives as technical issues are decided. The project managers may not make the decision, but they should be knowledgeable enough to steer the interactions between team members, make sure project data (e.g., architectural platform constraints) are fully understood by the team, and keep the team on track in making timely technical decisions.

Furthermore, project managers must champion technical excellence because therein lies the key to adaptability and low-cost iteration that drives long-term product success. Project managers are jugglers, always keeping multiple balls in the air. They must be aware, for example, of the point at which their team starts tipping the balance from technical excellence to perfection. They must be aware when the product manager pushes too hard for speed and features over adaptability. Helping project teams find and maintain these balance points is nearly impossible unless the project manager has the necessary technical background. The project manager doesn't have to *be* a technical guru, but he has to know enough to recognize and converse with one. That said, if the project manager isn't a technical guru, he better have one in the form of a chief engineer or developer.

Customers and Products

Delivering customer value—product features produced within the target timeframe—is a cornerstone of APM, and the customer drives the process. In order to innovate in delivering that value in an effective and timely fashion, agile teams employ iterative, feature-based delivery. Finally, to ensure that value gets delivered both today and in the future, that products can adapt to changing customer demands both during development and after initial deployment, project managers and teams need to create an environment in which technical excellence is viewed as a critical priority.

Chapter 3 will cover the next set of guiding principles, those related to management and organizational issues.

Guiding Principles: Leadership-Collaboration Management

Management Style

Sitting in the local Java Jerry's, Herman picked up his conversation with Maya. "Agile practices like iterative delivery sound okay, but I'm having a problem with the management style. I mean, 'egalitarian workplace' sounds like some liberal, socialist conspiracy."

"Don't get me started on politics, Herman. What I heard him ask was why, if we think it's important for our government to operate as an egalitarian democracy, we'd accept an authoritarian hierarchy in our workplace? It's the old command-control versus collaboration argument."

"But projects aren't democracies. They're dictatorships. We don't vote on critical issues. If I don't make the decisions, they don't get made."

"Keep your team on their toes, huh?"

"Every day."

"You're inch-pebble tracking already? Are they completely incompetent?" Maya asked.

"No, they're pretty sharp, just undisciplined … got to keep after them. My team seems to wait around for me to tell them what to do."

"Maybe you have to keep after them because you keep after them."

"What?"

Maya almost bit her tongue when she saw the look of surprise on Herman's face. The guy was clearly a micro-manager, but if she wanted to continue this conversation, she'd better find a gentler way to make her points.

"If you don't mind me saying, they might seem undisciplined because you've trained them that way. I know I can count on one hand the number of times I've had to implement an inch-pebble approach. My team divvies up the work among themselves. Micro-managing isn't my thing."

"And people actually do what they should be doing, when they should be doing it, without you laying it out for them, and without hounding them?"

"95% of the time."

"Maybe, and one day pigs will fly. So, how does work get assigned?" asked Herman.

"Well, when the team is running smoothly, they assign work to themselves. But sometimes in the beginning I 'suggest' assignments. I try to mix people with different skill levels, but I also want to encourage the most experienced people to work on the most difficult problems, the good performers on other problems. I put the poorest performers, as long as they last, on compliance work."

"Don't they hate that?"

"Of course they do, but this actually accomplishes two goals. First, the poorer performers can't screw up the product. Second, while we are flexible, fundamental responsibilities come with that flexibility. Technical expertise, excellence, and team behavior matter."

"But," Herman muttered, "doesn't process help make up for lack of skill? That's what process proponents have been preaching for years— install comprehensive processes and then utilize less skilled individuals."

"Well, that might work for unskilled labor or clerical-type jobs," said Maya. "But the idea that you can substitute process for skill is bull. A process helps us organize work, but if my team is designing an electronic sensor and they don't have any electrical engineering skill or experience, the chances of being successful are nil."

"Everyone on my team has reasonable skills. It's just judgment they lack."

"And that's why processes work. If you can trust them to make good decisions most of the time, then you can trust them to do the job. We look for raw talent leveraged by training and experience. We place those talented people in a loose process framework and let 'em rip," said Maya.

"Well, I need to get back and pack. May I call you after the conference?" Herman reached into his coat pocket and handed her his business card.

Maya picked up her PDA from the table. "We can sync, or you'll have to be patient while I dig around for a business card."

"I can wait. But I really would like to chat later."

Maya pulled the cards out from under the jumble of stuff in her briefcase and handed him one. "Feel free to call. I'm not sure that what works at Geo-Tech will work at…" Maya glanced at his name tag again, "Great Mid-West Insurance, but I can share what has worked for us."

Herman put her card into his day planner, then packed up his briefcase. Extending his hand, he said, "Thanks, Maya. It's been fun, but this stuff will be a tough sell."

Watching him hurry from the coffee house, Maya looked forward to talking. She had a feeling that the conversations might be intense, but they'd also help her clarify her thinking about these concepts and keep her sharp.

The Business of APM

What does a business executive want from a product development and project management process? She wants three key things. First of all, she wants the process to be *reliable*—to produce innovative results project after project. Second, she wants the process to be *predictable*—so she can effectively plan and manage such business activities as financial management, staffing, and product launches. Third, she wants *dependable*, reality-based information, because visions can be wrong, business models can be wrong, people may hit blocks they can't get past, and progress is not always smooth. If the project needs to be terminated, she wants to do it earlier rather than later. Dependable progress reports enable managers to take appropriate actions early.

Note that the word "repeatable" isn't in the agile lexicon. Implementing repeatable processes has been the goal of many companies, but in rapidly changing environments, repeatability turns out to be the wrong goal; in fact, it turns out to be an extremely counterproductive goal. Which brings us to the critical difference between reliable and repeatable. Repeatable means doing the same thing in the same way to produce the same results. Reliable means meeting targets regardless of the impediments thrown in your way—it means constantly adapting to meet a goal.

Confusion about reliable and repeatable has caused many organizations to pursue repeatable processes—very structured and precise—when exactly the opposite approach—mildly structured and flexible—works astonishingly better for new product and service development. If your goal is to deliver a product that meets a known and unchanging specification, then try a repeatable process. However, if your goal is to deliver a valuable product to a customer within some targeted boundaries, when change and deadlines are significant factors, then reliable processes work better.

Reliable, Not Repeatable

Failure to differentiate between highly uncertain and highly certain project environments causes much of the confusion about measuring project performance. This confusion stems from two sources—the definition of scope and the difference between estimates and constraints.

Repeatable processes reduce variability through measurement and constant process correction. The term originated in manufacturing, where results were well defined and repeatability meant that if a process had consistent inputs, then defined outputs would be produced. Repeatable means that the conversion of inputs to outputs can be replicated with little variation. It implies that no new information can be generated during the process because we have to know all the information in advance in order to predict the output results accurately. Repeatable processes have severe problems with product development projects: precise results are rarely predictable, inputs vary considerably from project to project, and the input-to-output conversions themselves are highly variable.

Reliable processes focus on outputs, not inputs. Using a reliable process, team members figure out ways to consistently achieve a given goal even though the inputs vary dramatically. Because of the input variations, the team may not use the same processes or practices from one project, or even one iteration, to the next. Reliability is results driven. Repeatability is input driven. The irony is that if every project process was somehow made repeatable, the project would be extremely unstable because of input and transformation variations. Even those organizations that purport to have repeatable processes are often successful not because of those processes, but because of the adaptability of the people who are using those processes.

Even at best, a repeatable process can only deliver what was specified in the beginning. A reliable, emergent process can actually deliver a *better* result than anyone ever conceived of in the beginning. An emergent process can produce what you wish you had thought about at the start if only you had been smart and prescient enough.

Herein lies a definitional issue with project scope. With production-style projects, those amenable to repeatable processes, scope is considered to be the defined requirements (and constraints). But in product development, requirements evolve and change over the life of the project, so "scope" can never be precisely defined in the beginning. Therefore, the correct scope to consider for agile projects isn't defined requirements but the articulated product vision. Project managers may be worried about specific requirements, but executives are concerned about the product as a whole—does it meet the vision of the customer or product marketing? When management asks the ever-popular question, "Did the project meet its scope, schedule, and cost targets?" the scope part of the answer should be evaluated according to the vision, value, and totality of the features delivered, not on the set of specific features defined at the start of the project.

Another source of confusion arises from viewing cost and schedule as estimates rather than constraints. For a repeatable manufacturing process, the costs and schedule estimates are predictive; the actual results should approximate the estimates. But what happens when the project is volatile and initial estimates are very likely to be wrong? Does this mean executives shouldn't expect predictable results, that they should just accept results as they unfold?

Let's look at an example to answer the question. The project team develops a release plan with the best estimates it can make early in the project. Let's assume that the team estimates the project will take 15 months and cost $4.5 million. Product marketing then counters, as always, "That will never fly, we have to have the product in 9 months, for no more than $3.0 million." Vigorous negotiation, further refinement of feature definitions, and feature reduction establish a "plan" that both engineering and product marketing agree on for 11 months and $3.5 million. Everyone understands that significant changes will occur during the project—features will change, technology will become better understood, and hundreds of other changes will occur. However, the product vision remains, and the 11 months and $3.5 million remain as constraints—a target rather than a prediction.

When things change, decisions need to be made and tradeoffs must occur. The product's vision, schedule, and cost become boundaries to guide these change decisions. As long as the project remains within its constraints, swapping one feature for another doesn't change the project "scope." When the product manager comes up with an exciting group of new features, he has to determine which others can be deferred in order for the project to remain within the constraints. In an agile project, he can no longer scream, "These new features have to get into the product. We're lost without them—just find a way!" He has to be a part of finding the way, which could be going back to the executive sponsor with a change to the project constraints.

Agile project management is both reliable and predictable—it can deliver products that meet the customer's evolving needs within the boundary constraints better than any other process for a given level of uncertainty. Why does this happen? Not because some project manager specified detailed tasks and micromanaged them, but because APM establishes an environment in which people want to excel, meet their goals, and do the best they can.

The last paragraph raises another issue, identified in the phrase "for a given level of uncertainty." While APM is reliable, it is not infallible, and it cannot eliminate the vagaries of uncertainty or the surprises encountered while exploring. APM can shift the odds toward success. If executives expect projects to deliver on the product vision, within the constraints of specified time and cost, every time, without fail—then they should be running an assembly line, not developing products.

Finally, neither the best project manager nor the best team performance can trump organizational politics. Nor can any methodology make up for outrageous fantasies or dictatorial edicts. These traits make for what Ed Yourdon (1999) calls "death march" projects—projects that have failed before they begin and go downhill sharply from there. Agile project management can't deliver on fantasies, and its management style is at the opposite end of the spectrum from dictatorial edicts. Agile methods won't help you on death march projects. The only useful strategies for such projects are (1) to get out—now; (2) if you can't get out, hide; and (3) if you can't hide completely, tell managers exactly what they want to hear—because it's exactly what they deserve.

Progress Reporting

APM is not abdication of control; it's an endorsement of accountability and a revised definition of "what" to control. Project teams should be accountable for performance, for results that they have had a part in planning. Periodic progress reporting assists the project community—executives, project manager, and team—in controlling the project and determining when to take adaptive action. Because agile projects are often exploring areas of high risk and uncertainty, early recognition of issues and problems is essential to early adaptive action. By employing short, timeboxed iterations and reviewing working features that demonstrate real progress (or lack thereof), APM provides the tools needed to identify problems early, when there is a wider set of adaptive actions available, including project termination.

A manufacturing process operates on known information. A product development process essentially purchases information. The uncertainty of product development turns a project into an information discovery process in which money and time are spent gathering requirements, trying out designs, building features (or models), and testing alternatives. At the end of each iteration, additional information is known about the product. The project team, managers, and executives access the progress information, compare it against targets, decide if the project is still viable, determine if new targets are needed, and identify adaptive actions. They are essentially asking the question, "Was the information generated worth the money and time we spent on this last iteration?" This is a very different question than, "Did the project conform to plan?"

Production-style project management begins with deterministic, predictive plans and then exercises control over those plans, so it can be characterized as having a "conformance to plan" control mentality. APM begins with project plans that adapt over time to changing conditions. In order to have both predictability and innovation, we have to broaden our controls from conformance to plan to conformance to vision and value. Conformance to value recognizes the critical nature of the business outcome of a project. If we produce a product that's on schedule, on budget, and meets specifications but doesn't sell in the market, we have not been successful.

The saying "The map is not the territory" should be emblazoned on project progress reports, as some measurements often hide real progress. Working product (or simulations and models, in some cases) are the ultimate in reality-based, verifiable, dependable progress measurements.

Features are done—finished and acceptance tested by customers—or they are not. Measuring feature completion closes the gap between the map and the territory.

Progress reporting helps the project community determine if the project is still moving in the right direction and whether the customer feels that she is getting value for the money. If the customer or product manager confirms that value is being delivered, the project proceeds to the next iterative delivery cycle. If value has not been delivered, then the project is terminated or adaptive action is initiated. At the end of an iteration the customer may say, "I thought I understood what I wanted four weeks ago, but now that I see the results, and based on recent business information, we now need to change direction." Or, the development group may deliver a set of features, but for some reason it missed what the customer intended. In either scenario there is little blaming, and the response is, "Now that we know what we now know, how do we best move forward?"

Leadership-Collaboration Management

Most projects are overmanaged and underled. Admiral Grace Hopper once said, "You cannot manage men into battle: You manage things ... you lead people." What is the difference between project management and project leadership? Although there is an elusive line between them, the core difference is that management deals with complexity, while leadership deals with change. Without adequate management, complex projects rapidly descend into chaos. Plans, controls, budgets, and processes help project managers stave off potential project-threatening complexity. However, when uncertainty, risk, and change are prominent, these practices are insufficient.

Project managers should be both managers and leaders, with the importance of the latter escalating rapidly as the exploratory nature of projects increases.[1] Good leadership contributes significantly to project success. As authors Carl Larson and Frank LaFasto (1989) point out, "Our research

---

1. The terms "project manager" and "team leader" are commonly used. I will use these terms also, but I will emphasize the leadership characteristics of the project manager's role.

strongly indicates that the right person in a leadership role can add tremendous value to any collective effort."

Leaders are leaders not because of what they do, but because of who they are. Authoritarian managers use power, often in the form of fear, to get people to do something their way. Leaders depend for the most part on influence rather than power, and influence derives from respect rather than fear. Respect, in turn, is based on qualities such as integrity, ability, fairness, truthfulness—in short, on character. Leaders are part of the project team, and although they are given organizational authority, their real authority isn't delegated top down but earned bottom up. From the outside a managed team and a led team can look the same, but from the inside they feel very different.

Project managers who are effective at delivering in complex situations—planning in detail, creating organizational positions and roles, monitoring through detailed budget and progress reports, and solving the myriad day-to-day project problems—don't like change. Change leads to paradox and ambiguity, and these managers spend enormous energy trying to drive ambiguity and change out of their projects.

Leaders, as opposed to managers, encourage change—by creating a vision of future possibilities (which are usually short on details), by interacting with a large network of people to discover new information that will help turn the product vision into reality, and by creating a sense of purpose in the endeavor that will motivate people to work on something outside the norm.

Projects, like organizations, need both leaders and managers. Unfortunately, it is often difficult to find both skill sets in the same person. And since creating a project budget is more tangible than, say, resolving the ambiguity that arises when trying to satisfy conflicting customer groups, project management training tends to focus on tangible practices and tools. Growing leadership skills in managers is clearly possible, but it requires a dedication to understanding the differences between the two roles.

As authors Phillip Hodgson and Randall White (2001) observe, "Leadership is what crosses the frontier between what we did yesterday and what we'll do tomorrow. We'll argue ... that the real mark of a leader is confidence with uncertainty—the ability to admit to it and deal with it." The authors pose six questions that illustrate the damaging illusions of our 20th-century approaches to management:

- Why do you believe you are in control?
- Why do you behave as if you can predict the future, its consequences and outcomes?
- Why do you think that because you've done it before and it worked that it will work again?
- Why do you believe everything important is measurable?
- Why do you think that words like leadership, management, and change have the same meaning for everyone?
- Why do you think that reducing uncertainty will necessarily increase certainty? (Hodgson and White 2001)

Agile project managers help their team balance at the edge of chaos—some structure, but not too much; adequate documentation, but not too much; some up-front architecture work, but not too much. Finding these balance points is the "art" of management. While books like this can help readers understand the issues and identify practices that help, only experience can refine a manager's art. High exploration-factor projects are full of anxiety, change, ambiguity, and uncertainty that the project team must deal with. It takes a different style of project management, a different pattern of project team operation, and a different type of project manager. I've labeled this type of management *leadership-collaboration.*

A leadership-collaboration management style creates a certain kind of social architecture, one that enables organizations and teams to face the volatility of their environment. Such a social architecture blends performance and passion, results and egalitarianism. As I've written elsewhere, "Commanders know the objective; leaders grasp the direction. Commanders dictate; leaders influence. Controllers demand; collaborators facilitate. Controllers micro-manage; collaborators encourage. Managers who embrace the leadership-collaboration model understand their primary role is to set direction, to provide guidance, and to facilitate connecting people and teams" (Highsmith 2000). The values of APM resonate with concepts such as egalitarianism, competence, self-discipline, and self-organization. A leadership-collaboration management style creates a social architecture in which these values flourish.

Jim Collins (2001) has a similar concept that he refers to as a "culture of discipline," meaning self-discipline, not imposed discipline. In discussing company growth and the frequent imposition of "professional management" to control that growth, Collins says, "The company begins to hire MBAs and seasoned executives from blue-chip companies. Processes, procedures, checklists, and all the rest begin to sprout up like weeds. What was once an egalitarian environment gets replaced with a hierarchy. They create order out of chaos, but they also kill the entrepreneurial spirit. The purpose of bureaucracy is to compensate for incompetence and lack of discipline."

Or, as Dee Hock (1999) so eloquently puts it, "In the Chaordic Age, success will depend less on rote and more on reason; less on the authority of the few and more on the judgment of the many; less on compulsion and more on motivation; less on external control of people and more on internal discipline." So, the last three guiding principles of APM address how to achieve a leadership-collaboration management style—Encourage Exploration, Build Adaptive (Self-Organizing, Self-Disciplined) Teams, and Simplify.

Encourage Exploration

Change is hard. While agile values tell us that responding to change is more important than following a plan and that embracing rather than resisting change leads to better products, working in a high-change environment can be nerve-wracking for team members. Exploration is difficult; it causes anxiety, trepidation, and sometimes even a little fear. Agile project managers need to encourage and inspire team members to work through the difficulties of a high-change environment. Remaining calm themselves, encouraging experimentation and learning through both successes and mistakes, and helping team members understand the vision are all part of this encouragement. Good leaders create a safe environment in which people can voice outlandish ideas, some of which turn out not to be so outlandish after all. External encouragement and inspiration help teams build internal motivation.

Great explorations flow from inspirational leaders. Cook, Magellan, Shackleton, and Columbus were inspirational leaders with vision. They persevered in the face of monumental obstacles, not the least of which was fear of the unknown. Magellan, after years of dealing with the entrenched Spanish bureaucracy trying to scuttle his plans, launched his five-ship fleet on

October 3, 1519. On September 6, 1522, the *Victoria*, last of the ships, sailed into port without Magellan, who had died in the Philippines after completing the most treacherous part of the journey—establishing a route around Cape Horn and sailing across the vast Pacific Ocean for the first time (Joyner 1992).

Great explorers articulate goals that inspire people—goals that get people excited such that they inspire themselves. These goals or visions serve as a unifying focal point of effort, galvanizing people and creating an esprit de corps among the team. Inspirational goals need to be energizing, compelling, clear, and feasible, but just barely. Inspirational goals tap into a team's passion.

Encouraging leaders also know the difference between good goals and bad ones. We all know of egocentric managers who point to some mountain and say, "Let's get up there, team," when everyone else is thinking, "Who is he kidding? There's not a snowball's chance in the hot place that we can carry that off." "Bad BHAGs [Big Hairy Audacious Goals], it turns out, are set with *bravado*; good BHAGs are set with *understanding*," says Jim Collins (2001). Inspirational leaders know that setting a vision for the product is a team effort, one based on analysis, understanding, and realistic risk assessment, combined with a sprinkle of adventure.

Innovative product development teams are led, not managed. They allow their leaders to be inspirational. They internalize the leader's encouragement. Great new products, outstanding enhancements to existing products, and creative new business initiatives are driven by passion and inspiration. Project managers who focus on network diagrams, cost budgets, and resource histograms are dooming their teams to mediocrity.[2, 3]

Leaders help articulate the goals; teams internalize them and motivate themselves. This internal motivation enables exploration. We don't arrive at something new, better, different without trial and error, launching off in

---

2. This sentence should not be interpreted as saying these things are unimportant, because, properly used, each can be useful to the project manager. It is when they become the focal point that trouble ensues.

3. Ken Delcol observes, "Most PMs are not selected for their ability to inspire people! Leadership and business influencing skills are hard to establish in an interview. Most managers have a difficult time identifying and evaluating people with these skill sets."

multiple new directions in order to find the one that seems promising. Magellan and his ships spent 38 days covering the 334 miles of the straits that now bear his name. In the vast expanse of islands and peninsulas, they explored many dead ends before finding the correct passages (Kelley 2001).

Magellan's ship *Victoria* sailed nearly 1,000 miles, back and forth—up estuaries that dead-ended, and back out—time and time again. Magellan (his crew, actually) was the first to circumnavigate the globe. But he would probably have driven a production-style project manager or executive a little crazy, because he surely didn't follow a plan. But then, any detailed plan would have been foolish—no one even knew if ships could get around Cape Horn; none had found the way when Magellan launched. No one knew how large the Pacific Ocean was, and even the best guestimates turned out to be thousands of miles short. His vision never changed, but his "execution" changed every day based on new information.

Teams need a shared purpose and goal, but they also need encouragement to experiment, explore, make mistakes, regroup, and forge ahead again.

Shared Space

"The biggest single trend we've observed is the growing acknowledgment of innovation as a centerpiece of corporate strategies," says Tom Kelley (2001), general manager of IDEO, one of the world's leading industrial design firms. IDEO uses a combination of methodologies, work practices, culture, and infrastructure to create an environment conducive to innovation. Its methodology includes understanding the issues, observing real people, visualizing through the use of simulations and prototypes, evaluating and refining the prototypes, and implementing the concept. The use of prototypes, simulations, and models has a profound influence on IDEO's entire product design process.

"Virtually every significant marketplace innovation in this century is a direct result of extensive prototyping and simulation," says Michael Schrage (2000). His investigation into the world of prototypes—starting with his work at the Media Lab at MIT—led him to a startling conclusion: "You didn't have to be a sociologist to realize that the Lab's demo culture wasn't just about creating clever ideas; it was about creating clever interactions between people."

Innovation cannot be guaranteed by some deterministic process—innovation is the result of an emergent process, one in which the interaction of individuals with creative ideas results in something new and different. Demos, prototypes, simulations, and models are the catalysts for these clever interactions. They constitute the "shared space" (Schrage's term) in which developers, marketers, customers, and managers can have meaningful interactions.

Shared space has two requirements—visualization and commonality. One of the common problems in the product development field has been that requirements documents had neither quality. When engineers moved to conversations with customers around prototypes and working features rather than documents, the quality of the interactions increased dramatically. Visualization drives industrial design today. For example, Alias Systems, whose software builds special effects for today's movies—*Lord of the Rings, Spiderman, Harry Potter*—also provides sophisticated software to industrial designers who need to visualize their products early in the development process.

Commonality means that the prototype needs to be understood by all parties that have a stake in the development effort. So, for example, while electrical circuit diagrams might help electrical and manufacturing engineers communicate, they wouldn't create a shared space for marketing or customer representatives. Project leaders need to be aware, at each stage of the project, of who needs to interact at that stage and what the shared space needs to be in order for that to happen.

Project teams need encouraging leadership that may come at various times from the project manager, a technical architect, or a team member. Delivering tangible features at frequent intervals—creating this shared space that drives the team to creative interactions—is a key tool of encouraging innovation.

Encouragement Isn't Enough

Encouragement extends beyond rousing speeches to providing the mechanisms for innovation. As Tom DeMarco (2003) advises, if you want to invent something new, don't also try to wrest every minute of time from your team. They need time to think, to experiment, to brainstorm. "People under time pressure don't *think* faster," comments Tim Lister.[4] Management needs to set some time to do this outside of a project's time constraint, particularly for key technology feasibility studies.

Inspiration needs to be primed with policies and practices. For continually delivering new, innovative products—decade after decade—no company bests 3M. The company backs up its core ideology of constant innovation with specific mechanisms, such as a long-standing policy that gives researchers a percentage of their time to investigate ideas of their own. 3M also has a series of prestigious award programs that recognize entrepreneurship, dissemination of technology, stimulation of new technology, and cross-fertilization of ideas across the company (Collins and Porras 1994).

Year after year IDEO wins more design competitions than any other firm. General manager Tom Kelley outlines the team environment he thinks builds "Hot Teams":

- First, they were totally dedicated to achieving the end result.
- Second, they faced down a slightly ridiculous deadline.
- Third, the group was irreverent and nonhierarchical.
- Fourth, the team was well rounded and respectful of its diversity.
- Fifth, they worked in an open, eclectic space optimal for flexibility, group work, and brainstorming.
- Finally, the group felt empowered to go get whatever else it needed (Kelley 2001).

While there seems to be a contradiction between DeMarco's and 3M's "give them time" and Kelley's "slightly ridiculous deadline" advice, I think they are actually compatible. Astute project managers know that meeting a tight deadline may be achieved by reducing the day-to-day pressure rather than constant harping on the team. In a pressure-cooker environment, people have, or at least perceive that they have, no time to think; they just have time to do. With less pressure and more encouragement to interact with each other, teams can actually go faster in the long run by slowing down today.

Looking at Kelley's list, we see that innovation comes from breaking down rigidities—interpersonal, space, organizational—while concentrating

---

4. Quoted in (DeMarco 2003).

on the end result and its key time constraint. Managers who want to build innovative products, who want to inspire their teams to greatness, need to constantly strive for a well-defined goal and create a fluid team environment.

Developing great products—particularly new, version 1.0 products—requires exploration, not tracking against a plan. Magellan had a vision, a goal, and some general ideas about sailing from Spain down the coast of South America, avoiding Portuguese ships if at all possible, finding a way around Cape Horn, then tracking across the Pacific to once-again known territory in the Southeast Asia archipelagoes. Great new products come from similarly audacious goals and rough plans that often have large gaps in which "miracles happen," much like the miracle of finding the Straits of Magellan.

Build Adaptive (Self-Organizing, Self-Disciplined) Teams

Adaptive teams form the core of APM. They blend freedom with responsibility, flexibility with structure. In the face of inconsistency and ambiguity, the team's goal is to consistently deliver on the product vision (including adaptability) within the project's scope. Accomplishing this requires teams with a self-organizing structure and self-disciplined individual team members. Building this kind of team is the core of an agile project manager's job.

A simple definition of a team is that it has a defined goal, consists of two or more people, and requires coordination among those people (Larson and LaFasto 1989). Beyond this definition, there are numerous variations in team composition and structure, but the self-organizing team seems best fitted for exploratory work. In a self-organized team, individuals take responsibility for managing their own workload, shift work among themselves based on need and best fit, and participate in team decision making. Team members have considerable leeway in how they deliver results, but they are accountable for those results and for working within the established flexible framework.

Self-organizing teams are not, as some perceive, leaderless teams. Any group left to its own devices will self-organize in some fashion, but to be effective in delivering results, it needs to be steered in the right direction. Self-organizing teams aren't characterized by a lack of leadership, but by a *style* of leadership. There is a big difference between the terms "self-organizing" and "self-directing." Self-directing usually implies self-led, as various team members assume the leadership role depending upon the situation. The self-directing model runs counter to much research that indicates good leaders are a major ingredient of project and organizational success (Larson and LaFasto 1989).

Creating a self-organizing framework entails:

- Getting the right people
- Articulating the product vision, boundaries, and team roles
- Encouraging interaction and information flow between teams
- Facilitating participatory decision making
- Insisting on accountability
- Steering, not controlling

In Michael Kennedy's (2003) wonderful book on the Toyota lean product development system, he states, "This book is about the interaction of people and how to manage or influence that interaction." Ultimately, APM is also about people and their interactions and about creating an environment in which individual creativity and capability erupt to create great products. It's people, not structure, that build great products.

Getting the Right People

The organization, through the project manager or other managers, has the responsibility to staff the project with the right people. At the team level, getting the right people means finding those with appropriate technical and behavioral skills. At the project level, the project manager works to ensure that the right leaders are assigned to each team. The project manager should have the authority to reject any team member that other managers might want to assign, unilaterally, to the project.

The agile value of people over process drives the need to get the right people. Process proponents argue that a good process will compensate for less capable staff, and therefore getting the right people isn't as critical to success as getting the right process. Agilists believe that process can provide a common framework within which people can work effectively, but it cannot replace capability and skill. Products are built by capable, skilled individuals, not by processes. Effective project managers focus on people, product, and process—in that order. Without the right people, nothing gets built. Without a laser focus on the product, extraneous activities creep in. Without at least a process framework, there can be inefficiency and possibly a little chaos.

Getting the right people (which implies, of course, getting rid of the wrong ones) and the right managers determines project success more than any other factor. (I will cover the issue of getting the right people in more detail in Chapter 5.)

Articulating the Product Vision

The project manager ensures that every individual understands the product vision and his or her role in the project. The vision might include a vision box (described in Chapter 5) and an architectural overview to help team members grasp the big picture, as well as component descriptions and interface definitions to help them get a sense of their piece of the product. In addition to understanding product responsibilities, individuals need to understand their roles with respect to the others.

Comprehending the product vision also includes understanding the project's boundary conditions. For example, the project manager (or product manager) needs to help the team grasp not only the actual schedule, but also why the dates are critical. She needs to convey to the team a sense of what the few high-priority areas are and why they are high priority. The better the team members comprehend the reasons for project constraints, the better they can help in meeting those constraints and making tradeoff decisions in their day-to-day work.

Articulating the product vision is not a one-time activity. Products evolve. New people are added to a project. In the heat of daily activity, visions become blurred. Articulating the vision, the end result desired, should be an ongoing task of project and product management.

Encouraging Interaction

The capability of self-organizing teams lies in collaboration—the interaction and cooperation of two or more people to jointly produce a result. When two engineers scratch out a design on a whiteboard, they are collaborating. When team members meet to brainstorm a design, they are collaborating. When team leaders meet to decide if a product is ready to ship, they are collaborating. The result of any collaboration can be categorized as a tangible deliverable, a decision, or shared knowledge.

The quality of results from any collaborative effort is driven by trust and respect, free flow of information, debate, and active participation—bound together by a participatory decision-making process. When any of these components is missing or ineffective, the quality of the results suffers. In a collaborative team, one of the key leader roles involves facilitating, coaching, cajoling, and influencing the team members to build healthy relationships.

At the core of healthy team relationships is trust and respect. When team members don't respect the knowledge and capabilities of others, meaningful debate falters. The line between confidence and arrogance can be awfully narrow, and individuals sometimes bluster to cover up lack of knowledge. The project manager melds a group of people into a working team by working through these types of issues—and getting the wrong people off the team when necessary.

Complex systems, such as large project organizations, thrive on interaction and information flow. The project management team should be constantly asking questions such as, "Are the right people coordinating with each other about the right things at the right times?" and "Is the right information available at the right time?" These are critical questions whose answers can help the team operate smoothly or bog the team down. The design engineer who fails to include the ideas of the manufacturing engineer ends up with products that are too expensive to make. Software engineers who fail to work closely with QA build code that is difficult and expensive to test. Too little coordination and information, and teams will diverge so far that integration becomes a nightmare (hence the need for frequent integration). Too much coordination and information flow, and teams become mired in constant meetings and information overload.

Project managers need to focus on interaction, collaboration, and coordination first and appropriate documentation second, because documentation discourages conversation. One of the problems with serial product development, and one reason why companies have moved to cross-functional teams, is that it tends to discourage people from interacting by suggesting, implicitly at least, that documentation provides the information they need. Complex, tacit information is primarily conveyed by interaction and conversation (probably in the range of 70% to 75%) and only secondarily by documentation (25% to 30%). Understanding, not documentation, is the goal of information transfer. Documentation-heavy teams will have difficulty achieving agility.

Although collaboration and interaction drive effective agile development, not all engineers (and other team members) are effective communicators.[5] This fact gives rise to another key role for agile project managers and team leaders: coach. Agile project managers will assist team members in developing the interaction skills they need to become effective collaborators.

Participatory Decision Making

Decision making is the heart and soul of collaboration. Anyone can sit down and chat about a product design. Collaboration means working together to build a feature, create a design, or write a product's documentation. Collaboration is a joint effort. So whether you are designing with another individual or struggling with feature priorities or deciding if the product is ready to ship, there are literally thousands of decisions, large and small, to be made over the life of a project. How a team makes those decisions determines whether the team is a truly collaborative one. Some teams are driven to quick decisions by a senior technical individual, while others are driven by those with the loudest voice. Neither situation is conducive to true collaboration.

Several years ago, I wrote an article on distributed decision making. In researching that article, I reviewed six books on project management and found only one paragraph on decision making. Many, if not most, process-centric approaches to both product development and project management seem to spend no time on decision-making processes. But for all the general neglect, team decision-making capabilities are absolutely critical to successful project management, agile or otherwise. From feasibility go/no-go decisions, to whether or not to release a product, to each and every minute

---

5. Ken Delcol makes a sobering point about collaboration. "Most people in product development are not collaborative; they do not like to talk to each other. Innovation requires interactions and exchange of ideas, and if you don't like talking to people, this becomes difficult. Companies need to develop environments, both physical and cultural, that prompt/demand/expect collaboration. Part of the reason for lack of collaboration is the education system for technical people."

design choice—the way teams make decisions will have a major impact on their performance.

Leadership is also critical to good decision making. In innovative product development work there are thousands of decisions to be made—and the information available to make those decisions often remains fuzzy. Customer preferences may be fuzzy. The new technology being used may be untried, and therefore fuzzy. For every clear decision to be made there are ten others that require "fuzzy" logic. Teams can become paralyzed by this fuzziness and oscillate back and forth over decisions. When all the discussion, debate, and dialogue have reached an impasse—when the ambiguity of the situation overwhelms the decision-making capability of the team—the leader often has to step in and say, "Well, the direction isn't abundantly clear, but we're going East." An effective leader "absorbs" the ambiguity, takes responsibility for the decision, and allows the team to get on with its work. Knowing when and how to carry this off is one mark of an effective leader.

There are two words that engineers seem to hate most, maybe because they see a relationship between the two—politics and compromise. Compromise results from win-lose thinking, in which I am right and you are wrong. An alternative model is win-win thinking, in which reconceiving replaces compromise.[6] Reconceiving means combining ideas to create something better than any individual could create on her own. It isn't giving up, but adding to. Innovation and creativity are emergent, not causal, properties of teamwork. There is no set of steps that guarantees innovation; it *emerges* from a melding of gradually expanding ideas that are the results of interaction. In this process there are pieces of your ideas, and pieces of mine, that contribute to the eventual solution. This process of melding ideas, of subjecting them to discussion, of analyzing them in the light of our product's vision and constraints, is not a process of compromise, but one of reconceiving. Compromise polarizes. Reconceiving unites.

However, win-win or reconceiving should not imply consensus decision making. Participation doesn't mean consensus either. Self-organizing teams have managers who make unilateral decisions on occasion, but their primary style is inclusive, to encourage wide participation in decision making in order to make the best decisions. Self-organized teams have a lot of discretionary

---

6. Colleague Rob Austin originated the use of the word "reconceive" in this way.

decision-making authority, but it is balanced with that of the project manager. As in other areas, balance is the key to agility in decision making.

Insisting on Accountability

Responsibility and accountability create self-organizing teams that work. When an individual commits to delivering a particular feature during an iteration, he accepts accountability for that delivery. When the team commits to a set of features by the end of the second project milestone, all members of the team accept accountability for that. When the product manager is involved in iteration planning, she has agreed to be accountable for providing requirements information to the team. The project manager agrees to be accountable for resolving impediments to team progress. When a team member commits to provide some information to another the next day, he has agreed to be accountable for that action. When team members commit to each other, when the team commits to the customer, when the project manager commits to provide the team with a particular resource, they are all agreeing to be held accountable. And it is incumbent on each and every team member and the project manager to hold each other to those commitments. Trust is the foundation of collaboration, and meeting one's commitments is core to building trust.

Steering, Not Controlling

Leaderless teams are rudderless teams. Managers who want to create an adaptive, self-organizing project teams steer rather than control—they influence, nudge, facilitate, recommend, assist, urge, counsel, and, yes, direct in some instances. They view themselves as teachers (Larson and LaFasto 1989).

Micromanagers will always have to micromanage, complaining the whole time about staff members who are unwilling to take responsibility. But what about individuals and teams that don't have experience working in a self-organizing manner? Surely they need a heavier managerial hand until they are self-disciplined enough to fulfill their part of the freedom-responsibility bargain, right? Alas, destructuring rarely follows structuring. Managers whose fundamental beliefs tend toward structure rather than flexibility rarely give up the power and control necessary to create an adaptive organization.

To achieve an adaptable, self-organizing team, the project manager grants the team as much autonomy as possible, destructures to the extent possible, and then coaches individuals and gets rid of those who don't fit.

Steering is not abdication of decision making. Self-directing (as opposed to self-organizing) teams—those that theoretically don't have a single leader—tend to drift and procrastinate, which is not appropriate for fast-moving product development teams. Steering means the manager makes unilateral decisions at times and makes decisions with team involvement at other times, but primarily delegates decisions to the team.

Self-Discipline

Self-discipline enables freedom and empowerment. When individuals and teams want more autonomy, they must exercise greater self-discipline. One of the acute dangers of process-centric development and project management is that they remove any incentive for self-discipline. When managers impose discipline through detailed processes—"follow this process or else"—they stifle initiative and self-discipline. These same managers then turn around and complain, "Why doesn't anyone around here take any initiative or accept any responsibility?" Imposed-disciplined teams gets things accomplished. Self-disciplined teams accomplish near-miraculous things.

Self-disciplined individuals:

- Accept accountability for results
- Confront reality through rigorous thinking
- Engage in intense interaction and debate
- Work willingly within a self-organizing framework
- Respect colleagues

Dialogue, discussion, and participatory decision making are all part of building self-discipline. A series of words scattered throughout Jim Collins's book *Good to Great* (2001) creates an image of the rigorous thinking and debate that are core to self-discipline—truth and brutal facts; dialogue and debate, not coercion; a penchant for dialogue; questioning. Collins found that individuals in great companies were extremely interactive, engaging in debates that often lasted a long time.

Self-discipline is also built on competence, persistence, and the willingness to assume accountability for results. Competence is more than skill and ability; it's attitude and experience. Get the right people involved, and self-discipline comes more easily. Get the wrong people, and imposed discipline creeps in, destroying trust, respect, and the egalitarian atmosphere. "The point is to first get self-disciplined people who engage in very rigorous thinking, who then take disciplined action within the framework of a consistent system," says Collins (2001). One reason would-be agile teams don't succeed is that they fail to realize the self-discipline required. There is no binary switch to go from no discipline to self-discipline; it's a journey that some individuals get right away, while others need to take a longer trip.

Simplify

If you want to be fast and agile, keep things simple. Speed isn't the result of simplicity, but simplicity enables speed.[7] If you want to be slow and rigid, pile on the bureaucracy. A friend who once worked for NASA relayed the story of his team's unique software design criterion—least impact on documentation. The documentation revision process was so onerous and time consuming that minimizing the documentation changes became the major design objective. This is a clear example of how compliance work not only impedes delivery by draining away engineering time, but also undermines technical design decisions.

When you simplify processes by taking out the detailed tasks and compliance, you force people to think and to interact. Neither they nor their managers can use structure as a crutch. While some structure aids agility, the overabundance of structure in many organizations gives people an excuse not to think, or bludgeons them into not thinking. Either way, people feel their contributions are devalued, and they lose any sense of personal responsibility or accountability for results.

---

7. Colleague Luke Hohmann has a speed-oriented catch phrase that he shared with me: "When you want your boat to go fast, it is easier to cut anchors than add horsepower."

GUIDING PRINCIPLES: LEADERSHIP-COLLABORATION MANAGEMENT

Generative Rules

The epitome of simple rules lies within Nordstrom's employee handbook—a 5×8-inch card that outlines Nordstrom's goal of providing outstanding customer service and lists the company's rules:

> *Rule #1: Use your good judgment in all situations. There will be no additional rules* (Collins and Porras 1994).

Simple principles (or rules) are one facet of "swarm intelligence" from complexity theory. This is the idea that the right set of simple rules, applied within a group of highly interactive individuals, generates complex behaviors such as innovation and creativity. Jim Donehey, former CIO of Capital One, used four rules to help ensure everyone in his organization was working toward the same shared goals:

1. Always align IT activities with the business.
2. Use good economic judgment.
3. Be flexible.
4. Have empathy for others in the organization (Bonabeau and Meyer 2001).

Do these four rules constitute everything that Donehey's department needed to do? Of course not, but would a 400-page activity description get the job done? What Donehey wanted was bounded innovation—a department that thought for itself in a very volatile business environment, but also one that understood boundaries.

Principles do not define activities that a development group should accomplish. However, the right set constitutes the minimum set of rules that bound innovative and productive work. They create an innovative environment by specifying a simple set of rules that generate complex behavior. APM, for example, doesn't include a configuration control practice. It assumes that when a team needs configuration control, it will figure out a minimum configuration control practice and use it. Agile methods don't attempt to describe *everything* that any development effort might need in thousands of pages of documentation. Instead, they describe a minimum set of activities that is needed to create swarm intelligence.

Developing a useful set of rules is not a trivial exercise, since the right combination can often be counterintuitive. Apparently minor changes can have unforeseen results. Changing one practice, without understanding the interactions and the concepts of swarm intelligence, can cause an agile system to react in unforeseen ways. The guiding principles of APM, and its practices, constitute a set of rules that have been shown to work together well.

Barely Sufficient Methodology

When deciding on process, methodology, practices, documentation, or other aspects of product development, the admonition to simplify steers us toward a bare sufficiency, toward streamlining, toward implementing "a little bit less than just enough." Simplicity needs to balance the need for speed and flexibility with retaining enough stability to ward off careless mistakes. Barely sufficient does not mean *in*sufficient. It does not mean "no documentation" or "no process." Furthermore, barely sufficient for a 100-person project will be very different from barely sufficient for a project of only 10 people.

John Wooden's admonition to his basketball teams seems appropriate here: "Be *quick*, but don't hurry." As author Andrew Hill (2001) recounts his playing days with Wooden, he enriches the meaning of the phrase "Life, like basketball, must be played fast—but *never* out of control." In product development, lack of quickness results in competitive disadvantage, while hurrying causes mistakes. Balancing, one of the keys to agility, was part of Wooden's coaching technique. As Hill writes, "Wooden's genius was in helping his players find and maintain that razor's edge between quickness and hurrying." Finding that razor's edge isn't easy. If it was, everyone would be doing it.

An engineer who hurries to design a feature but fails to adequately review or test it creates defects that ultimately slow the project. Delivery activities done quickly and effectively speed projects, while overemphasis on compliance activities act as a speed break. Selecting the activities that absolutely, positively have to be done, and doing them well, contributes to quickness. Sloppy execution of those key activities can be the consequence of hurrying.

One of the competitive advantages of finding this balance, of being quick without hurrying, is that it often forces the competition into hurrying. This is actually one of the potential dangers of implementing agile project management and development approaches. Less disciplined organizations and teams may confuse quickness with hurrying and misunderstand the foundational work, experience, and dedication it takes to balance on the edge. Wooden used the fast break to increase the tempo of the game enough that the opponent was pressured into hurrying. Because of his team members' discipline and work ethic, they could play faster than opponents but still be in control. Project teams can use the same strategy.

New product development teams inhabit a world of growing complexity, developing ever more complex products while being bombarded with a bewildering array of information. Leaders who can coax simplifications out of the complexity, who can institute just enough process, who can find that razor's edge between quickness and hurrying have a much better chance of success.

Principles to Practices

Ultimately, what people *do*, how they *behave*, is what creates great products. Principles and practices are guides; they help identify and reinforce certain behaviors. In agile development the behaviors we want to encourage are *thinking*, *acting*, and *interacting*. We want knowledgeable people to glean new information from the product development process; apply that new information thoughtfully; and to interact with their peers to generate emergent, innovative ideas and apply those ideas to the building of real, demonstrable product components.

While principles guide agile teams, specific practices are necessary to actually accomplish work. A process structure and specific practices form a minimal, flexible framework for self-organizing teams. The next five chapters identify and describe the processes and practices of APM.

Chapter 4

An Agile Project Management Model

Principles and Practices

"Hi, Maya, it's Herman."

"Hi, dude, how's your project going?" asked Maya.

"Pretty well. Things are actually moving along. We've implemented a few of the agile practices. But you know, I'm just an action kind of guy. Just explain the practices to me. The principles stuff still seems like fluff."

"I thought they were fluff, too, at the beginning," Maya responded. "But once you've used APM for a while, you'll understand that it's the principles that make the practices flexible."

"OK, apply principles to iteration planning."

"Think about Deliver Customer Value. For us, this principle guides the selection of features. We're constantly asking ourselves whether one feature is more valuable than the next."

"But won't most of the features ship anyway?"

"Possibly, but we keep two things in mind. Sometimes we release incremental versions, and the goal of always having a releasable product really keeps us on our toes."

"Isn't early release unlikely?" Herman asked.

"Mostly, but last summer we had a customer with a critical problem. We were able to take a product that was three-quarters finished, do a couple of quick special features for the customer, and deliver it in three weeks. The customer was blown away, and this one spends megabucks."

"So, on to the Employ Iterative, Feature-Based Delivery principle. That seems redundant with the practice to me, but maybe that just reinforces its importance."

"That's the general idea. See, you already understand this stuff, Herman! You just don't trust it yet." Maya grinned to herself. She knew it was hard for Herman, who worked for a 75-year-old insurance firm, to break with the conservative, traditional approach that Great Mid-West had always taken to everything, but he was trying, and she gave him lots of credit.

"That's fine as far as it goes, but does this scale? You and I both know that any competent PM can complete a small, short-term project on force of will alone, but that all changes when you scale the whole thing up."

"Yeah, but that's where the Simplify principle comes in. It's how you scale everything up without tripping over yourself and your process. For example, on Jupiter, the new project I'm running, we have a big team. And to make matters worse, one feature team is distributed. Adopting a collaboration strategy was a given, but we also figured that we might need some additional documentation to keep everyone in sync."

Herman interrupted with a "See, I told you so."

"But the Simplify principle keeps it from turning into the pounds of paperwork you generate," Maya laughed. "We're bears about using the simplest documentation that accomplishes the goal. We work with just a few documents and keep them as informal as we can. Then we adapt them from time to time as we find what works and what doesn't."

"So, you use the principles to help adapt practices to specific situations," Herman said.

"Right. Without these guiding principles we could get hung up on the specific practices instead of understanding the intent of the practices. They keep us from going overboard."

"One I really get hung up on is Encourage Exploration," Herman replied. "This whole notion of responding to change over following a plan, of actually embracing change, is really foreign."

"That's a tough one," said Maya. "We can respond to change and deliver reliably. It's all in how you look at the relationship between uncertainty and time."

"My management doesn't care. They just want a commitment," said Herman.

"There is no way around the fact that the higher the uncertainty, the wider the potential schedule variation," said Maya. "It's too bad you aren't here—I need a whiteboard to draw this, but imagine that the probability curve of schedules is a skewed distribution curve, one with a long tail of possible very late delivery dates. High exploration-factor projects have a lot of possible dates based upon technology and requirements volatility."

"Everyone around here just assumes a project is a project is a project. There's no allowance for riskier projects—we just get the mantra 'on time, on budget, on scope' over and over. It's like a broken record."

"Don't remind me. Hopefully we're past that. In effect, the role of dates changes. In low-uncertainty projects, dates are predictions. For high-uncertainty projects, dates are boundaries, as in 'We will deliver as many features as possible by June.' Does that make sense?"

"I think I understand, but I'm not sure if the folks around here will get it," Herman said.

"It took us a while to work through it, too," Maya continued. "That's why the principle Encourage Exploration is critical to reducing people's anxiety. I have to keep encouraging people and reminding them that responding to change is part of our day-to-day work. We always have a few people from a conformance-to-plan type organization who get a little crazy at first. We project managers have to encourage them."

"Lots to think about," said Herman. "Bye for now."

An Agile Process Framework

Process may not be as important as people, but it's far from unimportant. Process has gotten a bad rap in agile circles (much of it deserved) as being static, prescriptive, and difficult to change. But process, per se, doesn't have to be negative, although in many companies the move to "improve process" leads down a slippery slope to standardization and certification, at which point the static, prescriptive, and difficult to change criticisms are generally accurate. Process, like anything else, must be tied to business objectives. If the business objective is repeatable manufacturing, then a prescriptive process may be completely justified. However, if the business objective is reliable innovation, then the process framework must be organic, flexible, and easy to adapt. An agile process framework needs to embody the principles described in the last two chapters. In addition to supporting business objectives, the framework needs to:

- Support an envision, explore, adapt culture
- Support self-organizing, self-disciplined teams
- Promote reliability and consistency to the extent possible given the level of project uncertainty
- Be flexible and easy to adapt
- Support visibility into the process
- Incorporate learning
- Incorporate practices that support each phase
- Provide management checkpoints for review

The APM model's structure—Envision-Speculate-Explore-Adapt-Close— focuses on delivery (execution) and adaptation (see Figure 4.1). It is based on the Speculate-Collaborate-Learn model first described in *Adaptive Software Development* (Highsmith 2000). In the APM model, the Explore phase replaces the Collaborate phase in the earlier model. Although collaboration practices dominate the phase, the "action" is better described by Explore. Similarly, while Learn reflects the monitoring portion of a feedback-gathering phase, Adapt completes the loop. Not only is the team learning, it is also taking action on that learning.

The APM phase names reflect both activities and results. For example, the Envision phase results in a project vision. Furthermore, the departure from traditional phase names—such as Initiate, Plan, Manage, Control— while subtle, is significant. First, "Envision" replaces the more traditional "Initiate" to indicate the criticality of vision. Second, a Speculate phase replaces a Plan phase. Words convey certain meanings, and those meanings arise from systematic use over time. The word "plan" has become associated with prediction and relative certainty. "Speculate" indicates that the future is uncertain. We know the future of any project, particularly high exploration-factor projects, contains uncertainty, but we still try to "plan" that uncertainty away. We have to learn to *speculate* and *adapt* rather than *plan* and *build*.

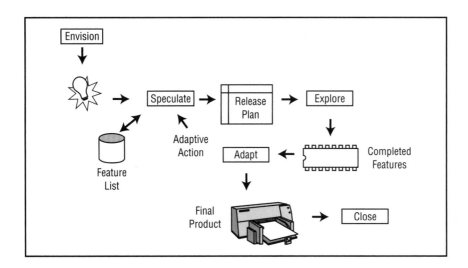

Figure 4.1
The APM Process
Framework

Third, the APM model replaces the common Manage phase with Explore. Explore, with its iterative delivery style, is *explicitly* a nonlinear, concurrent, non-waterfall model. Questions developed in the Speculate phase are "explored." Speculating implies the need for flexibility based on the fact that you cannot fully predict the results. The APM model emphasizes execution and the fact that it is exploratory rather than deterministic. Fourth, a team practicing APM keeps its eyes on the vision, monitors information, and adapts to current conditions—therefore the Adapt phase. Finally, the APM model ends with a Close phase, in which the primary objectives are knowledge transfer and, of course, a celebration.

To sum up, the five phases of agile project management are:

1. **Envision**: determine the product vision and project scope, the project community, and how the team will work together
2. **Speculate**: develop a feature-based release, milestone, and iteration plan to deliver on the vision
3. **Explore**: deliver tested features in a short timeframe, constantly seeking to reduce the risk and uncertainty of the project
4. **Adapt**: review the delivered results, the current situation, and the team's performance, and adapt as necessary
5. **Close**: conclude the project, pass along key learnings, and celebrate

Phase: Envision

The Envision phase creates a vision for the customers and the project team that covers what, who, and how. Absent a vision, the remaining activities in getting a project off the ground are wasted effort. In business-speak, vision is the "critical success factor" early in a project. First, we need to envision *what* to deliver—a vision of the product and the scope of the project. Second, we need to envision *who* will be involved—the community of customers, product managers, project team members, and stakeholders. And, third, the project team members must envision *how* they intend to work together.

Phase: Speculate

The word "speculate" first calls to mind an image of reckless risk taking, but actually the dictionary definition is "to conjecture something based on incomplete facts or information," which is exactly what happens during this phase.[1] The word "plan" has come to connote certainty and prediction, while the more useful definition of plan, for exploratory projects at least, is speculating or hypothesizing based on incomplete information. Colleague Ken Delcol makes a great observation: "People believe when they plan that they introduce certainty, which is far from the truth. What they introduce is something to gauge their performance by. Then, when the gauge does not reflect reality, they fail to replan." APM consists more of envisioning and exploring than planning and doing—it forces us to confront the reality of today's precarious business environment and highly volatile product development environment.

The Speculate phase, which is actually an extension of and interactive with the Envision phase, consists of:

- Gathering the initial broad requirements for the product
- Defining the workload as a list of product features

---

1. Encarta® World English Dictionary, © 1999, 2000 Microsoft Corporation.

- Creating a delivery plan (release, milestones, and iterations) that includes schedule and resource allocations for those features
- Incorporating risk mitigation strategies into the plan
- Estimating project costs and generating other required administrative and financial information

Phase: Explore

The Explore phase delivers product features. From a project management perspective there are three critical activity areas during this phase. The first is delivering planned features by managing the workload and using appropriate technical practices and risk mitigation strategies. The second is creating a collaborative, self-organizing project community, which is everyone's responsibility but is facilitated by the project manager. The third activity is managing the team's interactions with customers, product management, and other stakeholders.

Phase: Adapt

Control and correction are common terms applied to this lifecycle phase. Plans are made, results are monitored, and corrections are made—implying that the plans were right and the actual results, if different from the plan, are wrong. "Adapt" implies modification or change rather than success or failure. In projects guided by the philosophy that responding to change is more important than following a plan, attributing failure to variation from the plan isn't productive. A purely ad hoc process fails to learn from its mistakes, whereas the incorporation and retention of lessons learned are key pieces of APM.

After the Envision phase, the loop will generally be Speculate-Explore-Adapt, with each iteration successively refining the product. However, periodically revisiting the Envision phase may be necessary as the team gathers new information.

In the Adapt phase the results are reviewed from customer, technical, people and process performance, and project status perspectives. The analysis looks at actual versus planned, but even more importantly, it considers actual versus a revised outlook on the project given up-to-the-minute information. The results of adaptation are fed into a replanning effort to begin the next iteration.

Phase: Close

Projects are partially defined by the presence of both a beginning and an end. Many organizations fail to identify a project's end point, often causing perception problems among customers. Projects should end—with a celebration. The key objective of the Close phase, and the "mini" close at the end of each iteration, is learning and incorporating that learning into the work of the next iteration or passing it on to the next project team.

Judgment Required

Because of product and project management's long history of favoring serial development processes, any figure like that of Figure 4.1 can take on a serial appearance. However, while a project may follow the general sequence of Envision, Speculate, Explore, Adapt, and Close, the entire model should be considered fluid. The wording of production-style models implies linearity—Initiate, Plan, Manage, Control—while the APM terms were selected to imply iterative evolution—Speculate, Explore, Adapt.

An overemphasis on linearity leads to stagnation, just as an overemphasis on evolution leads to endless, and eventually mindless, change. With either model, development team members, customer team members, and executives need to exercise keen judgment in its application.

Project Size

The core values and principles of APM are applicable to projects of any size. Similarly, the practices described in the next few chapters are applicable to projects of any size. However, for project teams that exceed 50 or so people, additional practices or extensions to the described practices may be necessary—some of which are described in Chapter 9. As project teams get larger, more documentation, additional coordination practices, increased ceremony, or other compliance activities (financial controls, for example) are usually needed. However, even these expanded practices should still be governed by APM's values and principles. For example, the principle of Simplify still applies to a large project; it just means to employ the simplest practice that works for a team of 150 rather than one of 15.

A 500-person team can't be as agile as a 10-person team, but it *can* be more agile than a competitor's 500-person team. By focusing on delivery, self-organization, and self-discipline, even larger teams burdened with complex coordination issues can readily adapt to business, technology, and organizational changes.

Agile Practices

The next four chapters describe specific practices that align with the agile values and guiding principles for each of the APM framework phases. These practices should be considered a "system of practices," because as a system, they reinforce each other as they align with values and principles. But they do more than align; they implement. Principles without practices are empty shells, while practices without principles tend to be implemented by rote, without judgment. Without principles, we don't know "how" to implement practices—for example, without a Simplify principle we tend to overdo the formality and ceremony of almost any practice. Principles guide practices. Practices instantiate principles. They go hand in hand.

Aligning principles and practices prompts the realization that the holy grail of "best practices" is a sham. A wonderful practice for one project team may be a terrible practice for another. Practices are just practices—various ways of carrying out some goal. A practice is only good or bad within some context, which might include principles, problem type (e.g., exploratory), team dynamics, and organizational culture.

The practices in the following chapters have proven useful in a variety of situations. Some could be useful in production-style projects, just as practices not included may be very useful in agile projects. In selecting and using these practices, I've used these guiding principles:

- Simple
- Generative, not prescriptive
- Aligned with agile values and principles
- Focused on delivery (value adding), not compliance
- Minimum set (just enough to get the job done)
- Mutually supportive (a system of practices)

Few, if any, of the practices described in the following chapters are new. Some of them are variations on a theme of practices described by others. Some are well known; others are not so well known. For example, risk management practices are widely described in the project management literature, while others, like participatory decision making, are not. Therefore, common practices such as risk management will be briefly described and other resources will be referenced, while less well-covered practices such as decision making will be described in more detail.

Chapter 5

The Envision Phase

Get the Right People

"Hi, Maya," said Herman. "How's the world treating you these days?"

"Not too bad, but I'm up to my eyeballs on Jupiter."

"Sorry to bother you at home, but I'm in a bind. I asked for more people for my project, but you should see who they gave me. I think I may be worse off now than I was before," Herman moaned.

"How many turkeys did you get?" Maya asked.

"Three, but when you add them to my existing problems, I feel like I've got a high school basketball team when what I really need is the LA Lakers. Management does a terrible job judging their capability. I think it's a case of bravado winning out over humility."

"I hear you," Maya said in agreement. "With the wrong team you're either going to fail or underdeliver. That's what I like about APM. It helps expose staffing problems early. Of course that's why so many companies stick with their old project management methods—they don't really want to face reality. It's management by wishful thinking."

"So, what do I do? Hey, Maya, what's that noise? You have a motor running?"

"Oh, that's our project cat Hermione. And the answer to your first question is to set performance standards. Even Hermione, our project cat, has goals and objectives she has to meet."

"You're kidding, right?"

"Only a little. Hermione, my cat, comes to work with me about half the time, and she really is there to relieve stress. Petting a cat can be very soothing. But seriously, while I don't always get the people with the skill levels I need, I only have to keep people whose attitude lets them contribute to the project."

"So I take it if you can get a cat onto the project, you must always get the people you want, huh?"

"Of course not. I don't always get the people with the skill levels I need, but in this company I always get people with the right attitude."

"So you have the right to fire even if you can't hire?" asked Herman.

"It sounds draconian when you say it like that. But we do have a strong culture, and the team makes it clear to new folks that they either pull their own weight or they get out. I've mostly got self-starters who aren't waiting around for someone to manage them—they manage themselves."

"And how did you accomplish that, Oh Mighty All-Knowing One?" Herman asked.

"By making sure everyone shares the same vision—of the product, the project, and how we get work done."

"My management always talks about repeatable processes. They think that processes, procedures, sign-offs, and status reports will deliver results every time."

"And when they don't?"

"Well, they just figure we didn't adhere closely enough to the process."

"Like, it didn't work the first time, so we'll just do more of it," Maya teased. "People aren't machines, and product development isn't a cookie cutter process. The problem with product development, as opposed to product manufacturing, is that we can't control the inputs—every project is different. Our process is reliable, not repeatable."

"Hmm. Reliable rather than repeatable. I'll have to mull that one over for a while. Next time," said Herman.

Phase: Envision

It is rare to discover anything in the realm of human behavior that occurs with great consistency.... Therefore, it was surprising to find that in every

case, without exception, when an effectively functioning team was identi-
fied, it was described by the respondent as having a clear understanding of
its objective (Larson and LaFasto 1989).

It's the vision thing again! Visioning and goal setting have been identified time after time as key ingredients of project, and general management, success.

But how does this need for a clear vision jibe with the exploratory nature of product development, which we have just gone to great lengths to describe as volatile and fuzzy? This apparent dichotomy is resolved by the fact that while the details of requirements and design can be volatile and fuzzy, the overarching business goal or product vision must be clear. In fact two critical aspects of a vision are clarity and an elevating goal that makes a difference and conveys a sense of urgency to the project (Larson and LaFasto 1989). Absent a clear vision, the exploratory nature of an agile project will cause it to spin off into endless experimentation. A clear vision must bound exploration.

If everyone knows that creating a clear, compelling vision is so critical to project success, then why do so many teams suffer from lack of vision? The answer is that creating a clear, compelling vision is hard—it takes work, and it takes leadership. In the process of developing a new product there are so many options that creating a clear path forward can be daunting. This is one activity in which effective leaders lead—they help cut through the ambiguity and confusion to create an effective vision. Compounding the problem is the fact that there is no fixed rule for creating a good vision statement. It's one of those "I'll know it when I see it, but I can't describe it" phenomena, in part because the essence of a good vision is the leader's articulation of it.

The purpose of the envisioning phase is to clearly identify what is to be done and how the work is to be accomplished. Specifically, this phase answers the following questions:

- What is the customer's product vision?
- What is the scope of the project and its constraints (including the business case)?
- Who are the right participants to include in the project community?
- How will the team deliver the product (approach)?

For small projects, much if not most of the work of the Envision and Speculate phases can be accomplished in a single "kickoff" week. For larger projects, requirements gathering, additional training, resource procurement, and architectural work may take longer and can be included in an Iteration 0 (see Chapter 6). For large- to medium-sized projects there is normally a debate and discussion period required in order to obtain agreement about the product vision. During the Envision phase the vision constantly evolves based on new information. After the Envision phase it needs to be reviewed periodically to ensure that the team continues to understand the vision.

Depending upon the situation, the information available to an Envision phase will vary, but the key outputs remain constant: product scope, project objectives and constraints, project participation, and project approach. While there are other important aspects of initiating a project, such as budgets, staff organization, and reporting needs, without a commonly held vision the project will falter.

Envisioning begins in whatever feasibility study initiates the project. Because the APM model as shown is not a portfolio or total product lifecycle model, it uses information provided by the feasibility study and extends it. Many companies conduct feasibility and marketing studies prior to initiating development projects, while others use only brief project requests.

Figure 5.1 depicts the evolution of a project plan—from vision, to scope, to features—utilizing three simple but powerful practices: the vision box, the project data sheet, and the iterative feature plan (accomplished in the Speculate phase). Each of these artifacts is simple in concept, powerful, and low ceremony (informal), and each operates on the principle of limited "real estate." The vision box exercise forces the team to condense information about a product vision onto the limited space of a box. The project data sheet forces the team to condense key project scope and constraint information into a single page. Feature cards force the team to condense the key information about a feature onto a single 4×6-inch index card. Limiting the space in which we record information requires focus and selection—it demands collaboration and thinking, and it compels the team to make effective tradeoffs.

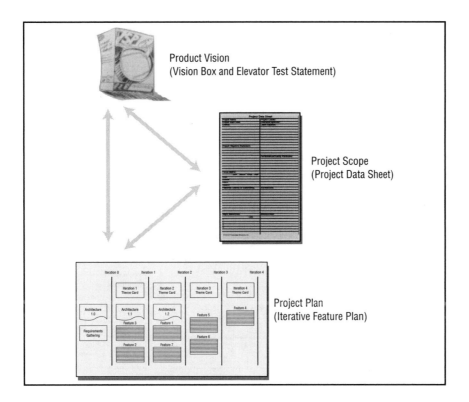

Figure 5.1
Evolution of a
Project Plan

Product Vision
(Vision Box and Elevator Test Statement)

Project Scope
(Project Data Sheet)

Project Plan
(Iterative Feature Plan)

In the Envision and Speculate phases of APM it is particularly important to remember that:

- The team members should constantly ask the question, "What is the barely sufficient process and documentation that we need?"
- All the practices related to "how" a team delivers are subject to tailoring and adaptation to improve performance as the project progresses.
- The project community and its processes and practices will evolve. For example, as the product architecture evolves, the team structure may need to evolve also—nothing is fixed.

Figure 5.2
Envision Phase
Practices

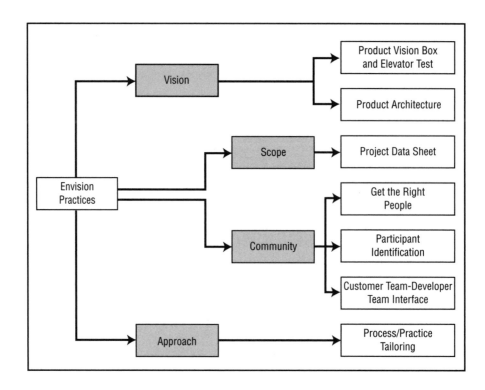

The practices explained in this chapter fall into four categories: visions for product, project, community, and approach (see Figure 5.2).[1]

Product Vision
- Product vision box and elevator test statement
- Product architecture and guiding principles

Project Scope (Objectives and Constraints)
- Project data sheet

Project Community
- Get the right people
- Participant identification
- Customer team-development team interface

Approach
- Process and practice tailoring

---

1. For additional information on project envisioning, see (Highsmith 2000), Chapter 4.

Practice: Product Vision Box
and Elevator Test Statement

Objective

The product vision box and elevator test statement galvanize members of the product team into focusing their often disparate views of the product into a concise, visual, and short textual form. These two project artifacts provide a "high concept" of the product for marketers, developers, and managers.

Discussion

Innovation, or creating emergent results that we cannot predict, requires an evolutionary process that can accommodate exploration and mistakes. A good product vision remains relatively constant, while the path to implement the vision needs room to wander. Emergent results often come from purposeful accidents, so managers must create an environment in which these accidents can happen. Mountain climbing is a good analogy for this process. The goal remains getting to the top of the mountain, a fixed point. The goal may also have constraints, such as only having food for nine days. Every climbing team has a route plan for gaining the summit. Every climbing team also alters its route plan on the way to the top—sometimes in minor ways, sometimes in major ones—depending on conditions.

Similarly, every product needs a marketing theme, a crisp visual image and feature description whose intent is to draw potential customers into further investigation. In this design-the-box exercise (developed originally by colleague Bill Shackelford), the project and customer teams, with other participants, create a visual image of the product. (Vision does imply "visual," after all.) For software and other small products, the image should be the product package. For larger products—automobiles or medical electronics equipment, for example—the vision could be a one- to two-page product brochure or one to two Web pages.

In the design-the-box activity, the entire team, including customers, breaks into groups of four to six people. Their task is to design the product box—front and back. This involves coming up with a product name, a

Figure 5.3
Product Vision Box
Example

graphic, three to four key bullet points on the front to "sell" the product, a detailed feature description on the back, and operating requirements. Figure 5.3 shows a sample vision box developed during a workshop session.

Coming up with fifteen or twenty product features proves to be easy. It's figuring out which three or four would cause someone to buy the product that is difficult. Usually this involves an active discussion about identifying the real customer. Even with a simple product example, the product vision boxes can vary quite a bit among three to five teams. Presentations by each of the groups are then followed by a discussion of how the different focal points can be reduced to a few that everyone agrees upon. A lot of good information gets generated by this exercise—plus, it's fun.

In addition to the vision box, the team concurrently develops a short statement of the product's positioning using an "elevator test statement"—a couple of sentences that indicate target customer, key benefit, and competitive advantage:

> *For midsized companies' distribution warehouses <u>who</u> need advanced carton movement functionality, <u>the</u> Supply-Robot <u>is a</u> robotically controlled lifting and transferring system that provides dynamic warehouse reallocation and truck loading of multisized cartons <u>that</u> reduces distribution costs and loading time. <u>Unlike</u> competitive products, <u>our product</u> is highly automated and aggressively priced.*

The elevator test statement—an explanation of the project to someone within two minutes—takes the following format:

- For (target customer)
- Who (statement of the need or opportunity)

- The (product name) is a (product category)
- That (key benefit, compelling reason to buy)
- Unlike (primary competitive alternative)
- Our product (statement of primary differentiation) (Moore 1991)

Every product and project needs a core concept from which details can flow. Without a core concept, team members can spend time investigating blind alleys and racking up costs without contributing to the project's success. Particularly with new products for which the risk and uncertainties are high, having a core concept, a vision, is critical to keeping down the cost of exploration.

The product vision box and elevator test statement vividly depict a product vision. They emphasize that projects produce products. Some projects (e.g., internal IT projects) may not create products for the external market, but viewing them as products for an internal market keeps the team grounded in a customer-product mindset. Whether the project results involve enhancements to an internal accounting system or a new digital camera, product-oriented thinking reaps benefits.

Finally, with several hours of active product vision discussion recorded on flipchart paper, the team can construct a good outline for a complete one- to five-page product vision document. This might include the mission statement, pictures of the "boxes," target customers and each of their needs, the elevator test statement, customer satisfaction measures, key technology and operational requirements, critical product constraints (performance, ease of use, volumes), a competitive analysis, and key financial indicators.

For a four- to six-month project, this visioning exercise might take half a day, but it will pay big dividends. Recently, a client reported that spending three to fours hours for a visioning session brought a group with widely different ideas about product direction into alignment. The more critical the delivery schedule and the more volatile the project, the more important it is that the team have a good vision of the final desired outcome. Without this vision, iterative development projects are likely to become oscillating projects, because everyone is looking at the minutiae rather than the big picture.[2]

---

2. Ken Delcol comments, "This statement is true regardless of the development approach. The big picture is key for both, and the joy of the iterative approach is that if you are lacking one, it should become obvious sooner than in the case of the traditional approach. The traditional approach creates the illusion that a vision exists for a number of months before someone figures out what is going on."

Figure 5.4
A Product Vision
(Courtesy of Alias
Systems, Inc.)

Companies doing NPD have a range of other "visioning" tools available to them, some of which significantly reduce the cost of experimentation and cycle time. One example is Studio Tools, a graphics software product from Alias Systems, which industrial design firms use to "sketch" new product ideas. The use of Studio Tools precedes (and feeds) CAD/CAM tools, providing the ability to explore product possibilities visually, as shown in Figure 5.4.

The next step, a prototype or working model, is the realm of companies such as Stratasys. Its fused deposition modeling (FDM) system creates plastic models simply by downloading a 3D drawing (analogous to a 3D copy machine that creates plastic parts). Figure 5.5 shows an example of the parts produced. In operation, a liquefier melts and extrudes the plastic in ultrafine layers. The model is built layer by layer from the bottom up. These parts can be used to construct working models quickly and cost effectively. Bell &

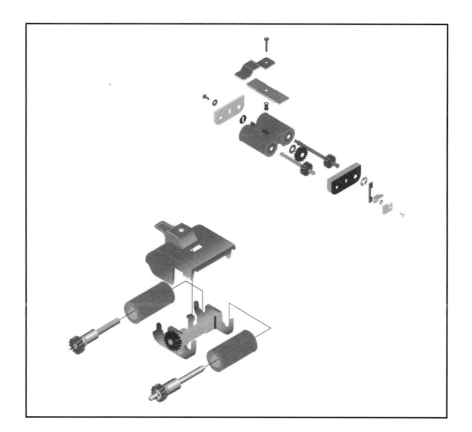

Figure 5.5
A Plastic Prototype
of a New Scanner
Design (Courtesy
of Stratasys, Inc.)

Howell used FDM to create a new top-of-the-line scanner, building working prototypes from parts created by FDM. Both the design cycle and product part count were reduced by 50%. Using early lifecycle visioning tools such as Studio Tools that can feed data to automated prototyping tools such as FDM (which might be employed in either the Envision or early in the Explore phase) can greatly reduce cycle time and experimentation costs.

While these practices provide a high-concept vision of the product, for complicated projects the vision may need to be supplemented with additional concept documents and financial analyses. However, without a high-concept vision, these other supporting practices tend to grow large and unfocused. A 25-page vision document subverts the whole meaning of a concise vision. For larger products and projects, an overall product vision can also be supplemented with vision statements for the major components. Each component team should participate in this visioning process for its own area.

Practice: Product Architecture

Objective

The objective of product architecture is to depict the internal plumbing of the project—a design that facilitates exploration and guides ongoing product development. Product architecture guides both the technical work and the organization of people who carry out the technical work.

Discussion

Product architecture may seem like an odd practice to put into a project management toolbox, but a product's technical architecture, together with the overall size of the project, has significant implications for project and product success. For example, the organization of components and modules may impact decisions about outsourcing or about distributed development and how to manage distributed groups. Similarly, if a team is building a complex product with both hardware and software components, the interface specifications may have a major impact on the change management process. In agile development, architecture is a guide, not a straightjacket. It is intended to communicate the larger context to the development team, not lock in a design.

While in general agile practices encourage change and adaptation, certain changes have greater impact and require careful coordination. For example, in automobile design, the transmission and drivetrain components have a certain

Figure 5.6A
Software Feature
Breakdown Structure
for a CRM Application

> - **Sales Management (Business Subject Area)**
>   - ° Prospecting (Business Activity)
>   - • Create sales person log on (Feature)
>   - • List leads for the sales person
>   - • Display individual lead detail
>   - ° Territory Management
>   - ° Sales Analysis
> - **Marketing**
>   - ° Lead Generation
>   - ° Lead Follow-Up
>   - ° Advertisement Placement
>   - ° Call Center Service

Figure 5.6B
Hardware Feature
Breakdown Structure
for a Mass Spectrom-
eter (Courtesy of
MDS Sciex)

- **KIT Vacuum Pump (Group)**
- **Control Panel**
- **Electrical**
  - ° Power Cable Assembly
  - ° Vacuum System (Component)
    - • Tray (Feature)
    - • Base Unit
    - • Fan
    - • Vacuum Chamber
    - • Card Cage
  - ° Gas Control
- **System Electronics**
  - ° Vacuum Gage Model
  - ° System Control Module
  - ° Exciter Module
  - ° Amplifier Module

well-defined interface. Changes within the component, which don't change the interface, can be handled less formally than those that affect the interface. It is not a matter of control—who gets to make the decisions—as much as it is a matter of coordination—making sure the team understands the total impact of a change and which groups are affected. A poor technical architecture makes this change coordination job difficult. Astute project teams will recognize when excessive time spent on cross-component coordination or integration points to poor architectural decisions that need to be remedied.

In general, technical architectures utilize some combination of platform, component, interface, and module elements. A new sport utility vehicle may begin with a "truck" or a "car" platform. A software product may utilize a Windows or a Mac platform, or both. The SUV has components such as a body, drivetrain, and engine. A software component may have application programming interfaces (APIs) that specify how other components are to interact with it. A multifunction PC device may have printer, scanner, and faxing components, each of which has subordinate modules (which in this case include integrated circuit boards).

A feature breakdown structure (FBS) can be used to depict a product architecture (see Figures 5.6A and 5.6B). There are other architectural representations that are useful for technical teams, but the FBS serves to communicate between customer and development teams and acts as a bridge between the Envision and Speculate phases. The FBS identifies a backlog of features from which an iteration plan will be developed.

One of the reasons project managers need technical domain experience as well as project management skills is that they need to understand the interactions among technical architecture, project organization, and planning. Poor technical structures can cause severe organizational problems, just as poor organizational structures can sometimes result in bad technical decisions.

Finally, in many projects, the project team structure and the technical architecture are decided upon in the beginning and are thereafter fixed. Colleague Mike Cohn comments, "This is a real problem with staffing large projects too quickly. If you have 20 people on a project that needs 5 to start with, you have a tendency to want to find work for the other 15 so as not to be inefficient. This means that the system gets partitioned along the skill sets of the 20 developers rather than along boundaries appropriate for that project."

A better model would be for the human organization and the technical architecture to co-evolve over the life of the project. (Technical architecture evolution is a difficult concept for engineers whose experience has been to design and fix the architecture early in the development process.) It may appear beneficial, with a large project, for the project subteams to be aligned with the major product components. In automobile design we might have body, frame, drivetrain, engine, and electronics subteams. While this organization may be useful later in the project, a core team of all disciplines may work better in the beginning. The core team develops the overall architecture and, very importantly, the interfaces. Once the interfaces have been specified through interaction and debate, component-based subteams may work better. The core team may evolve into a part-time architecture and integration group that coordinates changes among subteams. Another advantage of this approach comes from the cross-functional relationships that are built in the early project stages, which facilitate coordination as people are dispersed from their initial assignments into various subteams.

Guiding Principles

A second piece of the architectural guide is, appropriately enough, a set of guiding principles (GPs) to assist development teams in "molding" the product to meet customer preferences. Just as agile values and principles guide people in their efforts, guiding "product" principles assist in steering the product's evolution in the desired direction.[3] GPs are usually not measurable requirements or constraints but conceptual guides. For example, defining the ubiquitous phrase "user friendly" in measurable terms may be difficult. However, a GP stating that "The target user for this medical device, an entry-level medical technician, should be able to use the basic features of the product with minimal training" would help steer a development team in its user interface design. A guiding principle for this book was to focus on delivery rather than compliance practices.

GPs can be used early in a project before specific requirements or design decisions have been made. For example, an early GP might be, "Maximize the employment of reusable components and services to speed development." That GP could then be used as a consideration in design, where it might, for example, encourage the selection of a technology platform. An early GP may evolve into a specific requirement later. In the case of the medical device mentioned above, after several iterations of experimenting, the minimal training GP might be supplemented with specific user interface design requirements and measurable training objectives.

Although some GPs may be developed during project envisioning, they often emerge over early development iterations. Each principle should be described in a sentence or two, and the total number for a project, at any one time, should not exceed around ten.

Practice: Project Data Sheet

Objective

The objective of a project data sheet is to convey the essence, in terms of scope, schedule, and resources, of how a project will deliver on the project vision.

Discussion

A project data sheet (PDS) is the second major visioning practice in the evolution of a project plan (Figure 5.1). While the *product* vision is an expansive view of what the product could become, the *project* vision limits product development to the confines of current scope, schedule, and cost constraints. To keep these two elements separated, I usually refer to the *product*

---

3. Colleague Kevin Tate introduced me to this idea of guiding principles.

vision and the *project scope*. Colleague Mike Cohn defines product vision as the "should haves" and the project scope as the "will haves." Eventually the product "should have" 234 features; however, for this project (release 1.0), it "will have" 126 features. A PDS, as shown in Figure 5.7, is the minimum documentation for a project's scope and constraints.

> *A project data sheet (PDS) is a single-page summary of key business objective, product specification, and project management information. It is a document to help focus the project team, management, and customers. The PDS's simplicity belies its power to convey quickly these key project elements. It is one of those simple practices with a powerful impact. Not only does its condensed format appeal to stakeholders who might not be fully involved in the project, and remind those who are fully involved about the most important aspects of the project, it also plays a part with those who develop it* (Highsmith 2000).

Sections of the PDS might include some combination of the following, depending on organization and project type:

- **Clients/customers**: a list of the key clients or customers
- **Project manager**
- **Product manager**
- **Project objective statement (POS)**: a specific, short (25 or fewer words) statement that includes important scope, schedule, and resource information from the tradeoff matrix
- **Tradeoff matrix (TOM)**: a table that establishes the relative priorities of project scope, resources, schedule, and defects—with one and only one of these established as the highest priority
- **Exploration factor**: a measure (1 to 10) of the risk and uncertainty of the project
- **Delay cost**: the daily, weekly, or monthly cost of project delay (particularly useful when schedule is the highest priority)
- **Features**: a list of the key features
- **Client benefits**: the key benefits and/or selling points of the product
- **Performance/quality attributes**: a list of the key performance and quality attributes of the product
- **Architecture**: key architectural components of the product (platform, component, interface, module)
- **Issues/risks**: factors that could adversely impact this project

Project Data Sheet

Project Name: CRM Development	Project Manager: Braxton Quivera
Project Start Date: 3/1/2004	Product Manager: Roger Jones
Clients:	Executive Sponsor: Andrian Poledra
Marketing	Client Benefits:
Call Center	Better customer service
Sales	Reduce paperwork
Accounting	More accurate order processing
	Better customer account management
Project Objective Statement:	Performance Attributes:
The objective is to build a web-based CRM	Call Center volume of 3,500 calls per day
application that includes sales tracking, order	Worldwide web access
management, sales management, and marketing.	<1/2 day training required
The system needs to be operational by 6/30/05 and	No severity 1 defects
cost less than $2.5 million.	

Trade-Off Matrix:

	Fixed	Flexible	Accept	Target	
Scope		x		12,500 FP	Product Architecture:
Schedule	x			=/– 6 weeks	Interface with ERP system
Resource			x	+/– $.5 M	Windows XP, SQL Server, .NET
Stability			x		

Project Delay Cost per Month: $50,000	
Exploration Factor: 8	
Business Subject/Activity:	
Sales Management	
Sales Analysis	
Prospecting	
Territory Management	
Marketing	
Lead Generation	
Lead Follow Up	Issues and Risks:
Advertisement Placement	Development costs are difficult to calculate.
Call Center Service	Sales staff reluctant to embrace new system.
Order Management	Requirements agreement among user groups
	may be difficult.
* See the Feature Breakdown Structure for details,	
including the individual features	

Major Project Milestones:

Marketing except Call Center	9/30/04
Call Center	1/15/05
Sales Management	3/30/05
Order Management	6/30/05

Figure 5.7
Project Data Sheet

Figure 5.8
Tradeoff Matrix

	Fixed	Flexible	Accept
Scope	X		
Schedule		X	
Stability			X
Resources			X

Tradeoff Matrix

The tradeoff matrix is an agreement among the project team, the customer (product manager), and the executive sponsor that is used to manage change during the project. The TOM informs all participants that changes have consequences and acts as a basis for team decision making.

The rows of a project TOM, as shown in Figure 5.8, depict the key dimensions that create a product's value—scope, delivery schedule, stability (defects), and resources. The columns display the relative importance of each dimension and are labeled Fixed, Flexible, and Accept.[4] Fixed means that the dimension, schedule for example, is fixed or constrained and that tradeoff decisions should not impact performance in that dimension. Fixed also connotes that the dimension in question has the highest priority. Flexible is one step down from Fixed; the dimension is still very important, but not important enough to trade off for the Fixed dimension. Accept indicates that the dimension—cost, for example—has a wider range of acceptable tolerance. In fact, as the importance goes from Fixed, to Flexible, to Accept, the tolerance for variation increases.

In the matrix, columns one and two can each contain only one entry. If the highest priority is scope (Fixed), then everything else takes lower priority. Schedule might be designated as the second-highest priority (Flexible). Similarly, the team would strive to maintain *acceptable* (Accept) defect levels

---

4. Finding the right names for these column headings has proved tricky. Lynne Nix has used Excel, Improve, and Accept, indicating a dimension in which to strive for excellence, a dimension to improve as long as the Excel dimension doesn't suffer degradation, and a dimension whose performance could be acceptable. Ian Savage suggested Fixed, Flexible, and Free to me in an e-mail message, and I've adapted from his and Lynne's usage. Sometimes it is simpler to think of priority 1, 2, and 3.

(within some specified tolerance level; for example, 5 sigma) and to stay with a reasonable tolerance on total project cost (possibly +/–15%).[5]

Many managers and executives consider project success to be on time, on budget, and on scope. They define each characteristic with no tolerances and then fantasize that the project team can respond to all manner of change without tolerances. Software engineering metrics guru Capers Jones (1994) points out that it is common for customers "to insist on costs and schedules that are so far below US norms that completion on time and within budget is technically impossible." If these three characteristics—plus a fourth, quality—are all top priority, then how do teams make hard tradeoff decisions? Executives and customers put teams into an impossible position by demanding that they respond to change, while failing to give them reasonable tolerances for dealing with those changes.

If a customer executive asserts that the delivery schedule is of paramount importance, then he should also be willing to prioritize other characteristics—to say, for example, that cutting features would be preferable to slipping the schedule. The team strives to meet all the goals, but it also needs to know the relative importance of the key characteristics in order to make informed day-to-day and end-of-iteration decisions.

Another powerful piece of information that can assist teams in making project decisions is delay cost. I once worked with a project team for which the calculated delay cost was nearly a million dollars a day in lost revenue. Knowing this cost drove much of the decision making on the project and helped ward off the constant flow of new features from marketing. When stakeholders insist that schedule is the most critical element of a project, having them calculate a delay cost puts the criticality of the schedule in perspective.

Exploration Factor

An exploration factor acts as a barometer of the uncertainty and risk of a project. Big projects are different from small projects; risky projects are different

---

5. Some might argue that there are no tolerance levels for defects, that the agile principle of technical excellence precludes any tradeoffs for defects. While this may be the case at a module level for engineers, from an overall product perspective there can be levels of emphasis on, for example, extensive QA testing. A video game won't have the same "proof of quality" demands as a CAT scan machine. Balancing between excellence and perfection can be tricky for engineering teams.

from low-risk ones. One issue in selecting project management practices and processes is the particular problem domain in which the project team has to operate. An exploration factor of 10 indicates a highly exploration-oriented (high-risk) problem domain, and a 1 indicates a very stable problem environment. It is important to identify the various problem domain factors, but it is even more important to tailor processes and practices to the problem and to adjust expectations accordingly.

The exploration factor is derived from a combination of the volatility of a product's requirements and the newness—and thus uncertainty—of its technology platform. The exploration factor matrix shown in Figure 5.9 shows four categories of requirements volatility: erratic, fluctuating, routine, and stable. "Erratic" requirements depict a situation in which the product vision is understood, but the business or product requirements are fuzzy. An example would be a version 1.0 NPD effort in which features are unfolding as the project goes forward. In this case, the requirements might change drastically as the project proceeds, not from poor requirements gathering but from evolving knowledge of the product. Fluctuating requirements would be one step down in uncertainty. While an erratic problem space might experience a requirements change of 25% to 50% or more, a fluctuating one might be more sedate at 20% to 25%. A routine categorization would apply to a wide range of projects in which up-front requirements gathering yields a reasonably stable baseline for further work, while a stable environment might be something like a federally mandated change to a payroll system that is well defined and unlikely to change.[6]

The exploration factor's technology dimension also has four categories: bleeding edge, leading edge, familiar, and well known. "Bleeding edge" would involve a technology so new that very few people have experience with it. With bleeding-edge technology, learning by trying is the only strategy because no one else knows how to use it either. In the early 2000s,

---

6. Ken Delcol comments, "This guides the PM in both how the project and individual requirements should be managed. For example, erratic requirements need a more iterative approach and should be planned that way up front regardless of the overall state of the remaining requirements. Not all requirements fall into the same bucket. The trick is to realize which requirements are key to overall product success—there is no point rushing forward to specify the stable requirements when critical, high-risk requirements are erratic or fluctuating!"

Product Requirements Dimension	Product Technology Dimension			
	Bleeding Edge	Leading Edge	Familiar	Well Known
Erratic	10	8	7	7
Fluctuating	8	7	6	5
Routine	7	6	4	3
Stable	7	5	3	1

Figure 5.9
Project Exploration Factors

Microsoft .NET or nanotechnology might be examples of bleeding-edge technologies. Leading-edge technology is relatively new, but there are pockets of expertise to turn to—although the cost and availability of these experts might be an issue. Projects employing bleeding- or leading-edge technology have much higher risk profiles than those using familiar or well-known technologies. Development teams should carefully evaluate in what parts of the product technology risk is justified, because even within a single product, not all components should be bleeding or leading edge.

Combining these elements, we might find that an erratic requirements, bleeding-edge technology problem space receives an exploration factor of 10, whereas a stable requirements, well-known technology project receives a factor of 1. A project with fluctuating requirements and leading-edge technology receives a factor of 7. By determining the exploration factor, project and customer teams can now discuss projects from the perspective of the overall "uncertainty" of the problem space. An 8, 9, or 10 project will require a very agile approach since the uncertainty and risk are high. Short iterations, feature-driven planning, frequent reviews with customers, and a recognition that plans are very speculative are imperative for solving problems in this domain. In contrast, projects with a 1, 2, or 3 rating will be relatively stable and low risk. Plans could be more deterministic, iterations could be somewhat longer, and additional up-front requirements gathering and design time can be cost effective.

Without the recognition of different problem domains, one-size-fits-all project processes and practices seem justified. With such a recognition, customization and tailoring to specific problems will enable project teams to be successful.

Practice: Get the Right People

Objective

The objective of team staffing, and the subsequent organization of teams, can be summed up in four words: Get the Right People.

Discussion

Author Andrew Hill (2001) once asked basketball coach John Wooden who he thought were the best coaches he faced. Without hesitation Wooden replied, "The ones with the best players." Hill continued, "So many top-level managers feel they can make do with mediocre employees. What I learned from Coach is that you must have top-notch talent to succeed."

In product development, as in most endeavors, getting the right people involved is *the* critical success factor. "Right" consists of both having the appropriate technical ability (or domain expertise) and exhibiting the right self-disciplined behavior. Getting the right people doesn't necessarily mean getting the most talented and experienced people, just the appropriate people for the job.

That said, there *are* reasons for getting overqualified people, especially in product development projects in which effectiveness and speed are so important. In his classic book *Software Engineering Economics*, Barry Boehm (1981) offers his Principle of Top Talent: "Use better and fewer people." As Boehm summarizes, "The top 20% of people produce about 50% of the output." If you plan to take on difficult, demanding projects, you need the best talent. If you take on less-demanding projects, you'll still do better with better-than-average talent. People sometimes counter this argument by saying, "But, you have to understand that half the people are below average." My response is twofold: "One, that might be true, but it doesn't have to be true for my company or my project. Second, nearly everyone has the potential to be above average at something. It's a manager's job to help them find that something."

Author Jim Collins (2001) is adamant not only about getting the right people "on the bus," but also that getting those people is even more important than figuring out where the bus should go. He declares, "The 'who' question comes before 'what' questions—before vision, before strategy, before tactics, before organizational structure, before technology." Everyone understands the notion that casting is critical in theatre or the movies. As authors Rob Austin and Lee Devin (2003) observe, "It is also clear that no matter how good you get at repeating a play, you can't replace Dustin Hoffman or Sigourney Weaver with a less-experienced beginner and expect to maintain quality."

As I said earlier, two factors determine whether or not a team has the "right" people—capability and self-discipline. There was much ado during the last decade about how having the right process could make up for having the wrong people (after all, the reasoning went, we can plug just about anyone into a well-defined process). In reality, having a reasonable process can help the right people work together effectively, but it can't make up for having the wrong people.[7]

Jim Collins (2001) aptly expresses this point with his analogy of getting the right people on the bus: "Most companies build their bureaucratic rules to manage the small percentage of wrong people on the bus, which in turn drives away the right people on the bus, which then increases the need for more bureaucracy to compensate for incompetence and lack of discipline, which then further drives the right people away, and so forth." This observation fits right into the delivery-compliance dichotomy—the right people focus on delivery, while the wrong people generate extra compliance work.

Collins's ideas are intended for organizations as a whole, but many of his ideas apply at the project level. Part of getting the right people involved, from a capability perspective, is having some idea of the project and the required skill set to carry it off. A group's capability should influence what products or projects are appropriate to pursue. More people are coming to the understanding that *process isn't a substitute for skill.* Process may be an

---

7. Larson and LaFasto (1989) articulated these ideas before Collins. Their research indicated that "it was imperative to select the right people." Secondly, they defined the right people as those with the necessary technical skills and personal characteristics (working well within a team).

enabler, it may prevent reinventing the wheel, but it is not a substitute for skill. Process may assist a group of skilled people in working together more effectively, but the fundamental capabilities, the fundamental skills, must be present in the team.

Several years ago I participated in a project retrospective with a software development team. The project was an outsourced Web project, and the customer ended the project unhappy with the technical architecture because the application was difficult to change. The team admittedly did not have sufficient capability in the new Web technology; however, to mitigate the risk, it had established an architectural review process. Unfortunately, none of the reviewers had any experience in the technology either—they had instituted a process without a sufficient capability.

The second aspect of getting the right people involves finding (and developing) those with the self-disciplined behavior described in Chapter 3. Rigorous self-discipline differs from ruthless imposed discipline. One is generated from internal motivations, the other from authoritarian admonitions, usually playing on fear.

Getting the right people extends to the product management or customer team as well. I often get asked questions like, "What if we don't get the right customer involvement on our project?" The answer is easy—don't do the project—although implementing it in most organizations is not. Not doing a project when the fundamental reality is that the team doesn't have the right customers or the right staff is part of the rigorous discipline required to succeed. Undisciplined organizations go ahead; they ignore reality or convince themselves through bravado that they can succeed in the face of information that indicates otherwise.

There is a difference between getting the right person and getting the perfect person. Your team may need an expert geophysicist but may not be able to obtain one with the exact skills and experience desired. If you find one with the right self-disciplined attitude and sufficient technical skills, she will figure out how to obtain the right information. If, on the other hand, you find a pharmacologist and expect him to make the jump, that would be wishful thinking. The right person is the one who has the required capability or enough capability to grow—with coaching by the project manager and the team's technical specialists—into what is needed for the project. Similarly, the right person from a self-discipline perspective will have enough motivation to learn the behaviors that create a well-functioning team.

Practice: Participant Identification

Objective

The objective of participant identification is to identify all the project participants so that expectations can be understood and managed.

Discussion

Project participants comprise any individuals or groups that are part of the project community: from customers of the product, who can influence the project and determine requirements; to executives who provide funding and assume some managerial oversight of the project; to the core project team members who work to deliver the product.

There are three broad categories of participants: customers (which could include end users, their managers, the product manager, and the executive sponsor), project team members, and stakeholders.[8] In this book, the term "stakeholder" will be used for internal participants, such as managers who are not direct customers of the product, and external participants such as vendors.

From a broad-brush perspective, customers provide requirements, project team members build the product, and stakeholders contribute constraints. Customers are those participants who use the product to create value for themselves or their organizations. Project team members are the developers and managers who are actively involved in delivering the product. Stakeholders provide constraints, compliance requirements, and resources (vendors). For example, the audit staff dictate certain process and control compliance requirements, while the financial department may require certain reports from the team. External regulatory agencies may impose product testing constraints.

---

8. Some people may be concerned that customers aren't included in the project team. They are part of the overall "team," but they have different responsibilities from the delivery team. In the final analysis, whether you think of customers and developers as a single team or two teams isn't nearly as important as the degree of collaboration and interaction between them.

Author Rob Thomsett proposes three levels of participants (whom he calls "stakeholders"), each with a different potential degree of impact on a project:

- **Critical**: These are the participants who can prevent your project from achieving success before or after implementation; in other words, the showstoppers.
- **Essential**: These participants can delay your project from achieving success before or after implementation. In other words, you can work around them.
- **Nonessential**: These participants are interested parties. They have no direct impact on your project, but if they are not included in your communication, they can change their status to critical or essential (Thomsett 2002).

Identifying a project's participants is a project management task that is very easy to talk about and often most difficult to do well. Project team after project team has been blindsided by unidentified participants coming forth to bury the project with unforeseen information or political agendas.

But identifying and managing participants has another subtle, but important justification—it helps improve teamwork. According to Carl Larson and Frank LaFasto (1989), "external support and recognition" of the team by the organization contributes to success, or more precisely, lack of that support is a cause of failure. A development project doesn't operate in a vacuum; it operates within a larger organizational environment. When that wider organization withholds recognition, resources, or support, development teams will feel isolated and abandoned—not an atmosphere that makes for effective work.

A list of project participants might include:

- **Executive sponsor**: the person (or group of people) who champions the product and makes key decisions about the product's goals and constraints
- **Project manager:** the person who leads the team charged with delivering the results
- **Product manager**: the person who leads the team responsible for determining what results to deliver
- **Lead engineer**: the person who guides the technical aspects of the team's delivery

- **Management**: a potentially wide range of individuals who can be in charge of participant organizations; may have budget or technical decision-making authority or influence over the project outcomes
- **Customer team**: the individuals, both full and part time, who are charged with determining features that need to be built and prioritizing them
- **Project team**: the individuals, both full and part time, who are charged with delivering results
- **Suppliers**: external companies or individuals who provide services or product components
- **Government**: regulatory agencies that require information, reports, certifications, and more

Nearly all of the above roles are self-explanatory or, as in the case of project and product managers, are explained throughout this book. However, one role does need a further bit of explanation here—the lead engineer role. Any role like that of project manager or lead engineer can be interpreted from a perspective of either a command-control or a leadership-collaboration management style. Since many people have less experience with the latter, they tend to interpret the words "lead" and "manager" from a hierarchical, control-oriented perspective. But the lead engineer's role is much like the project manager's—to guide, to steer, to facilitate knowledge sharing, to encourage collaboration, to participate in team decision making, and, periodically, to be the final arbiter of critical technical decisions. The same person may also fill both the lead engineer and project manager roles when he or she has the right combination of skills and experience.

The more complex the participant group, the more time project managers must spend managing expectations, getting critical project decisions made, and keeping the project from being pulled in too many directions. Identification is the first step in integrating various participants into the project community.[9]

9. Identifying the right project participants in product development efforts, and getting them involved at the right time, is critical. For example, software licensing decisions can impact design, so waiting until the later stages of a software project to include the legal department can cause delays at the end. A great reference on this topic for software product developers is (Hohmann 2003).

Practice: Customer Team-Developer Team Interface

Objective

The objective of this practice is to define the collaboration interface between the customer team and the development team.

Discussion

A significant number of project failures are caused by poorly defined customer-developer interfaces. While customers and developers are often on the same "team," they are often not on the same subteam. When this interface—which is defined by information flows, accountabilities, and responsibilities—is ill defined, project failure looms close by.

Every project should have a project manager and a product manager. One of the key reasons internal IT projects fail, or underperform, is misunderstanding the nature of these two roles. Product groups often do a decent job of differentiating these roles, but IT projects often miss the product manager role. At one level the responsibilities of the product manager and project manager are simple—the first is responsible for "what to build" and the second for "how to build it." In practice each role, each person, has input and influence on the entire project—both the what and the how.

This brings up another wider issue. Roles are not static descriptions that we slavishly follow; roles are instantiated by individuals, and every person who fills a role plays it differently. Just as every actor playing Macbeth brings his own talents, interpretation, and experience to the play, every person who fills a product or project manager role (or any other role) plays it differently. One product manager may have extensive technical experience, another less. To tell the first person that she shouldn't have any input to the technical decisions would be throwing away a valuable resource. To tell a product domain-experienced project manager or developer that he will have no input to the product vision or specifications would be an equal waste of talent.

Project management books and company job descriptions often contain specific role narratives that include decision-making authority. While role

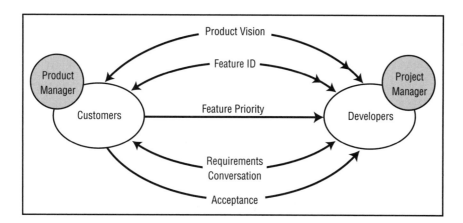

Figure 5.10
Creating a Customer-
Developer Interface

boundaries are important, in practice a role should be flexible, adapting to the specific person who fills it. At best, a role takes a page of description. Roles are finite. People are infinite. Role descriptions are merely a starting point for actual product and project managers to build relationships that will quickly transcend static roles. How each individual interprets his or her role and how he or she interacts with others who are interpreting their own roles results in a richness of relationship that transcends our feeble attempts at role descriptions. Trying to force people into a fixed role description is not only ultimately impossible, it is counter to agile principles. People are not only more important than process, they are more important than roles.

Getting back to the interface issues, there has long been a controversy in IT circles about where project managers should come from—customer or IT departments. Because of failed interactions on projects, companies have attempted to push project responsibility onto the customer by having someone from the customer organization be the project manager. Unfortunately, these individuals often don't have the time, project management skills, or technical knowledge required for the job. The real customer-developer problems get lost in this shuffle, because there is no differentiation between product and project management. All too often customer-side project managers try to do the job of both project manager and product manager in addition to their full-time job and end up failing at all three.

Figure 5.10 shows the outlines of a solution to this problem of who is responsible for what. Within any project there should be a development team and a customer team. The development group should be headed by a project manager and the customer group by a product manager. So who gets the final say? In most cases, the product manager does. Either manager can of course appeal decisions to the executive sponsor, but if the product and project managers can't work out most conflicts, the project risk escalates rapidly.

For a small project, the product manager may also be the primary customer. For an IT project for which there are ten customer departments, spread across six cities, with 150 users providing requirements input, a product manager should be appointed to coordinate the customer information flow and decision making. For a product development organization, the product manager—who often resides in the marketing department—coordinates the gathering of information from thousands or even millions of retail customers, condenses them into a usable form, and then coordinates the decision-making process.

While any decisions made without interaction and debate between the customer and development groups will be poor ones, ultimately the "what" decisions are made by the customer team and the "how" decisions are made by the development team. Good development groups have a wealth of knowledge about the product domain and should have significant input into the "what" decision. Product managers and other customer group members often have significant input into "how" a product might be designed. In the end, however, each group has its own responsibility—and projects fail because these responsibilities aren't clear.

The responsibilities of each group and the interactions between the two groups are key to success. In the early Envision stage of a project, both groups are involved in creating a product vision, but the product manager is responsible for the final decisions. During the Speculate and Explore phases, the groups interact to analyze requirements, to identify features, and then to prioritize those features into development iterations. Customers define feature requirements and help the project team make day-to-day refinements. Larger projects may have many customers, who often have conflicting needs and priorities. No single person may have knowledge of all the feature requirements. For these larger projects, or for projects with wide-ranging needs for customer information, it is important to consolidate multiple voices into a consistent "customer voice," a task that is ultimately the product manager's responsibility.

Without a strong product manager, the worst situation arises—prioritization fails, and the development team, in order to keep the project from bogging down, begins making the priority decisions itself. This degenerates into a no-win situation, as the customers can always fault the decisions and then use that failure as an excuse to reduce their involvement further. When a project loses its partnership relationships and parties abdicate their responsibilities, that project is in big trouble. This problem sometimes occurs in companies because product managers tend to wear both a marketing hat and a development hat. The marketing role takes up so much time that they have little left over for working with development.

One of the fallacies of serial development methodologies is the idea that complex information can be transferred from one group to the next via documentation alone. Most NPD efforts utilize cross-functional teams because company managers realize they cannot depend on documentation to convey complex information. Documented requirements, at some level, are necessary but insufficient. Without interaction between the customer and development groups, requirements documents will be sterile husks. Agilists believe that critical understanding comes from interaction and discussion rather than documentation. In many cases, the agreement and understanding need to be documented, but not the churn that was created in order to get to the agreement and understanding.[10]

The final interaction shown in Figure 5.10 is acceptance. It is the customer team's job to accept the product by verifying that it meets requirements. This acceptance can be done through a combination of formal testing and customer focus groups. A technical quality assurance group may assist the customers and product manager in this effort, but ultimately the responsibility for acceptance lies with the customer team.

As with many other practices, defining the customer-developer interface presents different challenges when you are using it with a team of 10, or 100, or 1,000. Trying to corral 100 customers from disparate business departments is much more difficult than working with a single one. Similarly, working with a group of 100 engineers creates more headaches than working with 2. However, the basic interactions shown in the customer-developer interface diagram and the responsibilities of the roles as

---

10. For additional information, see (Cockburn 2002).

described above don't change with size. The means to the ends will be different, but the outcomes should be consistent.

Practice: Process and Practice Tailoring

Objective

The objective of this practice is to tailor a process and practice framework—driven in part by a self-organization strategy—that defines the approach the team members will take in working together.

Discussion

One of the characteristics that defines high-performance teams is their approach to doing their work. Approach rivals vision and objectives in importance because it determines how a team will execute, how it will deliver results (Katzenbach and Smith 1993). Since APM stresses execution, the team's approach to that execution becomes vital. Part of the self-discipline required of a team is that it agree on an approach and then actually use it. Either failure to agree or failure to execute indicates lack of self-discipline.

Process and practice tailoring defines the approach that the project team will use to deliver a product. This approach starts with the organization's standard framework, and then the project manager and team tailor it to their needs within the framework's constraints. For example, a company might use the APM high-level process framework with organizationally mandated checkpoints (approvals) at each phase. Within this process framework, the company identifies a set of required practices and deliverables (a streamlined set). The team then tailors the required practices and adds additional ones it deems necessary.

Self-organization strategy concentrates on how people work together, how they collaborate, and the mechanisms for that collaboration. Processes and individual practices concentrate on what people actually do. Although the strategy and process seem to overlap, they are actually complementary.

For example, the practice of daily team integration meetings describes the concepts and mechanics for conducting short daily meetings to coordinate team activities. But if there are multiple subteams, the project needs a strategy for using these meetings effectively in larger groups.

Finally, processes and practices evolve. In the Envision phase the team may develop a general plan for its use that will undoubtedly be revised as the release plan details are developed in the Speculate phase. Then, as each iteration and milestone reaches completion, the processes and practices will be adapted to the feedback from the project itself. Nothing is static in APM—neither the product nor practices. Teams are encouraged to adapt everything except the bare essential policies and process framework to the reality of the actual situation as it unfolds.

Self-Organization Strategy

The term "self-organization strategy" sounds like an oxymoron, because self-organization implies that "stuff happens" without planning and forethought. Some consultants and practitioners have interpreted the ideas of complex adaptive systems to mean that self-organization happens magically within groups of people. All groups self-organize, but if we want *effective* self-organization, we have to think carefully about how to create this type of environment.

Project managers often perpetuate a hierarchical, command-control management philosophy in their project organizations by focusing on organizational charts, detailed process and activity identification, and documentation requirements. Thinking about a self-organizing strategy attempts to break this mindset by having the project manager and project team focus *first* on interactions—how everyone associated with the project will play together. The strategy establishes the team's approach to communications, coordination, collaboration, decision making, and other individual-to-individual and team-to-team interactions. Teams need to ask questions such as:

- How will we collaborate with customers?
- How will members from different feature teams collaborate with each other?
- How will the team in Atlanta collaborate with the team in Seattle, or Bombay?

Once we figure out how people are going to collaborate, then, and only then, should we figure out the organization, processes, and practices that will support that collaboration.

Most project management approaches include a communications plan. The Project Management Institute's *A Guide to the Project Management Body of Knowledge* (Project Management Institute 2000) includes communications management as one of its key knowledge areas. However, communications is not enough. Communications is basically one way—I send you information (even if you send some back). Collaboration is much more than communication; it involves interaction to produce some "joint" result. Collaboration integrates your ideas and mine into a whole. We communicate status reports to management. We collaborate among project team members using practices such as whiteboard brainstorming sessions to create a design. Throughout the product development world, in industry after industry, the rising tide of cross-functional teams speaks to the need to collaborate.

When formulating their self-organization strategy, teams should ask the following questions:

- Who needs to talk to whom when?
- How are these people who talk to each other going to make decisions?
- Who is accountable for what?
- What practices are they going to use to facilitate the above?

While this early focus on self-organizing strategy may appear to be a throwback to a serial approach to project management, the fact is that anything and everything in an agile project should follow the philosophy of start quick, do something, get feedback, and adapt. The practices in the Envision phase, this one included, are no different. The larger the project, the more time will be spent in developing a self-organizing strategy, but implementing and adapting the strategy in subsequent phases will ultimately be the critical success factor.

Process Framework Tailoring

Even in an agile project, the broad process framework will be shaped by the organization. For example, product development organizations often employ some type of stage and gate lifecycle framework that products must follow. At each stage certain information, features, or artifacts must be available and approved. In order to balance structure and flexibility, this common framework should be as streamlined as possible, enabling a degree of consistency from a senior executive perspective with flexibility at the project team level. The APM process framework, shown in Figure 4.1, should be integrated with the company's broader product development lifecycle. However, if the company's product lifecycle is overly prescriptive, approval oriented, and documentation-centric, integrating the APM framework will be difficult.

The process framework should strive to identify the barely sufficient (or minimum acceptable) standards for an organization for the project, although "minimum" may be different for large projects than for small ones. The greater the "weight" of this framework—number of process elements, number of required artifacts, number of decision gates, greater documentation formality—the less agile the project team can be.

Because this guiding framework should be designed using the "barely sufficient" criteria, there shouldn't actually be much tailoring by the project team. When project teams begin approaching management with requests for exceptions to the standard framework, it should be a strong signal that the framework has crossed the threshold from bare sufficiency to bureaucracy.

Practice Selection and Tailoring

Agile development and project management are built on an underlying premise that individual capability is the cornerstone of success, and furthermore, that individuals are unique contributors. It follows from these premises that rather than molding people to a set of common processes and practices, processes and practices should be molded to the team itself. While an organization might insist that project teams follow a guiding framework, there should be flexibility as to what individual practices are used to meet the needs of each phase. The team should discuss what practices are going to be used or not used. Just because a practice is a good one doesn't mean it needs to be used in every project. There should always be a discussion about how to approach each iteration; what was done in one may not be required for the next one. With individual practices, each team will tailor them in different ways according to the capabilities of the team members, the size of the project, the number of customers, and many other factors.

There are four fundamental questions the team should ask itself about the practices they select and tailor for a particular project:

- What practices are required?
- What supplementary practices do we need?
- What modifications do we need to make to the selected practices?
- What level of formality or ceremony should be used for documentation, approvals, changes?

In addition to a barely sufficient process framework, organizations may also specify a set of barely sufficient practices for each project phase. For example, developing a feature-based, iterative release plan is a requirement, not an option, for a company applying APM, although the practice can be tailored for characteristics such as iteration length. The practices in this book can be viewed as an initial cut at a barely sufficient set of practices. There may be supplemental practices that teams need to employ, but the 18 practices discussed in this book approach a minimum set.

The 18 practices of APM focus on delivery activities, but as previously noted, every organization also has compliance activities and deliverables that need to be added to the set of required delivery practices. While project managers can attempt to reduce these as much as possible, at some point the team just has to accept some level of compliance work and add those practices to the required set.

The best trigger for implementing supplementary practices is to note when something isn't working through an iteration or two. If problems or risks are getting lost, for example, an issues recording and monitoring practice may need to be instituted, although project teams may add this to the supplementary list during the Envision phase. Team members and project managers need to fight the tendency to add supplementary practices early— they need to wait until a specific and significant need arises.

"Significant need" is an important qualifier. Too often, reasonable mistakes (after all, innovation requires both successes and mistakes) are followed by knee-jerk reactions to add controls or new reports or new restrictions on the development team. For a large number of these "mistakes," much more time and energy goes into processes and procedures to prevent them from occurring again than would be spent on a "fix on occurrence" strategy.

As with adding supplementary practices, teams should usually wait to modify practices until after they've tried them for an iteration or two. If the practice itself has been defined using the barely sufficient principle, it will usually get the team started. In large projects, the team may determine early that a practice isn't sufficient and enhance it.

The implementation of documentation and approvals is often what separates bare sufficiency from bureaucracy. The breadth of things that are documented, the formality or ceremony of that documentation, and the review and approval processes for the documents can determine whether a practice, or process, is streamlined or not. For example, a change control practice (which in traditional projects often becomes a change resistance practice) can be a simple activity of discussing changes and documenting them minimally, or it can be an elaborate process of documentation, analysis, and review that eats up both time and paper. Author Michael Kennedy (2003) relates the view of documentation in the Toyota product development system: "At Toyota, specifications are the documentation of the results, not a recipe of the plan."

When tailoring their documentation practices, teams should consider distinguishing between permanent documentation (which is consistently updated because a budget has been established) and working papers (which don't need to be updated). They should also contemplate the level of ceremony they need—rough notes work fine for many, many documents.[11] In order to use key engineering staff effectively, project managers should offload nearly all compliance documentation to administrative staff. The issue isn't zero or burdensome documentation, it's first what documentation contributes to delivery (today and in the future) and second what documentation is required for external compliance (regulations, for example). Colleague Lynne Nix has a great mantra for documentation: "A little documentation goes a long way if it's the right documentation."[12]

In the early to mid-1990s knowledge management practices placed an emphasis on explicit (written) knowledge, but in more recent years the pendulum has swung toward an emphasis on people and tacit knowledge— knowledge shared through interaction. When the critics of agile approaches

---

11. For example, new Xerox copiers can take hand-written notes, create a photocopy, and e-mail it to you. This is a nice way of getting electronic document and storage with little or no effort.
12. For additional information, see (Rueping 2003).

decry the "lack" of documentation, it's enough to make one scream, "The issue is *not* documentation; the issue *is* understanding." Understanding requires a blend of interactive conversations and documentation. The agile philosophy is that when documentation is used to replace conversation, it is misused. When it is used to complement conversation, it is used correctly.

Early Planning

There are always activities that need to be identified, and often planned, prior to the Explore phase. For example, end-of-iteration customer focus group reviews require the attendance of customers who may not work with the project team on a day-to-day basis. It therefore behooves the project team to schedule these review sessions early (at least for the first three to four months). Waiting until a few weeks before the session to invite participants usually results in poor attendance. The team needs to review all of the practices in the Speculate and Explore phases to ascertain if any "preplanning" needs to occur.

Envision Summary

Envisioning goes beyond project initiation. Initiation conjures an image of administration, of budgets and detailed schedules. And while these artifacts may be necessary, they need to flow from a well-articulated, discussed, and agreed-on vision. The four components of vision were expressed as questions early in this chapter:

- What is the product vision?
- What is the purpose of the project (objectives) and its constraints?
- Who will be included in the project community?
- How will the team deliver the product?

For some projects this Envision phase can be accomplished in a day, or several days. For others, particularly those that haven't gone through a feasibility study of some kind, it may take longer—not necessarily in effort, but in the calendar time it takes for the vision to jell within the project community.

Envisioning doesn't stop after the Envisioning phase. At the beginning of each iteration (or milestone), as the team meets to speculate about the next iteration, team members need to revisit the vision. This revisiting can be for the purpose of modifying the vision or to remind the team, amid the hectic daily grind, of the purpose of their endeavors.

Chapter 6

The Speculate Phase

Scope Evolution

"Hi, Dudess, how's it going?" Herman's voice boomed cheerfully in Maya's phone.

"Hermie, who you been hanging with lately?" Maya retorted.

"Just my team. I guess they're beginning to rub off on me a little. They're kind of cool when you get to know them."

Maya laughed. "Well, don't go changing too much, or I'll think the body snatchers got you. But seriously, how's it going with APM?"

"Good and bad. We're trying to use iterations and features, but I can't get around management's fixation on scope control," Herman replied. "They read the reports on project failures from scope creep, so we've got stringent change control procedures."

"Have they worked?" Maya asked. "My experience has been that strict change controls usually freeze requirements. The customers get so frustrated with the procedures that they just stop asking for needed changes."

"Well, we have managed to stabilize our project, but I'm not sure our customers are very happy. I think our concerns about destabilization have caused rigidity. There's a middle ground with how much change makes sense, but I admit I haven't found it yet."

"That's because it's always changing. An assumption that made sense at the beginning of the project clearly won't work by the time you're in the middle. We've found that you need to accommodate normal scope evolution rather than just try and control change."

"But I don't see any options; you either control scope or you don't," Herman said.

"Not quite," Maya responded. "Let's go back to one of the basic definitions of agility as 'the ability to balance stability and structure.' I look at it as trying to create a both/and situation rather than an either/or one. We think we can do both, and the secret is self-discipline. In the past, we've had both customers and developers who have made changes on a whim…"

"Oh, we have that all the time. First the customer wants one thing; two weeks later he wants the opposite. The project teams feel whipsawed back and forth. Unfortunately, they react by ignoring the customers."

"Right. We used to have similar problems, which were exacerbated by developers wanting to add features willy-nilly. They got away with it for a while because we were so scared about being rigid; we went overboard the other way for a time. Now we analyze changes fast within the team and document them with informal notes. It's really about attitude change—from change resistant to encouraging change. Change control is about coordination, not denial."

"Do you differentiate between minor and major changes?" asked Herman.

"Well, if the change impacts the overall boundaries of the project, we talk with the executive sponsor. Previously we found that minor changes based on a whim were destabilizing to our projects. Once we became self-disciplined about changes, even major changes tended to stabilize the project at the same time we were adapting to the change. It sounds weird, but that's how it worked for us."

"I don't know," said Herman. "You seem to be saying that self-discipline is the key. If I'm understanding you, undisciplined flexibility descends into chaos, while undisciplined stability creates rigidity."

"That's a good way to put it. To create real agility, we balance flexibility and structure through the application of rigorous self-discipline," Maya said. "Hey, I kind of like that! Gotta go. Next time."

Phase: Speculate

Plans are guides, not straightjackets. Agile teams plan, but they recognize that reality always intrudes. Plans in this context serve as a vehicle for embracing change, not blocking it. Plans have to adapt because the customers' understanding of their requirements changes, because estimates of work effort vary because of unknowns, because people arrive or depart from the project team, and for a variety of other reasons. Plans are both conjectures about the future—our best guess at what will occur given the information we have—and guides to the future—determining what we want to occur and making it happen. Development generates new information that in turn creates the need to replan.

Planning is an important activity, but speculating is a more appropriate term as uncertainty increases. Speculating establishes a target and a direction, but at the same time, it indicates that we expect much to change over the life of a project. As I mentioned in Chapter 4, speculating isn't wild risk taking but "conjecturing something based on incomplete facts or information." Plans are always conjectures about the future. When we "plan," we expect the actual project result to conform to that plan, and then deviations become project team mistakes or a sign of the team's failure to work hard enough. When we "speculate," we view the actual results positively—it's the plan we suspect was wrong. The plan, or speculation, is a piece of information, but it is only one piece that we will examine in order to determine our course of action in the next iteration.

The product of the Speculate phase is a release plan that outlines, to the best of the project team's initial knowledge, a plan that is based on features delivered rather than activities. The release plan utilizes information about the product's specification, platform architecture, resources, risk analysis, defect levels, business constraints, and target schedules.

There are two crucial components of an iterative planning and development approach—short iterative timeboxes and features. For software projects, iterations are generally two to six weeks in length. Hardware projects will have longer iterations and greater variation—electronic devices will generally have shorter timeboxes than, say, automobiles. Short iterations act to accelerate projects. By keeping timeframes short, teams have to figure out faster ways of accomplishing every aspect of development. For example, in serial development, major quality assurance activities are performed once toward the end of the project. In iterative development, QA activities are completed every iteration. The QA staff has to figure out how to be more effective and efficient because they perform these activities six, eight, or ten times rather than once.

Feature-based development is not a software-only technique. Many hardware product development efforts are driven by first creating a product structure and then an extensive list of the features. In addition, since more and more products include embedded software, hardware and software features are both candidates for this feature-driven approach.

The first goal of feature-based planning and development is to make the process visible, and understandable, to the customer team. All too often product development planning has concentrated on making the technical work understandable to the engineering team. Customers and product managers had to wade through lists of technical activities, many of which made little sense to them. A software development task such as "Create a normalized data schema design" means little to most customer teams. However, a hardware feature such as "Develop a DVD feature that will play sections of movies" resonates with customer teams. Customers understand products, components of products, and features of those components. They can attach significance (value) to these and therefore can make priority decisions about them. The engineering staff can then translate from a customer-facing view to a technical view in order to design and build the product.

Features act as the interface between development engineers and customer teams—a medium for shared understanding. This shared space takes the form of a feature card. The front of this hand-written index card contains feature information for planning purposes, while the back of the card contains technical task information to enable the team to estimate effort and manage its work.

Using this style of planning, product managers control which features are included in the product. Development engineers control how features are designed and implemented. Product managers wouldn't have the authority to say, for example, "We're running behind; let's cut testing time." Instead, they could only say, "We're running behind; let's cut features 34 and 68." Similarly, the development team couldn't arbitrarily add a feature because "it would be way cool." Obviously this delegation of responsibilities undergoes discussion and debate, as product managers may have suggestions about (but not final authority over) how products get built, and development engineers may make suggestions (but not final decisions) about potential features.

Agile project speculating helps the project team:

- Determine how the product and its features will evolve

- Balance anticipation of features and design with adaptation as the project unfolds
- Focus on the highest-value features early in the project
- Think about the project, business goals, and customer expectations
- Provide necessary budget and schedule information to management
- Establish priorities for tradeoff decisions as changes occur
- Coordinate interrelated activities and features across feature teams
- Consider alternatives and adaptive actions
- Provide a baseline for analyzing events that occur during the project

Everyone accepts the premise that our business world constantly changes. However, we still shrink from the implications of those changes. We still anticipate that plans won't change, at least not very much. We still view change as something to be controlled, as if we have some power over the world outside our projects. We still believe the way to reduce the cost of change is to anticipate everything at the beginning of the project.

The only problem is that this approach doesn't work. If we constantly measure people's performance against the plan, then adaptability will suffer. If we want adaptability, flexibility, innovation, and responsiveness to customers as they learn new information, then we need to reward the team's responsiveness to these changes, not admonish team members for not "making plan."

Through their actions, performance measurements, and vision, agile project managers constantly need to encourage teams to learn and adapt as projects evolve. Evolutionary projects are difficult—full of ambiguity, change, and uncertainty—but the rewards for adapting in order to deliver business value are great.

The practices explained in this chapter fall into two categories, as shown in Figure 6.1:

Feature Breakdown Structure
- Product feature list
- Feature cards
- Performance requirements cards

Release Planning
- Release, milestone, iteration plan

The final release plan can take several forms, such as a release plan spreadsheet (Figure 6.4), a feature card layout (Figure 6.5), a project "parking lot" (Figure 6.7), or some combination of these.

Figure 6.1
Speculate Phase
Practices

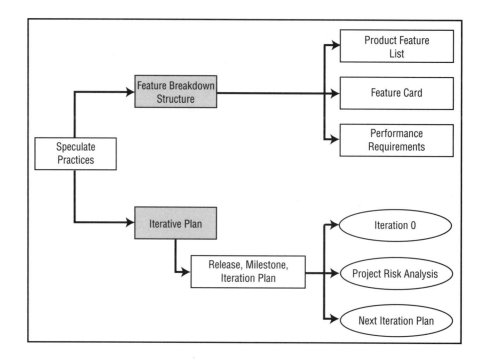

Practice: Product Feature List

Objective

The objective of this practice is to expand the product vision, through an evolutionary product requirements definition process, into a product feature list (similar to a manufacturing parts explosion list).

Discussion

A product feature list, an expansion and refinement of the one developed in the Envision phase, identifies and documents the features gathered for a product from feasibility or marketing studies, initial requirements-gathering efforts, and/or product visioning. For existing products, customers, developers, product managers, and customer support staff are constantly making suggestions about product enhancements. Part of a product manager's job is to constantly sift through this list and sort it (with customer involvement) into priority order. This list and the accompanying feature cards are the major inputs for release, milestone, and iteration planning.

Feature details evolve over the development phases. In the Envision phase the team creates a preliminary feature or product breakdown structure in which features are identified and structured (as shown in Figure 5.6). In the Speculate phase, the team expands this list, and for each feature creates an index card that contains basic descriptive and estimating information. During the Explore phase, in the specific iteration in which the feature is planned for implementation, the feature requirements are determined in detail, and the feature is built and tested.

There are tremendous differences between developing an automobile, an electronic instrument, a software application, or an airplane, and so the specifics of analyzing and specifying requirements and features vary widely. Some products will require more early requirements specification than others based on the cost of altering designs late in development. Since software is more malleable than nearly any other product, an evolutionary specification process will usually serve it best. However, as mentioned before, even the most sophisticated industrial products are undergoing evolutionary development via the use of simulations and modeling.

The results of the requirements specification process, whatever the engineering discipline involved, should be documented as a hierarchy of product features—product, component, group, and feature.[1] For business software products these categories could be product, business subject area, business activity, and feature (as explained later in this chapter). Small software products might use only the features level, while large industrial products with embedded software may use the entire hierarchy.

For a growing number of computer, instrumentation, and electronic products, a feature hierarchy will include both hardware and software features. Part of the design process will be determining whether low-level features will be implemented in hardware or software. Products that were once considered "hardware" products with rudimentary embedded software

---

1. Depending on the type of product, this "parts explosion" feature breakdown may be hierarchical, but it might also be nonhierarchical, particularly in the case of software.

now have such a large set of software features that they could be considered software products with supporting hardware. In just a few years, for example, cell phones have progressed from hardware with minimal software to hundreds of thousands of lines of software code that drive (or "support," depending on whether you are a hardware or a software engineer) all aspects of the hardware.

So what is a feature anyway? In general, a feature is defined as a piece of a product that delivers some useful and valuable functionality to a customer. Features for a software product (the ability to check a customer's credit rating) or an airplane (a comfortable seat for the passenger) will be very different, but they both focus on delivering value to the customer. In planning a product, however, some items that need to be delivered may not sound—at least to customers or product managers—as though they provide direct benefit. An interface component deep in the bowels of an electronic instrument may have minimal interest for an end customer but be a necessary "technology domain" feature.

For project planning and delivery purposes, teams need to include these technology features or components in the feature plan, where they are usually identified separately from customer-oriented features. However the project team decides to include these technical features, there is a danger in building too many technical or infrastructure components before building something that has direct meaning to the customer team. The longer the technical team "stays dark"—building techie stuff—the further off track the project can get before receiving feedback from the customer team. Getting off track like this can occur either because of the technical team's emphasis on infrastructure or the customer team's lack of adequate time to spend on the project. In either case, the project manager has to take action, even if it means halting the project until the issue can be resolved.

From the list of potential features, the product team and the engineering team will discuss prioritization and scheduling issues during the assignment of features to development iterations. One characteristic of APM projects is the volatility of the features on this list. For a more sedate project in which the requirements are firmly established in the beginning, this feature list becomes the input for a plan that becomes relatively fixed. In an agile project, the use of the list is much more dynamic. During the planning for each iteration, the list of features to be included in that iteration can change significantly from the original release plan.

Practice: Feature Cards

Objective

The purpose of feature cards is to provide a simple medium for gathering basic information about features, recording high-level requirements, and developing work estimates.

Discussion

Feature-based development is intended to be customer-facing development. Feature cards are used to identify, but not to define, features. Feature cards[2] act as agreements between customers and project team members to discuss (and document, to the extent necessary) detail requirements during an iteration. Discussion is critical to understanding, which in turn is critical to estimating. Feature cards identify features that the customer wants in the product. For large products, hardware component or business activity "group" cards (from the feature breakdown structure, or FBS) can be used to organize and plan individual feature lists. A group card may encompass 10, 15, or even 20 detail features.

Feature cards, as illustrated in Figure 6.2, are 4×6-inch index cards on which the project and customer team members record the information gathered in their requirements discussions. The critical piece is the discussion. As in other agile practices, the entire team, not the project manager alone, is responsible for interacting and producing the feature cards. The project manager facilitates the discussion and monitors action items, but agile planning is a team sport.

The cards themselves are important. They provide a mobile, tactile medium that team members can write on, shuffle about on the table, and have conversations around. Once data gets entered into a formal medium people are less likely to change it. The information on the cards becomes the product of the team's collaborative effort and a focal point for mutual understanding of the product at a detail level.

---

2. In Extreme Programming these are called story cards. Other agile software development methods may use similar terms—components, use cases, backlog items—although they are not identical concepts.

Figure 6.2
Sample Feature Card
(Requirements
Uncertainty Scale
refers to the explo-
ration factor cate-
gories; E=Erratic,
F=Fluctuating,
R=Routine,
S=Stable)

Feature Card	Planned Iteration: 3
Feature ID: 25	Feature Type: Cust
Feature Name: Establish Sales Territories	
Feature Description:	
Create US sales territories based upon states and standard metropolitan areas.	
Estimated Work Effort: 4.5 days	
Requirements Uncertainty (E, F, R, S): R (routine)	
Dependencies with Other Features: None	
Acceptance Tests:	

A few key items of information should be recorded on feature cards. Supplementary documents can be used for detailed requirements information. Typical items on feature cards are:

- Feature identifier and name
- Feature description: a sentence or two that describes the feature in customer terms
- Feature type (C=customer domain, T=technology domain)
- Estimated work effort: the estimated work effort needed to deliver the feature, including time for requirements gathering, design, coding, testing, and documentation[3]

---

3. Many project managers and team members are accustomed to estimating activities or tasks, not features. When estimating features, it is important to cover all the activities involved.

- Requirements uncertainty (erratic, fluctuating, routine, stable): an "exploration factor" for a specific feature
- Feature dependencies: dependencies that could influence implementation sequencing
- Acceptance tests: criteria the customer team will use to accept or reject the feature[4]

Often customer-recognizable features and technical activities provide orthogonal views of the same problem space. In planning the next iteration for a project (as I discuss later in this chapter), the team first turns the feature cards over and lists the technical activities required to specify, design, build, test, and document the feature. To progress from a customer-recognizable unit of work to a reasonable technical unit of work, there will probably be a reaggregation of that work. Technical activities from several customer features (e.g., multiple features displayed on a control panel) may be aggregated into a single technical work package. Design and technical architectures will influence this reaggregation.

For larger projects—those with 1,000 features, for example—the feature cards will probably require some form of automation for sharing among feature teams. While each individual team may use cards for its own planning sessions, sharing across multiple teams would prove difficult. Distributed teams and teams working under formal contracts may need to automate the cards—or more correctly, the information on the cards—even for smaller projects. As with other agile practices, the team should let the need dictate the use and formality of the documentation.

The level of requirements uncertainty and the technology risk factors will influence not only feature scheduling, but also the team's approach to implementing a feature. Generally, high-risk features (erratic or fluctuating) will be scheduled in early iterations so that the team can determine first, if the feature can be implemented at all, and second, if it can be implemented, if it will take more time or money than anticipated to implement it. If the requirements are difficult to gather or pin down, a series of discovery prototypes may be required. If the best design option isn't clear, a series of design experiments (simulations, quick throw-away implementations) may need to

---

4. These criteria could be implemented in specific test cases or included in a customer focus group review. Figuring out acceptance criteria compels the customer team to define what "done" means.

be conducted. Highly uncertain features may require additional research work before they can be planned at all. Even within a product there will be technology areas or features that run the gamut from low to high risk. Treating each with an approach geared to the level of risk will improve both effectiveness and productivity.

Practice: Performance Requirements Cards

Objective

Performance requirements cards document the key operations and performance requirements of the product to be built.

Discussion

While some performance requirements could be defined on a feature card and others could be covered as acceptance tests on a feature card, there are many situations in which a distinct, and very visible, definition of performance and operational requirements is necessary. For example, myriad design decisions—in fact the major design decisions—in aircraft design revolve around weight. Weight isn't a function of a single feature, avionics or engines, but a property of the entire plane. Similarly, the expected load on an Internet site is a function of the site, not an individual feature. In these cases it would be inappropriate to have the performance requirement be an acceptance test for an individual feature, although in the case of aircraft design, each subsystem team is given a weight target. If subsystems are too heavy, teams must coordinate by trading weight credits and negotiating other performance criteria.

Performance Card	Demonstrated Iteration: 6
Performance ID:	PC-12
Performance Name:	Flight Avionics Package Weight
Performance Description:	The weight allocated to the flight avionics package is 275 pounds, not including the display screens in the cockpit, which are included in the cockpit display package.
Difficulty in Achieving (H, M, L):	M (moderately difficult)
Acceptance Tests:	High-performance scale weights of all components beginning in iteration 3, followed by completed instrument package weighing in iteration 6.

Figure 6.3
Sample Performance Card

Performance cards—which can have a different color than feature cards—contain the name, description, and quantitative performance goals of the product, as shown in Figure 6.3. A card might be labeled, say, "Database Size" or "Aircraft Weight Limit" or "Training Time." Teams should focus on those performance attributes that will drive the design process. For example, weight, payload, range, and speed are critical aircraft design parameters; each would have a performance card (obviously backed up by more extensive documentation). Performance cards should also contain acceptance tests—how the team will demonstrate to the customer team that the product meets the performance criteria. These tests are essential when the performance criteria to be met involve critical real-world risks (e.g., planes falling out of the sky). Since some tests are very difficult to run until the product is fully built, creating interim tests (using simulations, prototypes, models, or historical calculations) should be considered.

Some performance attributes can be derived from the guiding principles established during the Envision phase. Others are well known by engineers who work with specific products. In any case, while feature specifications tell the engineering team what to build, performance requirements often have more relevance to the design process itself—they force design tradeoffs and often must be dealt with early in the project. They are a vital part of the information a product development team has to gather and analyze as it plans and implements features.

Practice: Release, Milestone, and Iteration Plan

Objective

A release, milestone, and iteration plan presents a roadmap of how the project team intends to achieve the product vision within the project scope and constraints identified in the project data sheet.

Discussion

As I discussed in Chapter 2, agile lifecycles are both iterative and feature driven. The feature-driven aspect changes the primary focus of planning and executing from tasks to product features. Most traditional project management plans utilize tasks to construct work breakdown structures (WBSs) to organize work.[5] Although experienced project managers concentrate first on deliverables and then on the work necessary to create those deliverables, work- or task-driven plans often degenerate into very detailed, prescriptive

---

5. Ken Delcol comments, "The WBS is really an extension of the PBS and hence closely reflects the product's architecture, which the engineers understand. This is critical when functions are allocated to the subsystems (i.e., the team determines which subsystems will support which customer features/functions). If the WBS is set up this way, then there is a stronger linkage between features and subsystems."

plans. Any product has a set of features that customers use for some purpose. The more quickly we can link those customers with the features they have requested and get feedback on them, the more likely the product development effort will be successful.

Seasoned project managers understand that how they break the project down into work breakdown structures can have a significant impact on how that project is managed and implemented. Each possible WBS has advantages and disadvantages. A feature breakdown structure (FBS) may strike some project managers as being more difficult to administer,[6] but it offers the significant advantage of increasing interaction between the project team and customers. Phase-based WBSs (requirements, design, build, test, etc.) may be easier to administer, but they don't match how engineers actually work.

Another advantage of basing plans on a product's features (and its architecture, which is instantiated by features) is that it keeps the project team and the customer team synchronized. It also focuses the team on delivering the product features rather than intermediate documentation artifacts.

The above statement isn't meant to minimize the importance of all forms of documentation; no one would consider building, say, an airplane or an automobile without extensive documentation. The problem is not documentation per se but that project teams often get lost producing intermediate artifacts that have little bearing on the team's real progress toward a final product. All too often, deliverables are documents, and the WBSs define document delivery schedules. In hardware development the team might deliver detail drawings, assembly drawings, test cases, simulations, specification control drawings, and bills of materials—all of which are used by the either the manufacturing organizations or the vendors to produce the parts. These documents contribute to the value generation stream. Even so, value-generating documentation has a great tendency to morph into compliance documentation. Feature-driven planning and constant thinking about value generation help to overcome this problem.

However, many project managers can't fathom a twelve-month project broken down into two-week iterations, which is understandable. Once

---

6. With a task-based WBS, tasks are relatively permanent. With a feature-based WBS, features can be added or deleted during each iteration. This adding and deleting of features can cause resource plan management and reporting difficulties. One solution to this problem is to group features such that specific features can easily change while the *group* of features remains more stable.

projects go beyond four to five months, project participants usually need interim checkpoints between two-week intervals and the project's end. Larger projects that employ distributed teams or vendor-supplied components will have problems synchronizing every two weeks. Therefore many projects will require three levels of iteration. The longest period is the release cycle. Products are generally released to customers periodically— for example, once every year or eighteen months.

Iterations produce acceptance-tested features. The goal is to have a partial-feature product that could be deployed at the end of any iteration—that is, the features, tests, documentation, and other product deliverables could be packaged up and deployed. Actual deployment of the iterative results— referred to as incremental delivery—depends on a variety of factors (as I will discuss in the section on first feasible deployment).

A development team uses an iteration to concentrate on small increments of work. In software development, an iteration might be two to six weeks or slightly longer for some projects.[7] If you're building an airplane, the iterations will surely be longer (although early prototype analysis might use very short iterations). Features developed within a feature team (usually fewer than ten people who work on a group of features) should be integrated and tested by the end of the iteration.

Milestones are intermediate points, usually from one month to three months apart. Milestones can have both a project management function and a technical function. From a project management perspective, milestones provide a chance to review progress and make significant project adjustments. While some reviews should occur every iteration (e.g., a customer team review of the product), others might be appropriate at the end of a milestone (e.g., a mini-retrospective of the team's performance).

The more important use of milestones is as major synchronization and integration points. For a product that has hardware and software components, monthly (or even less frequent) synchronizations may be entirely adequate. A software product team utilizing an external vendor for a component might plan to integrate that component starting at milestone two (two months into the project) and at every other milestone after that.

---

7. Iteration length will vary considerably across product types. Even within a single product, iterations for the hardware and embedded software features may be of different lengths, but they must synchronize at milestones.

Biweekly synchronization with the vendor could be too costly. On the other hand, if less frequent synchronizations are going poorly, it might indicate that the synchronization should occur more often. Milestones can also be viewed as "intermediate" planning horizons.

Some components will invariably take longer, or appear to take longer, than one iteration to complete. Usually when teams are pressed to decompose a "big" component into bite-sized features, they figure out a way. Inability to break things down in this manner is usually an issue of lack of experience rather than a un-decomposable component. However, in the unusual situation in which a component's development spans two or more iterations, the project manager and team need to keep in mind the added risk involved in delaying customer feedback on it.

Two factors drive release, milestone, and iteration plans—customer value and risk. A feature may deliver high value but not be risky, or it may employ risky new technology that is invisible to the end customer. Normally the first priority in assigning features to iterations is delivering customer value as defined by the customer team, and the second priority is to schedule features that reduce risk early in the project.[8] Sometimes a technical risk takes top priority. For example, if an airplane has a performance criterion that it must fly 10,000 miles without fueling and the technology to do this is as yet unknown, then there is no point in having the customers prioritize features until the technical team has some degree of confidence that it can meet the performance requirement. All other scheduling considerations—resource availability, dependencies, and others—are subordinate to those of value and risk.

Iteration 0

Some people think agile development gives developers license to dive in and build (or code, in the software arena). They condemn agile methods, saying that such methods spend little or no time on early requirements gathering or architectural issues. On the other hand, there has been an equally negative reaction to projects in which months and months of planning, requirements

---

8. The value may need to be explicitly calculated for each feature or group of features. This topic is covered in more depth in Chapter 8.

specification, and architectural philosophizing occur before they deliver any customer value. There is a balance point, but the argument would lead you to believe that there is no middle ground. Iteration 0 is a practice that can help teams find that middle ground and balance anticipation with adaptation. The "0" implies that nothing useful to the customer—features, in other words—gets delivered in this time period. However, the fact that we have designated an iteration implies that the work is useful to the project team.

A project to develop a large business software application, one that must be integrated with other business applications, may require some data architecture work in order to adequately define the interfaces with those other applications. In the case of an electronic instrument, the team might find it useful to create a preliminary componentization architecture. Teams utilizing unfamiliar technology may need time for training prior to a project's launch. A customer may demand a requirements document prior to signing a contract. All of these examples indicate a need for some time expenditure prior to launching into actual iterative feature development. For each of these items, a feature card (which will usually contain an artifact—a shape architecture diagram, for example—rather than an implementable feature) should be created and placed in iteration 0. The need for an iteration 0 will usually be obvious before the project gets underway and will be planned as part of the Envision phase.

While the relevant issues may vary, the outcome is the same—some projects require more extensive initialization work than others. The key to effectively utilizing iteration 0 is to balance the possible advantages of further planning with the growing disadvantage of lack of customer-deliverable features. There are always tradeoffs. If the cost of a technical platform change is very high, then additional work to improve the odds of a correct initial decision may be justified. The timeframe of an iteration 0 for a next-generation jumbo jetliner will be much different than that for a portable CD player.

Iterations 1–N

For most projects, the team will need to create a plan that assigns features to iterations for the duration of the project in order to get a feel for the project flow and determine completion dates, staffing, costs, and other

Feature	10	11	12	13	14	I5/M1
Iteration Delivery Date	1-May	1-Jun	1-Jul	1-Aug	1-Sep	30-Sep
Order Management						
Order Entry—Basic		8				
Order Entry—Advanced				6		
Order Pricing		3				
Partial Order Handling			4			
Calculate Reorders					6	
Pricing Error Handling				6		
Lead Generation						
Create Prospect Database		4				
Create Lead Message		2				
Generate Leads			8			
Call Service Center						
Establish Call Center Disks				4		
Establish Product Profiles				3		
Establish Service Entries					2	
Provide Call Routing					5	
Administrative and Security						
Security and Control					2	
User Documentation				3	4	
Contingency and Rework			3	3	3	20
Technology and Domain						
Shape Architecture	6					
Create EJB Connectors			8			
Work Effort in Days	6	17	23	25	22	20

Figure 6.4
Summary Release Plan for the CRM System (Iteration 5 is the first major milestone.)

project planning information. The resultant plan can be viewed in a spreadsheet, as shown in Figure 6.4. The project team and key members of the

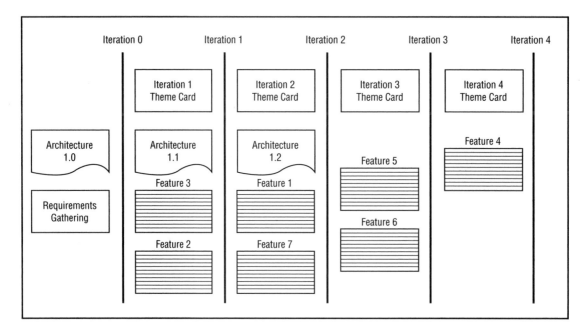

Figure 6.5
Feature Card Whiteboard Layout

customer team, including the product manager, do iteration planning. The activities involved in laying out the iteration plan include:

- Determining how identified risks will influence iteration planning
- Identifying the schedule target
- Establishing the milestone and iteration periods
- Developing a theme for each iteration (or milestone)
- Assigning feature cards to each iteration, balancing customer priorities, risks, resources, and dependencies as necessary
- Summarizing the plan in some combination of a feature-level spreadsheet plan (Figure 6.4), a feature card layout (Figure 6.5) (usually on a wall), or a project parking lot (Figure 6.7)
- Calculating an initial project schedule from staff availability and total feature effort estimates
- Adjusting the completed plan as necessary

While the product manager (together with the customer team) determines the priority of feature assignment to iterations, technical risk issues may influence her decisions. As previously discussed, customer value and risk are the primary drivers for feature scheduling. For example, in a project with an erratic requirements risk (the team realizes that requirements will be difficult to determine and volatile), the decisions on what features to implement early may be different than those for a project with high technical risk (the team has never used the technology combination before). There may be times when high-value features, which would normally be implemented first, will have to be deferred in favor of high-risk features, which need to be implemented early to reduce the risk. A risk list should be reviewed to determine what impact risk mitigation might have on the iteration plan, specifically the sequencing of features and the incorporation of high-risk items. Other considerations, such as feature-to-feature dependencies, may have some influence on scheduling, but customer value and risk are paramount.

Every project has some target delivery date selected by marketing, management, or a customer. A target establishes what someone outside the project team desires due to an understanding of the business. In the case of a co-product release (say Microsoft is releasing a new version of Windows, for which your company has a complementary product), a release date may be fixed. A target may also be used to ensure a fixed limit on development cost. While the rationale behind these dates can vary from a thoughtful analysis of the market to an off-the-cuff guess, they are important. Whether off-the-cuff or thoughtful, they represent the stakeholders' expectation. Every project also has a planned date, which the engineering team develops as part of the release planning process. Both of these dates will be used in the negotiation process, but the project team needs to understand the stakeholders' expectation, even if it is outlandish.

In many cases the target date becomes a constraint on the project. Let's say the best planning and negotiation still yield a date that the product manager, with executive concurrence, deems two months too long. The earlier date can be designated as the constraint date, provided everyone understands its purpose. Since there are many unknowns about the project, everyone—the development and customer teams and executives—works to resolve those unknowns such that the project is completed by the earlier date. For example, everyone looks to cut features in order to reduce the scope. At the earliest time that information indicates the earlier date cannot be achieved, a reevaluation of the project would occur.[9]

Iteration and milestone periods will vary considerably depending on the size of the project and whether it involves hardware and software, just software, or just hardware (rare today). As previously mentioned, milestones can be used for the purposes of both project management (status reporting) and technical synchronization (integrating hardware and software components). Hardware iterations may be longer than those for software, but the iterations should sync on milestone boundaries for integration testing.

For each milestone or iteration the team should develop and write a guiding theme. This is critical for focusing and ensuring that the team balances between breadth and depth of features. Theme development often evolves from the process of assigning features to iterations, but sometimes initial themes present themselves independently. These themes (e.g., "Demonstrate the basic instrument data acquisition capability"), or goals, help focus the team in ways that a list of individual features may not. Themes can also reflect risk abatement strategies (e.g., "Prove that our high-risk valve design is viable"). For large projects in which many features are being built each iteration, themes are particularly important. The best way to document the theme is on an iteration card, as shown in Figure 6.6. These cards can be used to organize feature cards on the table or wall and to record other useful information (such as assumptions) about the iteration.

One of the reasons index cards are an effective planning tool is that they can be easily shuffled during each iteration's planning session. For small projects the team may lay cards out on a table, while for larger ones cards may be taped to whiteboards. A summary spreadsheet can show a snapshot of the entire project and maintain resource summaries. While cards should identify features that are as independent from each other as possible, dependencies will occur and influence the order of implementation. It's critical that this information be captured on the card.

Other techniques can create a more reliable schedule. The first is to add time to each iteration for changes that are identified during an iteration review. One feature card entitled "Rework and Contingency" is placed in

---

9. This process of negotiating between target and planned dates will only work when all parties are working collaboratively to achieve a common goal. It will not work in a situation in which parties are being arbitrary and capricious.

Iteration Number: 3
Theme: To simulate the basic functions of the instrument circuit board
Comment:
Advanced functions will be addressed in iteration 7.
Assumption:
The simulations will be able to test 80% to 90% of the board functionality.

Figure 6.6
Documenting an Iteration Theme

each iteration. I've often seen plans with inspection or review tasks but without any time allotted for the changes that arose from those reviews! At the end of each iteration, an agile project goes through several quick reviews, both customer and technical. The planning phases of some agile methods imply that features are started and finished within a single iteration. Experience shows that most features actually evolve over two or three iterations as customer focus groups provide feedback. Including a rework and contingency "feature" card in each iteration (10%+ of the effort scheduled for the iteration) provides time for changes that are inevitable, even though the details aren't known.

A second technique for increasing the reliability of the schedule, particularly with high exploration-factor projects, is to set aside one or more "empty" iterations at the end of the project. These buffers are used to accommodate changes, new features, or other project alterations. Alternatively, features assigned to the last iteration or two should be those that can be dropped if necessary.

A final point about release planning needs to be made. Despite superficial appearances, this is *not* prescriptive planning. Even though a full release plan with features assigned to each iteration may *look* prescriptive, the plan is subject to review and revision at the end of each iteration and milestone.

Figure 6.7
Project Parking Lot
Plan

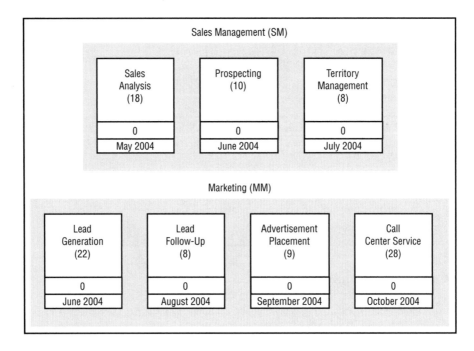

Component- or Business Activity-Level Planning and Reporting

For medium to large projects, feature-level planning is too fine grained, at least for many customers and managers. In automotive development, for example, a parts explosion (a type of FBS) for an entire car contains thousands of small parts. Similarly, a large software application may contain thousands of features. While the development team needs to plan and deliver at a detail level, customers and managers can be more effective at a coarser level of granularity.

In such situations, a practice derived from the work of Jeff DeLuca, one of the authors of Feature-Driven Development (FDD), can help. The FDD approach relies on a granular feature hierarchy. In a customer relationship management (CRM) application development project, the hierarchy might be business subject area (Sales), business activity (Sales Analysis), and feature (Generate a Territory Sales by Product Report). For an automobile project, the hierarchy might be platform (SUV Truck Body), group (Drivetrain), component (Transmission), and feature (Construct the Shift Lever). DeLuca uses a parking lot diagram, as illustrated in Figure 6.7, to plan and report at the component (hardware) or business activity (business software) levels.

Figure 6.7 shows a plan for a CRM system that includes two business subject areas (Sales Management and Marketing) and seven business activities, each represented as a box within each of those subject areas (e.g., Sales Analysis, Prospecting, and Territory Management under Sales Management). The numbers in parentheses under the activity names indicate the number of detail features identified for that activity (e.g., 18 for Sales Analysis), and the date at the bottom of the box indicates the month and year when that activity will be completed. Large applications, like those for CRM, might have 30 to 50 activities and several thousand features. In this approach to planning, the customer team is heavily involved in scheduling at the component or activity level, while the detailed scheduling at the feature level is left to the engineering team (with involvement from customers who may have detailed product or customer resource scheduling knowledge). This "two-tier" approach to planning can be very effective. It gives the customer team a dependable and reliable planning mechanism and the development team some flexibility.[10]

In the Figure 6.7 example, the Prospecting activity has been scheduled for completion in June 2004. Based on dependencies, resource availability, and other factors, the development team might schedule individual Prospecting features in April, May, and June. The features go through the same detail planning, development, and review process during their scheduled iteration as previously described. So, for example, if the development team scheduled a specific feature for April and it wasn't completed during its planned iteration, it would be flagged as late, even though the activity wasn't due for delivery until June.

---

10. In FDD (for software), DeLuca breaks the technology domain into User Interface, Database, and Systems Interface features. Scheduling these features is primarily the responsibility of the development team, which schedules them as required by the customer's scheduling of business activities. For industrial products, there could be similar categories of technology features that were scheduled primarily by the technical team.

Even with smaller projects, a hierarchy of activity and features can assist the team in thinking about a product. Listing features and then organizing them into activities, or starting with generic activities from a previous project or from product research and then identifying new features, can contribute to product understanding. In any case, the final artifacts from a planning activity include some combination of feature cards (or their electronic equivalent), an FBS (expanded upon from the product architecture practice), a feature card iteration layout, and a project parking lot.

Three Types of Iteration Plans

There are several ways to construct an initial project schedule. For example, the team can create an initial schedule by assigning features to iterations up to the target date and then determining if the scope (features that can be implemented) appears reasonable. Another approach would be to schedule all features and then compare the planned date (with all features) to the target date. Usually the target date precedes the planned date, and the engineering team, product manager, and sponsor must then negotiate, which also involves resetting expectations based on these new facts. Up to this point the target date was a desired date not grounded in an implementation plan.

However, for projects with high exploration factors, all these initial schedules can be very iffy. Depending on the degree of project uncertainty, teams might develop:

- A complete plan with features assigned to every iteration[11]
- A two-iteration plan utilizing only a next iteration and then everything after
- An iteration-by-iteration plan

Deciding upon one of these planning approaches will depend on the nature of the project and the expectations of customers and stakeholders.

---

11. Colleague Mike Cohn suggests another type of plan he calls a "buffered plan," which uses a critical chain–style estimating and buffering scheme. I would recommend that in doing a complete release plan, the team consider buffering, such as the rework and contingency cards, to match the uncertainty of the project.

The first, a complete plan, gives the team and other stakeholders a reasonable idea of how the entire project may unfold and a complete cost. This type of plan would be appropriate for a project with a mid- to upper-range exploration factor. In a two-iteration plan, the team decides on the features that will be implemented in the project as a whole and then selects the ones to be delivered in the next iteration. When there is a higher exploration factor, laying out all features into iterations may not be worth the time because of the overwhelming likelihood that much of the plan will change. The bulk of the features are scheduled in the "large" second iteration. With appropriate resource information, the team can make a stab at a planned delivery date.

For very high exploration-factor projects, the team may just select features for the first iteration, implement them, and then go on to the next iteration, with only a vague idea of how the overall project will unfold. If this strategy is employed, this "vision" of how to proceed should be discussed and agreed to in the Envision phase in order to establish reasonable expectations early on in the project. In this situation, the development team and management are learning about and managing risk based on the information discovered during each iteration. In any case, the plan remains a hypothesis about the future, not a prediction, and it will change over the life of the project. With projects of this last type, it will be very difficult to estimate a reasonable planned completion date, so a target date can be used as a constraint until a reasonable planned date can be determined.

Next Iteration Plan

Once the overall release plan has been established for the entire project, the team returns to develop a detail plan for the next (or the first, if it's the beginning of the project) iteration. The team takes each feature card and constructs a list of the technical activities required to implement the feature and records the activities on the back of the card. The team then reestimates the work effort based on the more detailed assessment and adjusts the features planned for the iteration if necessary.

Finally, team members sign up for features or activities based on their skills and/or desires. In some projects team members sign up for implementing whole features; in others they sign up for activities within features (and someone else signs up to make sure the whole feature is completed). Notice that the relevant words are "signed up for" not "assigned to" (i.e., by the project manager). Taking on the responsibility for getting the work done reinforces each individual's commitment to the project and thereby contributes to building a self-organizing team. Some teams may not have the experience or self-discipline to carry this sign-up off, but the project manager's and team's ability to make it work is a good indicator of their maturing into an effective, adaptive team.

Often in workshops or presentations the inevitable question arises, "Well, what happens if no one signs up for a particular task?" or "What happens when someone with the wrong skill set signs up for a task or feature that he is not capable of delivering?" Teams that are just learning the process might need to be coached with a gentle, "We don't leave the planning meeting until all tasks are taken." With experienced self-disciplined teams, the question never comes up—they understand task-level planning and the expectation that all tasks will be covered. In the second case, the project manager would "nudge" the team member into a different assignment, possibly pairing the inexperienced person with someone else.

First Feasible Deployment

Since there are significant benefits to early product deployment, one thing a product team can do is determine a first feasible deployment (FFD);[12] that is, the first iteration in which the product could potentially be deployed. For example, a company might be able to deploy early versions of a product to key customers who have been asking for such a product. The customers understand that the product only has certain features, but they are willing to work with that limited functionality. For the development team, early deployment might bring in both revenue and helpful product feedback. Early deployment has certain benefits but also potential costs, and high deployment costs would offset some of the benefits.

Teams contemplating an early deployment strategy need to think about it during initial release planning, as feature scheduling may be impacted. For example, an early deployment strategy might suggest scheduling all of the

---

12. For software products, this first feasible deployment is often called a "release candidate."

features in a particular area early such that the product would be rich enough in that one area to deploy. In the absence of an early deployment strategy, implementing features across functional areas might work as well or even better. Early deployment and beta test strategies also need to be considered together.

Iterative development creates *deployable* pieces of a product, whereas incremental development actually deploys pieces of the product. In some types of software development—Web-based systems, for one—each iteration can be an incremental deployment. With early deployment of partially completed products, early revenue can boost ROI, and early feedback from customers can enhance the development during subsequent iterations. Other products will be difficult to partially deploy. For example, if a competitor has a product on the market with a certain capability, it may not be feasible to deploy your product until it has comparable capability.[13] And needless to say, it would be inadvisable to deploy a partial airplane.

So identifying the FFD iteration provides both the engineering and customer teams with an idea of when the product might first be profitably deployed. If the FFD is toward the end of the project, it indicates a potential schedule risk or may even call into question the feasibility of the project itself.

Estimating

In nearly every presentation or workshop, I get the question, "How do you estimate an agile project?" The basic answer is "Using the same techniques you already employ." There are three subtleties underlying the "how to estimate" question:

- How to estimate the unknown
- How to estimate by features rather than activity
- How to do progressive estimation

---

13. On the other hand, Ken Delcol notes that "waiting for a full-featured product can be a mistake. Partial deployment forces you to identify which of the features are most important to your customers. Most software products have way too many features that the customer rarely uses. Partial deployment when the competition has a complete product may allow you to learn something about the customer that you and the competition do not know."

First, since agile methods are often used for high exploration-factor projects, the critical estimating question becomes "How do you estimate the unknown?" and the answer is "You can't." When there are unknowns, you are guessing, not estimating—and it's the best we can do. This is one reason why time and cost are often viewed as constraints, not estimates, in agile projects. Agile organizations learn to live with uncertainty rather than trying to demand certainty in a fast-changing world.

Second, agile projects are planned by features, whereas many project managers may be more familiar with task-based estimating. These managers have to learn to apply their experience to estimating tasks for each feature. For example, rather than estimate requirements gathering for an entire project, they will be estimating it on a feature-by-feature basis. Teams members who have spent several days identifying features and assigning them to iterations usually have a much better understanding of the product than those who have relied on task-based planning. So in most cases, feature-based planning provides better estimates.

Third, good project managers have always tried to employ progressive estimation practices (e.g., completing requirements definition prior to estimating the rest of the project), but they are often stymied by organizational demands for early numbers for budgeting purposes. Teams practicing APM can provide similar estimates for such purposes, but APM is fundamentally a progressive estimating and delivery process that mirrors the actual way product information unfolds over time.

As good project managers using task-based planning know, accumulating a project estimate from detailed estimates of either tasks or features can result in overestimating the entire project. Multiple techniques—bottom up and top down, comparisons to similar projects, using estimating tools—can help teams arrive at better overall project estimates, but they can't make up for uncertainty. While multiple techniques provide a better estimate for the entire project, team member estimates should be used for the next iteration plan. It is important for team development and cohesion that team members be responsible, and accountable, for these early iteration plans. As project iterations progress, the team members should get better at estimating for the next iteration, which should also improve the estimates for the rest of the project.

When estimating high exploration-factor projects, using distribution curves for estimates can help everyone—development team members, customers, and executives—assess the impact of uncertainty and risk. For example, for a given product scope, a skewed distribution curve would show the cumulative probability of delivering on a range of dates. The curve might show that the probability of hitting the target date is 75%, while the probability of hitting the target date plus two months is 85%.

As projects increase in size, estimation requires more than team members estimating features. While teams may have a reasonable idea of how long it will take them to develop features (at least for iterations early in the project), they will usually underestimate the workload involved in coordinating with other teams. As team size increases, productivity decreases, sometimes dramatically. For example, in software development a single small team with good tools might achieve a productivity rate of 50 function points (a sizing measure) per staff month, whereas a 100-person team would be highly unlikely to achieve even one-half of that. Understanding industry norms and using software tools in estimating can provide teams with sanity checks on team estimates. Even the best team is unlikely to deliver a product in one-half the time that anyone has ever done it before.

Scope Evolution

APM approaches scope management realistically. Scope creep isn't the problem, even though many observers lament the problems with escalating requirements. Reality is more complex than an admonition to "avoid scope creep" can handle. Some scope changes are inexpensive but valuable. Some scope changes are extensive and expensive but crucial to delivering customer value. Of course scope changes can be detrimental to a project if they are arbitrary and ill thought out. But in general, scope changes that are incorporated to meet evolving customer requirements and undertaken with an understanding, and approval, of their impact on the project increase the probability of project success.

At the XP2002 software development conference in Italy, Jim Johnson of the Standish Group presented some interesting information related to scope. First, Johnson discussed two federally mandated state child welfare projects—one in Florida and the other in Minnesota. The Florida project was begun in 1990 with an original budget of $32 million, a staff of 100, and a delivery date of 1998. As of the last review, the project was estimated at

$170 million and expected to be completed in 2005. The Minnesota system, with the same basic goals, began in 1999 and finished in 2000 with a staff of 8 who expended $1.1 million. Admittedly, many factors could be responsible for the differences, but a significant portion of the difference was attributed to "gold plating" requirements.

Gold plating is a type of scope creep that can be a significant problem, as the Standish and other studies (Jones 1994) show. Agile development encourages change that arises from evolving knowledge, while at the same time it discourages the gold plating and requirements bloat that often occur in traditional up-front requirements gathering. Johnson reported on two other Standish studies (one done for Dupont and another general study). In the first, Dupont estimated that only 25% of the features implemented in its software applications were actually needed. The Standish study estimated that 45% of software features were never used, and only 20% were used often or always. This points out another reason why partial deployment can be instrumental in ROI generation—it may keep you from building costly but unused features! If you were able to cut project sizes in half and project teams in half, wouldn't that greatly speed development and reduce costs at the same time?

Given these numbers, it's ironic that many traditional requirements-gathering practices decry the dreaded "feature creep" as a major problem in development. I would contend that it's faster and cheaper to let features evolve over the life of the project (within some limits, of course) than to hallucinate about what the requirements are in the beginning and then build them without constant customer involvement. A strategy of building minimum features and (a very important "and") a capability to easily and reasonably adapt to change can be very profitable.

Agile development is about focus and balance—focusing on the project's key vision and goals and forcing hard tradeoff decisions that bring balance to the product. Agile development plans by feature, in customer terminology, thereby concentrating the planning process on something the customer can relate to and prioritize easily. Because plans are adjusted each iteration based on actual development experience, not someone's guesses or wishes, nice-to-have features are pushed into later iterations and are often eliminated completely.

A product's scope should be driven by customer value, technical feasibility and cost, the impact on a product's adaptability, and critical business schedule needs. It should not be held hostage to a plan developed when our product and project knowledge was still in its infancy.

The short iterations in agile development, combined with end-of-iteration customer reviews, make the entire team—developers, customers, and managers—face reality. We can take a requirements document and "estimate" how long it will take to develop and test the code, or we can build a small set of features and measure how long it actually took to develop them. "Yes, we estimated that we could implement 25 features this iteration, but in reality, we only delivered 15. Now what?" We now have to drop features, add staff, and/or extend the project time. Note that we do this early in a project when there is still time to compensate. Traditional approaches delay these difficult decisions until the point at which adaptive action is nearly impossible. Short-cycle reality checks keep featuritis from getting out of hand.

Short iterations also keep developers focused. With a deadline approaching every few weeks, the tendency to "enhance" features diminishes. The prioritization previously discussed emphasizes reducing the number of features undertaken. Short iterations then act to limit the size of those features. Agile practices incorporate change into the development process, while at the same time reducing project size by constant and intense concentration on essentials.

Risk Analysis and Mitigation

Since APM was designed to handle high-risk, uncertain product development projects, a separate risk analysis may seem redundant. Redundant or not, it is crucial that risk analysis and mitigation become an integral part of every APM phase and process.

Until a final product emerges, the product development process is fundamentally one of gathering and processing information. A product's design evolves from understanding requirements and constraints and the underlying science or engineering. "Will this specialized chip do everything we specified? Will this titanium piece pass our stress tests?" Product development consists of answering hundreds, or even thousands, of such questions. Each answered question, each new piece of information, reduces the risk of project failure. Planning doesn't eliminate project risks; constant gathering of information systematically reduces them over the life of the project. Gathering information costs money, so we want to constantly ask what information has the highest value. The strategies we employ to gather information should be guided in part by our risk analysis—it's an integral part of the product development process and a critical component of iteration planning.

Rather than summarize what has been well documented by others about risk management, I will use some existing material to discuss how APM addresses different categories of risk. In *Waltzing with Bears*, their book on software risk management, Tom DeMarco and Tim Lister identify five core risks that dominate software projects:

1. Inherent schedule flaws
2. Requirements inflation (creep)
3. Employee turnover
4. Specification breakdown
5. Poor productivity (DeMarco and Lister 2003)

First, as these authors point out, "The best bang-per-buck risk mitigation strategy we know is incremental delivery." Inherent schedule flaws occur when the size of the product to be developed is either grossly misestimated or the engineering team is given a date based on fantasy rather than reality. For a highly uncertain product, failing to meet a schedule plan may not be a flaw but merely the impossibility of scheduling the unknown. In these cases, executives and product marketing (and the engineering team) have to understand what the process of exploration involves—and what are reasonable and unreasonable expectations. While APM addresses the issue of schedule flaws in a number of material ways, no process—agile or otherwise—can make up for an organization bent on the politics of fantasy.

APM techniques that address schedule risk are:

- Heavy team involvement in planning and estimating
- Early feedback on delivery velocity
- Constant pressure to balance the number and depth of features with schedule constraints
- Close interactions between engineering and customer teams
- Early error detection/correction to keep a clean working product

Requirements creep must first be differentiated from requirements evolution. Requirements evolution is inevitable in exploration projects; in fact it is desirable, because the cost of change remains low in agile projects, and therefore requirements evolution remains cost effective. Requirements evolution is a rational process in which the development and customer teams are constantly evolving the requirements of the product while considering other constraints such as time and cost. Requirements evolution is a joint effort in which all parties participate in deciding on features. Requirements creep occurs when there isn't a joint effort, when customers or developers add features indiscriminately. Requirements growth has acquired a negative connotation because of the high cost of change in many development efforts. Eliminate or greatly reduce that barrier, and evolving requirements become a virtue, not a vice.

Employee turnover, particularly losing a key person, remains a risk factor for any product development effort. The impact of turnover can be reduced by cross training (which rarely happens) and documentation (which conveys very little of the tacit knowledge that is so critical to success). Agile projects have built-in turnover mitigation because of the emphasis on collaboration. In software development, for example, the use of pair programming has demonstrated better knowledge sharing within the team, which reduces the impact of turnover (Williams and Kessler 2003).

Specification breakdown occurs when the customers or product managers fail to agree on specifications. For example, when an internal IT project has 10 customer departments and they can't decide on business process or business rules issues, the specification process breaks down. Unfortunately, in many serial projects, the project continues under the false assumption that the decisions will be made sometime later. The result of indecision—conflicting specifications or multiple near-duplicate features—can have devastating results for the project. APM lessens this risk by insisting on a product manager role. The product manager, aided by the executive sponsor, is charged with either stopping specification breakdown or halting the project until the specification process can be fixed. Creating a viable specification decision-making process is the responsibility of the customer team.

DeMarco and Lister's final risk of poor productivity arises from three sources: having the wrong people on the team, having a team that doesn't work well together, and poor morale. The APM practices of getting the right people on the team, coaching and team development, and forcing reality on the project help offset these risks. Similarly, using short iterations to focus on features, feature depth, and feature value often reduces the total amount of work on a product, which contributes to ROI, if not directly to productivity.

Colleague Ken Delcol contends technology risk should be added to the list for hardware projects, and colleague Donna Fitzgerald always includes it on her list of risks for software projects. The issue in both cases is that technology can't just be assumed. On some projects a high level of technology risk is appropriate, while on others it might border on foolishness.

In addition, NPD expert Robert Cooper lists four key failure areas for new products: poor marketing research, technical problems, insufficient marketing effort, and bad timing. Cooper's list indicates that much of the success or failure of a new product is outside the engineering team's control. However it's still within the scope of what the entire team—engineering and product management—should be constantly examining. Incremental delivery might mitigate some of these risks, but in general the development process itself won't make up for poor marketing research unless periodic reviews are held with the actual external customer (Cooper 2001).[14]

Agile development targets risky projects—those with high levels of uncertainty and short delivery schedules. Understanding the risks, within the context of a particular project, requires experience. Mountain climbers who get into the most trouble are those who don't understand the risks. Experienced mountaineers know their limits; they have a sixth sense about when to continue on—because getting to the top of major peaks requires pushing oneself and one's team to the edge, but not over the edge—and when to turn back. Project teams and managers need to be visionary and positive, and at the same time, brutally honest about the risks. For project teams operating at the edge on highly risky projects, there are no formulaic answers to managing risk. APM requires the project manager to stand back from the process and constantly ask questions and monitor the situation to get answers sooner rather than later.

Risk management is a tricky proposition for project managers. On one hand, they must be realistic about the dangers facing the project—denial leads to surprise, which leads to last-minute scrambling and firefighting. On the other hand, constantly harping on risks can demoralize a team. There are so many difficult questions about product development: Will it sell?

---

14. A good reference for risk management in product development is (Smith and Merritt 2002).

What exactly do the customers want? What are our competitors doing? Can we deliver it on time? Can we build it for the target cost? Will the new electronic control system be ready in time? And on and on. The project leader needs to project confidence in the positive outcome of the project without glossing over the dangers. Like most of the other aspects of leadership, risk management is a delicate balancing act.

Selection of an agile approach, particularly the use of iterative, feature-based development in and of itself, reduces some risks and increases others. For example, APM projects advocate less up-front planning, architecture, and requirements gathering because information is gathered for these as the project unfolds. Short planning and delivery iterations reduce the risks of losing customer involvement, wasting up-front work as project changes occur, encountering analysis paralysis, and delaying returns. On the flip side, too little initial planning increases the risks of major rework due to oversights and scope oscillation due to hurried customer interaction, plus the increased cost of frequent reviews and changes.

Every product development project gathers, analyzes, and generates information. Teams conduct product visioning exercises that begin to concentrate the gathering process. Product designers use the gathered requirements and constraints information to solve the problem of how to build the product. Product development projects generate incredible amounts of information—information that needs to funnel through a systematic, iterative, feedback-intensive process.

"A totally predictable process will generate no information," writes Donald Reinertsen (1997), an expert in industrial product design. Reinertsen believes that the design process is about producing economically useful information. With a product design, until the final manufacturing engineering plans are in place, no one knows for sure whether the product can be made to the specifications that customers demand. However, as a product gets closer and closer to the "release to manufacturing" stage, the more confident the development team should be. Product development is first and foremost about generating and processing information, not predictability. If a process is predictable, if all variations are accounted for, if the process is repeatable in a statistical quality control sense of the word, then it won't generate any new information. The ideal of statistical repeatability sought by "heavy" process proponents flies in the face of product development reality.

Speculate Summary

Product development hinges on managing information and how that information evolves over the course of a project as learning takes place. This progression of information requires a framework, or model, that assists in getting the right information to the right people at the right time, guides project participants, and monitors real progress.

There are three key activities that need to be completed prior to beginning feature development—articulating a product vision, defining the project's scope and constraints, and creating an iterative, feature-based delivery plan. The last of these is the primary deliverable from the Speculate phase. Once the release plan has been completed, other common project management planning artifacts—such as expenditure budgets—can be finalized. The fact is, when you get the feature list and release plan done, the rest is relatively easy!

While a Speculate phase may sound a little, well, speculative, in reality the practices presented in this chapter have proven highly reliable in extracting useful planning information early in development. Feature-based planning forces the engineering and customer teams to understand the product in ways that task-based planning rarely does. With the replanning that occurs at the end of iterations and milestones, plans and the product evolve as information is gained through experimentation and constant feedback.

Chapter 7

The Explore Phase

Individual Performance

"How was your climbing trip last weekend?" Herman asked as Maya answered the phone.

"Great. I redpointed a 5.12b and flashed an 11a," Maya responded.

"I don't have a clue about what you just said, but I'll assume it's good. I'll stick to golf," said Herman. "Now tell me about employee performance. With a flexible project management system like APM, how do I measure performance?"

"Well, my basic rule is measure effective effort, not conformance to the plan. The best example of this is a story my uncle told me. He played basketball for John Wooden at UCLA. According to him, Coach was an incredibly competitive man who wanted to win, but he never talked about winning. He focused on effort. According to Wooden, if everyone plays to their potential, that's the most he could ask."

"But isn't that the wrong thing? We always hear about how negative it is when a company focuses on activity rather than results. What else is effort except activity?" Herman asked.

"Maybe, but you gotta remember, Wooden's the best college basketball coach of all time," said Maya. "When we debrief at the end of each milestone, I ask the team if we did the best we could do. Did we work hard? Did we work smart? Did everyone make the effort to fulfill our goals?"

"Yeah, and I bet everyone just says they did their best."

"Actually, by focusing on effective effort rather than a plan, people are really more honest in their assessment. As they admit, they can always weasel out of a plan variance, but engineers tend to be brutally honest. If they slacked off a little, they tend to fess up."

"I don't think that would happen around here," Herman replied. "Can't the team just use 'we did our best' to shirk accountability for results?"

"Sure, with a less-disciplined team. Here, we're accountable," said Maya. "The team puts in extra effort, and they've always been honest about missing goals. Early on, teams tend to be optimistic. After an iteration or two, things get more realistic. You have to understand—the key isn't how closely we came to meeting schedule but how much value we created."

"So, let me ask you again. How do *I* improve performance on *my* team?" Herman asked.

"By being there for the team. I find that a lot of what I do is facilitate— sort of keep things on an even keel. A few members of my team tend to retreat to their cubes under pressure, and I encourage them to keep interacting. As to how to get the *team* to perform better, the answer is to ask them. After all, since they're the ones who make things happen, they're the ones who need to make the change."

"OK, gotta run. Call you next week," said Herman.

Phase: Explore

A complex adaptive system (CAS) is a collection of agents who explore to achieve a goal (fitness in a biological sense) by interacting with each other according to a set of rules. A CAS experiments with alternatives, selects and executes viable ones, compares the results against its fitness goals (the system's objectives), and adapts as necessary. Extending this metaphor to a project team, the project manager's job takes on new dimensions—to constantly help the team articulate and understand the goal and the constraints, to help the team interact effectively, to facilitate the decision-making process, to ensure appropriate feedback is being gathered and incorporated into the next iteration, and to keep score and deal with reality when things go off track, as every project does.

The CAS model defines a useful metaphor for a leadership-collaboration management style, one that encourages emergent (innovative), risk-taking behavior. Seen in this light, the key project management tasks become establishing a vision and creating a collaborative work environment. The practices in this chapter are focused on the latter objective. The purpose of the Explore phase is to deliver tested, accepted features. Rather than concentrate on the technical details of how to accomplish this goal, however, the agile project manager focuses on creating self-organizing, self-disciplined teams that can best deliver on the ultimate product goal.

Many individuals, even some in the agile community, think agile project management equates to less management. In my experience, adaptive, leadership-collaboration management may be different, but it is certainly not less time consuming. The people management aspects—decision making, coaching, facilitating, working with customers and stakeholders—are a significant load on the project manager's time. As authors Marcus Buckingham and Curt Coffman (1999) write, based on extensive research (interviews with over 80,000 managers during the last 25 years), "The manager role is to reach inside each employee and release his unique talents into performance."

The project manager, in her role as coach and team builder, contributes in six key ways to project success:

1. Focusing the team on delivering results
2. Molding a group of individuals into a team
3. Developing each individual's capabilities
4. Providing the team with required resources and removing roadblocks
5. Coaching the customers
6. Orchestrating the team's rhythm

The essence of an agile project manager's role is not creating Gantt charts or status reports (although doing that remains a part of her work); it is creating a high-performance exploration team from a group of individuals. Exploration and experimentation, the foundations of new product development, involve the risk of making mistakes—of failing—and then learning from those mistakes. Managers must respond by making risk taking, well, less risky. As authors Rob Austin and Lee Devin (2003) note, "Artful managers must also do their part; they must create conditions in which makers can work at risk. Willingness to work at risk is vital in artful making, in part because exploration is uncomfortable." While team members themselves must participate in these activities, the project manager's role is to make sure they happen. It is a difficult, never-ending, and ultimately rewarding role.

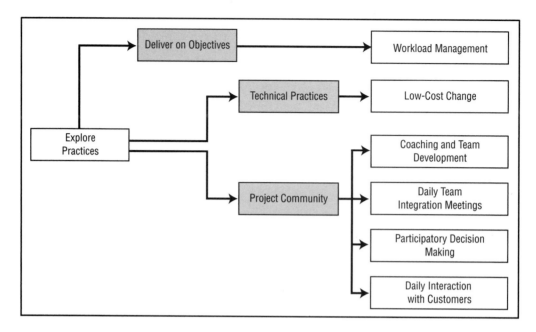

Figure 7.1
Explore Phase Practices

While all the practices in this phase are project management ones, two are geared to team members (workload management, low-cost change), while others are geared to project managers (e.g., coaching and team development). The Explore phase practices fall into three categories, as shown in Figure 7.1:

Deliver on Vision and Objectives
- Workload management

Technical Practices
- Low-cost change

Project Community
- Coaching and team development
- Daily team integration meetings
- Participatory decision making
- Daily interactions with the customer team

Practice: Workload Management

Objective

The objective of workload management is to have team members themselves manage the day-to-day activities required to deliver features at the end of each iteration.

Discussion

To the greatest extent possible, team members should manage their own workload. Each individual and the team as a whole are accountable to deliver the results they have committed to in the iteration plan. How they accomplish that goal (within the process and practice framework the team designed) and which team members take on which tasks should be left to team members collectively to decide. As with many of the agile practices, individuals and teams that exercise self-discipline can carry this off effectively—others can't.

In developing the next iteration plan, team members determine the tasks required to deliver planned features and sign up for those tasks themselves. Workload management also involves team members monitoring their own progress during an iteration (in part during daily integration meetings) and making necessary adjustments. This does not mean that the project manager or team leader abdicates his management responsibilities. When the team consistently meets its commitments, few interventions by the manager are required. However, when the team is implementing a new practice or technology, when new or less-experienced members join the team, managerial intervention—often in the form of coaching—may be necessary.

The project manager needs to monitor without micro-managing, primarily by establishing and monitoring performance goals (features, quality targets, required practices) rather than tasks. In some situations the difference between coaching and micro-managing is attitude. Micro-managers attempt to specify detailed activities and then constantly monitor whether or not those activities are completed on time. At their core, most of these managers view nonattainment of these micro-activities as a motivational problem. They believe that employees aren't working hard enough or fast enough.

Coaching managers, in contrast, understand that there will be motivational problems with only a small percentage of employees (they have tried to get the right people, after all). They approach performance as a capability issue and conclude that staff members who aren't performing don't have the information, tools, or experience for the task at hand. They see their role not as the hallway monitor, but as the teacher who helps with resources, information, or technical coaching. During an iteration, a coaching manager's attitude is reflected in the question, "How can I help you deliver results?" The micro-manager's attitude is reflected in the question, "Why isn't task 412 done yet?"

The project manager is in his position because of particular skills, abilities, and experience. It would be a waste of those capabilities for him to stand aside and let the team flounder. Project managers are expected to guide and coach to further develop the team's capability. Agile project managers steer rather than control; they nudge rather than bludgeon. However, continued intervention by the manager is an indicator of failure—too little progress, too little capability, too little self-discipline, or the wrong person in the role. Team members should manage their own workload—managers have their hands full with other activities.

Practice: Low-Cost Change

Objective

The objective of low-cost change when applied to technical practices is to reduce the cost of iterative development throughout the development and ongoing support phases of a product.

Discussion

Most technical practices are specific to the engineering domain of the product. However, there are several practices that can be applied generically to many types of products, particularly those with both hardware and software components. These generic technical practices are important to the goal of creating adaptable products—delivering customer value today and tomorrow. They are driven by the desire to keep the cost of change, the cost of experimentation, to a minimum, thereby greatly expanding the design possibilities. The four technical practices I will discuss in this section—simple design, frequent integration, ruthless testing, and opportunistic refactoring—also work in concert with each other. While there are many other technical practices, these four are critical to adaptability.[1]

But first, let's consider the phenomenon that makes these practices necessary: technical debt.

Technical Debt

When product development and support teams give lip service to technical excellence, when project and product managers push teams beyond quickness into hurrying, a technical debt is incurred. Technical debt can arise during initial development, ongoing maintenance (keeping a product at its original state), or enhancement (adding functionality). As shown in Figure 7.2, technical debt is the gap between a product's actual cost of change (CoC) and its optimal CoC. As I've said, the twin goals of APM are delivering customer value today and tomorrow. Managing technical debt helps achieve the *tomorrow* goal.

For software products in particular, the actual CoC curve rises slowly at first and then accelerates rapidly after a few years. With software that has been around 10 years or more, developers are loath to touch the now "fragile" code. Constant pressure to cut the time and cost of enhancements, no allowance for periodic refactoring, and poorly maintained test data all contribute to fragility and the increased CoC—which is exemplified by companies with 10- to 15-year-old products whose QA cycles extend for a year or more. Every product, software or otherwise, has a curve such as the one in Figure 7.2, but they will have different shapes and business implications.

---

1. This is not a book on engineering—software, electronic, mechanical, or otherwise—so it doesn't include specific technical practices. However, foundational skills in the various disciplines are critical to success. Software products don't get built without good software engineering skills. Electronic instruments don't get built without good electronic engineering skills. The four practices are adapted from *Extreme Programming Explained: Embrace Change* (Beck 2000).

Figure 7.2
Technical Debt
Results from
Hurrying

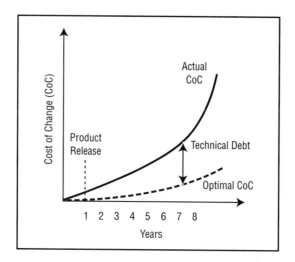

The bottom line is that increasing technical debt directly reduces responsiveness to customers. Customers and product managers, internal and external, don't understand why a seemingly simple enhancement takes months and months, or even years, to implement. Yet their relentless pushing for features, features, features, faster, faster, faster is often the root cause of the problem. Without a firm dedication to long-term technical debt management, development groups are pressured into the increasing technical debt trap. As the debt gets worse, the delays become greater. As the delays lengthen, the pressure increases, usually leading to another hurried implementation, which increases the technical debt yet again.

Exiting this downward spiral is very difficult, because the longer the technical debt cycle goes on, the more expensive it is to fix. And fixing it is a political nightmare, because after spending significant time and money, the product's functionality won't be any greater than before (although defects will be reduced). The bigger the debt, the more expensive it is to fix, the more difficult it is to justify, and therefore the death spiral continues.

Conversely, there doesn't seem to be much incentive for narrowing the technical debt early in a product's lifecycle (when doing so is inexpensive), because the delays are still short. Nevertheless, the secret to long-term technical debt reduction lies in doing it early and often while the cost is low. The smaller the debt, the less expensive it is to fix, the less difficult it is to justify, and this virtuous cycle reinforces itself. Reducing technical debt, keeping the cost of change low, has to become an ingrained technical strategy—part of an organization's dedication to technical excellence.

It must be noted that managing technical debt doesn't keep products from becoming obsolete. A technical debt strategy doesn't attempt to stave off eventual obsolescence but to keep the cost of change low so that customer responsiveness remains as high as possible during a product's life.

The historical approach to this issue was to get it right the first time and then hold on tight. Hold on tight, that is, to the original design or architecture, and resist meaningful change. When the pace of change was slower, this strategy may have worked, but in most product situations today, clinging to the past and resisting change don't work. Holding the cost of change down by *not* changing only means that when change has to happen, neither the product nor the people will be ready for it.

"OK," you may think. "This sounds good, but I'll never get my customers or management to invest the time or money in early technical debt reduction." I have three answers to this. First, the alternative will be to lose customers to competitors who are more responsive, especially new entrants into a market who are not burdened by old products. (Their time will come, but they will also steal your customers until then.) Second, a well-functioning agile team will work faster and at lower cost when practicing technical excellence. Third, even if practicing excellence costs a little more initially, the reduction in compliance work using APM will more than pay for the difference.

Simple Design

The objective of simple design is to keep the engineering team grounded in what is known rather than anticipating the unknown.

There are two fundamental approaches to managing change—anticipation and adaptation—and good design strategies encompass aspects of both. Anticipation involves planning for the future and predicting what kinds of change are probable. Adaptation means waiting until requirements evolve or changes manifest themselves and then building them into the product. Adaptation also means experimenting, selecting those experiments with the best results, and incorporating those results into the product. The lower the cost of change, the lower the cost of experimentation, the higher the likelihood of significant innovation.

Building a tax-rate parameter into a software payroll system *anticipates* future changes in federal withholding rates. Componentizing electronic instruments *anticipates* using the instruments in configurations not currently foreseen. If there is a high probability that something will change, we should design the system to easily incorporate that change. This is a *known* type of future change. In hardware design a lot of effort is spent defining interfaces; hence subsystems act as black boxes and can easily be swapped in and out provided the interface does not change. Also, a good design leaves some unused bandwidth for future opportunities; for example, a backplane that contains a few unused signal and data lines. Other examples include using recognized standards and protocols, which allow greater flexibility, and using chip mounts that allow easy upgrading of CPUs/memory to the next generation. Since the cost of change is higher for hardware, adaptability often requires a modicum of anticipatory design.

Conversely, there are changes to the business environment that are very difficult to anticipate. For example, IT organizations immersed in developing client/server systems in the mid-1990s had little inkling of the Internet boom that would rapidly overtake those efforts. Companies that spent hundreds of millions of dollars on enterprise resource planning systems during this same time were concerned with internal integration of applications, whereas a few years later integration across companies became critical. Today, anticipating changes in the biotechnology industry explosion would be impossible. Dealing with these unanticipated, and often unforeseeable, changes requires adaptation.

Simple design means valuing adapting over anticipating. (Anticipating or planning isn't unimportant; it's just less important than adapting.) This means designing for what we know today and then responding to what we learn in the future. If our objective is an adaptable product, we should be able to demonstrate its adaptability during development by responding to new information. However, the extent to which this approach is useful depends on the malleability of the medium we are working in; software is very malleable (with good design), while certain types of hardware are less so. The more malleable the medium, the lower the cost of change, the easier it will be to tip the balance of anticipation versus adaptation toward the latter.

So malleability depends on low-cost iteration, but some components, even in software systems, are not very malleable. Therefore the balance of anticipation and adaptation must swing back toward anticipation. Platform (and product line) architectural decisions, for example, are often expensive and time consuming to change, and thus they should be approached from an anticipation perspective.

But even with less-malleable hardware systems, the advent of highly sophisticated simulation and modeling technology provides hardware designers with nearly as malleable an environment as software designers—the design of the Boeing 777 being a good example. Of course changes immediately became more expensive when the 777 transitioned from design to construction, but until that point, Boeing employed simple design practices (to a certain degree) through their creative and extensive use of simulation.

Practicing simple design has the added advantage of pointing out bottlenecks in the development process. Say you are building an electronic test instrument. Every time you want to change the design, quality assurance complains that integration and regression testing is so expensive and time consuming that it cannot get the cycle time for this testing under four weeks. You've just discovered a bottleneck, one that resists change by making it too expensive and time consuming. Rather than accept the QA position and forgo design changes, the better strategy would be to examine how to bring QA cost and test time down.

The effectiveness of simple design and refactoring indicates to a product team how adaptable its development process can be. Barriers to these practices are barriers to reducing the cost of change. The key question isn't "How much does it cost to implement these practices?" but "Can you afford not to implement them?" Note that simple design doesn't mean simplistic design. Often coming up with understandable, adaptable, simple designs takes additional time. Doing less, by eschewing nonessentials and focusing on customer value, can free up the time required to do better—simple design.

Frequent Integration

The objective of frequent integration is to ensure that product features fit together into an integrated whole early and often during development in order to reduce both the high cost of late misalignment and the burden of testing. No matter what the product—from software to automobiles to industrial control systems—the less frequent the integration, the more susceptible the development effort will be to major problems late in the process and the more difficult, and expensive, it will be to find and fix them.

Consider some common problems with embedded software in industrial products. Hardware and software components never seem to be complete at the same time. Software engineers complain that hardware isn't available, while hardware engineers have the same complaint about the software. While software simulations and hardware prototypes can ease the situation for some products, they can both be expensive and oversimplify real-world situations. One company that was developing the embedded software for a cell phone ran into frustrating problems with hardware test equipment from a major vendor, slowing its testing efforts. An oil-field service firm found that simulations can't replicate all the variations of the real world, but "live" testing is also prohibitively expensive. Operating system and computer hardware developers seem to be constantly out of phase during development. At some level, integrating hardware and software will always be challenging and the problems only partially solvable. However, development teams need to strive for frequent integration to mitigate the problems.

Ken Delcol uses this approach at MDS Sciex in developing mass spectrometers. "We have just gone through this process. Our firmware group delivered firmware to the hardware group in iterations based on its testing schedule. Once sufficient functionality was confirmed, then the software group was brought in to add applications. With this approach we didn't need a fully populated digital board to begin firmware and hardware integration testing. We achieved a number of things (the best we have ever achieved): integration testing started sooner, hence issues were resolved more quickly (better schedule and cost); integration was continuous once minimal hardware was in place, hence no peak in resources; and communication was improved because all groups participated in the integration."

While companies establish cross-functional hardware teams, many software groups continue to operate separately. Again, if the development approach is a traditional, up-front, anticipatory one, this functional separation seems to make sense—the software group has its requirements and just needs to go do it. But this functional separation can be deadly to effective integration of software and hardware.

Changing to an agile development model can improve the flexibility of products containing both hardware and software. Figure 7.3 is an adaptation

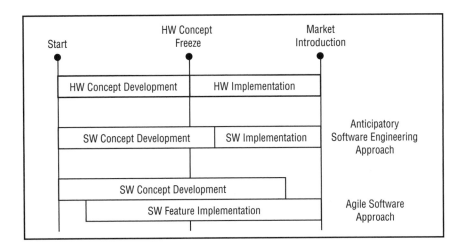

Figure 7.3
Model of Product Development Cycles (Adapted from Marco Iansiti, Technology Integration)

of a product development model from Harvard Business School professor Marco Iansiti. The diagram indicates that hardware development is typically broken into concept development, which at some point becomes frozen (at least for most purposes) because the cost and time delays of further design changes impact parts purchasing, manufacturing equipment acquisition, or downstream manufacturing set-up and hardware implementation.

Software development, on the other hand, can follow either a serial or an iterative approach. In the former, concept development (architecture, design, requirements) is frozen—somewhat later than the hardware development, but it essentially uses the hardware model. The agile approach, rather than attempting to limit (freeze) requirements, takes advantage of software's flexibility by overlapping the concept development and implementation activities and thereby extends the "software freeze" until much later in the product development process. This allows the distinct possibility that late-discovered hardware flaws (or new requirements) can be implemented in software. Furthermore, the flexibility of software features, and often inexpensive throwaway features, can be used to advantage in the testing of key hardware components.

Because of the constant pressure on new product development cycle time, hardware engineers have been forced into earlier and earlier purchase ordering for parts. Design changes that cause alterations to parts already in the purchasing pipeline can be very expensive and time consuming. How the product is ramped up to production and the size of the initial production run will be big factors in the team's ability to change that hardware. Since there are no physical inventory considerations with software (although there are testing, configuration management, and other issues), software engineers can often make late changes cost effectively.

Iansiti provides an example of how frequently hardware problems were solved by software solutions during a Silicon Graphics workstation development project. When hardware problems were found, software workarounds were used 70% of the time, the problems became "features" 10% of the time, a combination of hardware and software changed 10% of the time, and pure hardware changes were involved only 10% of the time.

In serial models, "a distinct separation exists between concept development and implementation," says Iansiti. "This model works well when technology, product features, and competitive requirements are predictable." In an agile approach (which Iansiti calls a flexible approach), "the key to the process is in the ability to gather and rapidly respond to new knowledge about technology and application context *as a project evolves.* Technology integration capability is central to meeting the challenges of such unpredictable change" (Iansiti 1998).

In an agile approach, control occurs not by conformance to concept-driven plans, but by constant integration and testing of the evolving feature sets as they emerge during the product development process. Having a product architecture is important, but having good technology integration is vital to success. For this reason, architects need to be heavily involved in product integration.

Ruthless Testing

The objective of ruthless testing is to ensure that product quality remains high throughout the development process.[2]

The old adage that quality can't be added on but must be built into the development process remains true. Extensive test instrumentation assists

---

2. The term "ruthless testing" comes from colleague Kevin Tate. While a growing number of software developers use "test-first development," ruthless testing is a better generic term that is widely applicable to all types of products.

development of everything from cell-phone chips to automobile engines. Ruthless testing contributes to the goal of creating adaptable products because finding faults early, when there is still time to correct them, reduces the cost of change. When product developers wait until late into the lifecycle to test, the testing process itself becomes cumbersome rather than streamlined. Furthermore, the lack of constant testing removes a necessary feedback loop into the development process. Wait too long, and designs solidify. Then when tests are finally run, the team is unwilling to make design changes—it's too expensive now! Constant ruthless testing, including acceptance testing, challenges the development team—no matter what the product—to face the reality of how its design actually works.

In software development, ruthless testing includes software engineers performing constant unit testing, integrating quality assurance and acceptance testing into each development iteration, and having a full range of those tests automated. The ultimate goal is to produce a deployable, limited-feature product at the end of each iteration.

Opportunistic Refactoring

The objective of opportunistic refactoring is to constantly and continuously improve the product design—make it more adaptable—to enable it to meet the twin goals of delivering customer value today and in the future.

A client was considering a multiyear, multimillion-dollar product redevelopment project for an existing software product—20+ years in its evolution—which contained several million lines of code. While the product had been instrumental to business success, it was also viewed as an anchor to future progress. Maintenance and enhancements were taking longer and longer to implement, and the costs of integration and regression testing had increased substantially. At the same time, the company's customers were increasingly asking for shorter response times. Replacement was seen as the solution to the problems of a creaky old system. My caution to them was that the new product would face similar problems within five years if they didn't include a systematic product-level refactoring discipline into their development process.

Refactoring involves updating a product's internal components (improving the design), without changing externally visible functionality, in order to make the product easier to enhance in the future. One unfortunate legacy of serial development is the idea that reducing the cost of change depends on getting correct architectural and design decisions in the beginning. Given the constancy of change and our inability to predict those changes with any accuracy, our designs should instead be based upon what we know today and a willingness to engage in redesign in the future. Since it is inevitable that product enhancements are sometimes "bolted on" without proper design considerations, a refactoring discipline encourages teams to revisit these decisions periodically and correct them.

Another client who implemented agile development had a software product they developed to coincide with another company's major platform announcement. Although they utilized refactoring and ruthless testing, the immutable delivery date caused them to "hurry" a little more than they would have liked. So upon the first release, rather than diving right back into the new feature enhancements marketing was clamoring for, they spent two months refactoring and getting their automated tests in shape. Only then, with a technically solid product in hand, did they resume developing features for the next release. I asked the product development manager if they would have taken that two months prior to implementing agile development, and his answer was "no." Living with the pain of another legacy product for which the "technical debt" had gotten away from them, the team members were determined it would not happen on this new product.

System- or product-level refactoring can have enormous benefits over a product's life. *Refactoring improves a product's design but does not add new functionality—it improves adaptability.* Adding new functionality usually entails redesign, and refactoring should precede that redesign. The greater the rate of change in a product's features, the more quickly the product's architecture or design will degrade. A large redevelopment project—whose justification relies on reducing the cost of change—has that very justification undermined when development and support teams (if they are separate) fail to instill an ongoing refactoring discipline.

The old axiom was "Get it right the first time to keep development cost down." The new axiom, one that makes more sense as business and product changes occur with greater frequency, is "No matter how good it is the first time, it's going to change, so keep the cost of change low." Refactoring should not, however, be used as an excuse for sloppy design. The objective isn't refactoring; the objective is to maintain a viable, adaptable design. This requires good design practices at every step.

Decisions about refactoring are difficult, because on the surface they appear to be technical decisions. But in fact they are product management and executive decisions, and they therefore need to be examined, and funded, from that perspective. Without the support of product managers, digging one's way out of a degraded product design will be nearly impossible. On the upside, however, I've found product managers amenable to investing in refactoring once they understand the situation. With customers clamoring for enhancements and development cycles lengthening because of technical debt, their current situations are often untenable.

In order to refactor, two factors are paramount—testing and persistence. One barrier to redesign and refactoring is the risk of breaking something that is already working. We reduce that risk by thoroughly integrating testing into the development process (not tacking it on at the end) and by automating testing to the greatest extent possible. Automated testing reduces the fear of breaking something that already works.

Which brings up the second factor—persistence. For software, it means considering doing a little code refactoring every time a change is contemplated—always trying to leave the code slightly better than before. It means thinking about redesign during every development iteration and allocating some time to implement redesigns. It means planning some level of refactoring into every new product release. It means slowly, but surely, building up automated tests and integrating testing into the development process. For hardware, persistence means applying these practices to development as fully as possible, particularly for those parts of the development process that are accomplished by simulations.

Every investment requires an adequate return. Refactoring itself takes time and money. It can degenerate into endless technical arguments about "right" designs. But many product teams understand that the status quo isn't working any more. From product managers who lament the unresponsiveness of their products to customer feature requests, to developers who struggle to understand designs that no one wants to touch, to QA departments who are viewed as bottlenecks because their activities take months and months and months, to executives who watch their products slip in the marketplace, the incentives to rethink this topic are real. Persistence involves a constant—iteration after iteration, release after release—investment in refactoring, redesign, and testing to maintain a product that is as responsive to change as the marketplace demands.

Practice: Coaching and Team Development

Objective

The objective of coaching and team development is to unleash the capability of the team by helping team members continuously improve their domain knowledge (technical, business), self-discipline, and "teaming" skills.

Discussion

This practice works in close conjunction with the Get the Right People practice. Many project managers view their job as getting the best utilization out of the staff assigned to them, but that's not enough. Ongoing staff development is every manager's job, whether she is a project manager or team leader. While project managers strive to get the right people, with both the right skill set and attitude, there is also a pervasive belief in agile projects that we can always improve performance, that we continually strive for excellence.

As I mentioned in the introduction to this chapter, the six key building blocks of coaching and team development are focusing the team on delivering results; molding a group of individuals into a team; developing each individual's capabilities; providing the team with required resources and removing roadblocks; coaching the customers; and orchestrating the team's rhythm.

Focusing the Team on Delivering Results

Every team member gets mired in details and forgets the goal—at least periodically. Good project managers remind the team about the goals from time to time by revisiting the key constraints and tradeoff parameters and by reinvigorating the group with the ultimate purpose of the project. This is part of encouraging exploration, which might be considered a leader's cheerleader role, but it's one that must be based in reality rather than fantasy. Team members want a boost every now and then, but they don't want meaningless rah-rah speeches. Team members want the facts, even negative ones, so they can help figure out how to deal with the situation.

One of the key motivators for individuals is understanding what is expected of them—but in terms of outcomes, not steps. Great managers and leaders manage outcomes, not activities. "Define the right outcomes and then let each person find his own route towards those outcomes," Marcus Buckingham and Curt Coffman (1999) recommend. If you have the right people, they want to know *what* needs to be accomplished and their role, but they want to figure out *how* to deliver the results. They want to understand why what they do is important, and they want to work with a team that is committed to delivering quality work.[3] Individuals assume accountability for delivering certain features, while the team as a whole assumes accountability for delivering all the features planned for an iteration. The project manager holds both individuals and the team as a whole to their commitments.

On large projects it is difficult to keep the end goal in sight without giving in to the worry "I don't know how we're ever going to finish this." Part of the value of an iterative approach, which needs to be reinforced by the project manager occasionally, is that it breaks very large development efforts into manageable chunks. While facing a two-year development effort seems daunting, trying to deliver a handful of features in the next few weeks doesn't. The project manager needs to help the team balance—understanding the end goal but working hard in the present iteration. She begins each iteration by reminding the team of the overall vision and constraints of the project and reiterating the vision box and project data sheet information. The vision provides a context for day-to-day decisions about current work. She then rapidly focuses on the next iteration and, in particular, the theme of the iteration.

The manager helps the team focus on both the overall goal of the project and the iteration themes. This may appear to be an easy task, but with the high rate of change and the pressure to deliver quickly, the task is a difficult—and constant—one.

---

3. According to Buckingham and Coffman (1999), these are two of the twelve core elements needed to attract, focus, and keep key employees.

Molding a Group of Individuals into a Team

Tom DeMarco and Tim Lister (1999) use the term "jelled team" to define when individuals make the transition from a group to a well-functioning team. But getting a team to jell isn't easy (few teams actually make the transition) because it involves four things that are difficult to achieve in any group of people: trust, interaction, satisfactory conflict resolution, and participatory decision making. Teams with little trust interact on only a superficial level. Lack of interaction fosters a focus on individual rather than team goals. Unsatisfactory conflict resolution reduces trust. Win-lose decision making undermines people's commitment to the team.

Trust is an easy word to bandy around, but it is a difficult thing to achieve. "Trust is the confidence among team members that their peers' intentions are good, and that there is no reason to be protective or careful around the group," says Patrick Lencioni (2002). Trust enables team members to share half-baked ideas without the fear of ridicule. Trust and respect are also closely tied together—it's difficult to respect those we don't trust, and vice versa—which is one reason that getting the wrong people on the team can have such a detrimental effect. Respect comes from understanding other people's roles on a project. Engineers need to understand how product marketing contributes to project success, and product marketing likewise needs to acknowledge engineering's contribution. Frequent interactions help generate understanding, which in turn can lead to respect and trust.

Managers have to trust also. Authors Buckingham and Coffman (1999) have an interesting twist on the common view of earning trust. They contend that great managers reject this view. "They know that if, fundamentally, you don't trust people, then there is no line, no point in time, beyond which people suddenly become trustworthy." Managers who fundamentally don't trust people will jump at the first failure to impose strict controls: "See, I told you we can't operate without rigorous controls." Conversely, managers who do trust people know some failures will occur because of human nature. For the few truly untrustworthy individuals, the great managers have a solution—get rid of them—instead of abusing the entire organization with burdensome controls. As I've observed, "Managers in organizations either have a fundamental trust of people or they don't—there is no middle ground" (Highsmith 2002).

Jelled teams often have fierce debates and conflict over technical issues. Part of the project manager's leadership role is to channel the debate so that it builds trust and respect rather than undermines them. The leader can facilitate this by focusing the discussion on the issues and not on individuals. Managing the "mood" of the team (mostly by managing one's own mood) is one of those "soft" leader skills that are so hard to do well. While self-discipline comes from within each team member, a leader can help the team build its discipline of debate, conflict, and decision making to further "jell" the team.

Interaction drives innovation. One of the tenets of adaptive organizations is that innovation emerges from the interaction of diverse individuals, each with ideas, who bring information and insight to the development process. Product development projects usually involve teams whose members possess a complex mix of information and talents. Engineers, product specialists, and scientists from diverse domains must consolidate their expertise into a consistent, high-quality product design. To accomplish this goal, individuals balance time alone to develop their particular piece of the product puzzle with face-to-face time with others to fit the pieces together. When team members don't interact, there is no synergy of ideas, and innovation suffers. Interaction can take many forms (brainstorming sessions, hallway chats, technical design reviews, online group discussions, and, in the software world, pair programming), but the objectives are the same: to share information, to co-create a product feature or development artifact, or to make a joint decision about an issue. Project managers must encourage this peer-to-peer interaction, particularly as pressure mounts and individuals have a tendency to "go dark."

There is more to successful interactions than talking. From time to time in any project team's development there are "crucial conversations," characterized by varying opinions, high stakes, and emotional intensity. These are the make-or-break conversations, the ones in which the character of the team is forged. Do these conversations degenerate into personal attacks and finger pointing, or do these conflicts help jell the team? There are a couple of things that determine whether the team has the self-discipline and character to have successful crucial conversations. First, each and every member must take the initiative to confront others when they are not performing, or behaving, according to team rules. This includes the administrative assistant calling the project manager on her actions when the situation dictates. No one should be exempt. Ignoring the problem, letting it fester, isn't acceptable behavior. The second critical thing is that the conversation be directed toward getting all the relevant information out on the table. Without this, crucial conversations cannot be effective. The process I describe in the section on participatory decision making is intended to do just this—extract relevant information that is devoid, for a while at least, of individual biases.[4]

Several years ago I was working with a project team that was under enormous stress—tight delivery deadlines, constantly changing requirements, and high pressure because of the revenue implications of the project's outcome. The team leaders and many staff members thought the ambiguity and anxiety within the project should somehow be mitigated, that the environment should be less chaotic and more stable. I pointed out that this kind of project was always borderline chaotic and, furthermore, that attempting to stabilize it—while it might make everyone feel better—was unlikely to lead to successful completion.

What ultimately helped the situation was to show the team leaders how they were making the situation worse by reflecting, rather than absorbing, the team's frustration. Each time a team member would come to a team leader and say something like, "Wow, things are really screwed up," the lead would counter with, "They sure are, and I wish someone would fix it." This exchange magnified the frustrations. While the team leaders needed to acknowledge the reality of the situation, they also needed to respond positively, to defuse the situation by remaining calm themselves. Just my telling the team leaders that a degree of ambiguity and frustration was a natural part of this type of project helped reduce their anxiety and kept the emotion and frustration level below a "constant crisis" level. They were then able to convey this new mood to team members.

Recent management research shows that mood or "emotional intelligence" in leaders has a much larger impact on performance than we may have imagined. "The leader's mood and behaviors drive the moods and

---

4. The research information in this paragraph comes from several sources, but the best is (Patterson 2002).

behaviors of everyone else. A cranky and ruthless boss creates a toxic organization filled with negative underachievers who ignore opportunities," say Daniel Goleman, Richard Boyatzis, and Annie McKee (2001). These authors describe how a leader's emotional intelligence is contagious, racing through an organization like electricity through wires. Researchers at the University of Michigan found that in 70 work teams in diverse industries, team members picked up the same moods within a couple of hours.

Project teams are groups of people who respond to emotions and whose emotions may experience wide swings—from despair to euphoria—over the life of a project. Encouraging appropriate moods and discouraging others can help create group interactions conducive to generating emergent results.

Finally, managers should assist the team in developing a set of "rules of engagement," ground rules for how team members are expected to treat each other. The team should participate in developing, enforcing, and adapting these rules over time—it is a part of being self-disciplined.

Rules of engagement are not meant to reduce conflict and contention but to direct them in positive ways. Great teams froth with tension, contention, and diverse ideas directed at delivering a high-quality result. Poor teams froth with tension, contention, and diverse ideas directed at each other.

These team norms can include such rules as:

- Everyone has an equal voice.
- Everyone's contribution is valuable.
- Attack issues, not people.
- Keep privacy within the team.
- Respect each other and your differences.
- Everyone participates.

The team should decide on the list of rules, post it prominently (especially during team meetings), and add to it freely during the project.

While making mistakes enhances learning, it only does so if those mistakes are identified. One of the most difficult tasks of working well within a team is confronting team members who violate behavioral or performance standards, but if they aren't confronted, the mistake isn't identified, and no learning occurs. Failing to address these issues head on is one of the greatest complaints against project managers (Larson and LaFasto 1989).

Developing Each Individual's Capabilities

Buckingham and Coffman have a nice little mantra that reflects the beliefs of great managers:

> *People don't change that much.*
> *Don't waste time trying to put in what was left out.*
> *Try to draw out what was left in.*
> *That is hard enough* (Buckingham and Coffman 1999).

Encouraging each individual's development is another of those key characteristics of great project managers. They try to understand people's inherent talents and build on those rather than trying to put in something that was left out. Developmental coaching comes in three flavors: technical, domain expertise, and behavioral. Project managers may not do the technical or domain coaching, but they facilitate its happening—often by pairing less experienced team members with more experienced ones or pairing people with different technical skills in order to broaden each person's technical capability. The leader also coaches individuals in how to help the team jell. The leader may help some overbearing team member lighten up, while encouraging reticent ones to participate more fully.

Individuals contribute by applying their technical skills and engaging in team-enhancing (self-organizing) behavior. This self-disciplined behavior includes:

- Accepting accountability for results (no excuses)
- Confronting reality through rigorous thinking
- Engaging in intense interaction and debate
- Being willing to work within a self-organizing framework
- Respecting colleagues

Not all of these behaviors come easily, particularly for engineers. However, developing the self-discipline to do these things is critical to creating jelled teams. Helping individuals learn these skills can be one of the highest-leverage activities a project manager can engage in.

Providing the Team with Required Resources and Removing Roadblocks

Project managers contribute directly to delivering results by making sure team members have the resources they need. When individuals are waiting for resources, they lose productivity, but more importantly, they lose time. Examples of resources include computers, lab equipment, and staff assistance. Providing resources can also include ensuring that critical dependencies between feature teams or with outside sources are well managed. Rather than doing the work, the project manager ensures that everyone has the resources to do his or her work. This style of project management is one of providing services to the team—an approach Robert Greenleaf called "servant leadership" (Frick and Spears 1996)—rather than having the team "work for" the manager.

Project managers also remove roadblocks that impede the team from working efficiently. For example, project managers need to quickly and effectively resolve impediments that are voiced in daily team integration meetings. Roadblocks can be things such as resources (the team doesn't have them), information (the team can't get it from a customer), or decisions (a stakeholder manager hasn't made them in a timely fashion).

Coaching the Customers

Another critical coaching job—that of coaching the customer team—goes to the product manager. Many internal IT projects have crashed on the shoals of poor customer involvement—for the last 30 to 40 years! The problem is simple, the solution complex. The fundamental problem is a poor customer-developer partnership caused by one of any number of factors:

- Development's lack of credibility in the eyes of customers
- Lack of customer involvement
- Poor accountability on the customer's side for making decisions and accepting the consequences
- Long development schedules, exacerbated by delivering meaningless (to the customer) intermediate artifacts
- Unrealistic project schedules based on poorly articulated requirements
- Lack of acceptance criteria and testing by customers

Individually, any one of these factors can doom a project. Collectively, they almost always lead to project failure.

Various APM practices and concepts address these issues, but just as engineers are accountable for building better partnerships, so are customers. Furthermore, just as the development team needs coaching in both technical and behavioral skills to meet their responsibilities, so do the customers. Customers may not know how to write acceptance tests or participate in requirements specification sessions or take part in the decision-making process of setting feature priorities. Just as the project leader facilitates the smooth running of the engineering team, the product manager must facilitate the smooth running of the customer team.

Consider an IT project that is building a business software application for multiple customer departments, each of which can identify requirements for the application. These requirements are gathered and documented, usually by a business analyst from the IT department. The analyst often inherits, because no one else wants it, the task of reconciling differences between multiple customer departments and trying to determine feature priorities. This approach leads to requirements bloat because the analyst has little power to say no to feature requests, and customer departments feel no obligation to make difficult priority decisions.

With a product manager appointed from the customer ranks, many problems are lessened because the customers, through the product manager, must accept accountability for identifying, defining, prioritizing, and accepting features. One of the product manager's jobs is to coach the customer team through this process. For industrial or consumer product development projects, the product manager has to work with (coach) internal "proxy" customers—marketing, executives—as well as gain information about the external customer base through periodic customer involvement, beta testing, and other means.

Orchestrating Team Rhythm

At times, the project manager's job mirrors that of a maestro, keeping the players in rhythm while bringing each into the music at the right time. At other times the team operates more like a jazz band, with each player improvising around a common structure. Working with the rhythms of agile projects can be a difficult transition for many individuals. People are used to linearity, at least in the way projects are usually planned. Execution is never linear, which is one reason people constantly complain that how they actually work never matches the plan.

Agile projects are rhythmic, not linear. Furthermore, there are rhythms within rhythms, which makes describing agile projects difficult to those who are used to seeing linear project task plans. There are the rhythms of iterations, which alternate between intensity and reflection as teams work to deliver features and then pause to reflect on the results. There is the rhythm of daily integration meetings and interactions with customers on feature details. There is the rhythm of peer-to-peer interaction as engineers meet at whiteboards to thrash through a design before retreating to more private reflection and work. There is the rhythm of constantly thinking, designing, building, testing, and reflecting on small increments of work. There is the rhythm of anxiety and euphoria as people try to solve, and then succeed in solving, seemingly intractable problems.

Project managers orchestrate the beat. They help team members learn to slow down to reflect after high-pressure delivery work, they help them find the right rhythm of working alone and working collaboratively, and they help them deal with anxiety and ambiguity. Creating task lists and checking completion boxes characterize one kind of project management—orchestrating rhythms characterizes another.

Practice: Daily Team Integration Meetings

Objective

The objective of daily team integration meetings is to coordinate team member activities on a daily basis.

Discussion

Normally the first agile practice my clients implement is the daily team integration meeting. These daily get-togethers (referred to as Scrum meetings in the Scrum methodology or daily stand-up meetings in Extreme Programming) focus on one objective: peer-to-peer coordination through information exchange (Schwaber and Beedle 2002). "Daily software builds are used to raise the visibility of development work and ensure that code modules integrate. Daily Scrum meetings serve the same purpose for people—raising the visibility of each person's work (to facilitate knowledge sharing and reduce overlapping tasks) and ensuring that their work is integrated. If daily builds are good for code, then daily 'builds' should be even better for people" (Highsmith 2002).

The daily integration meeting enables the team members to coordinate their work by monitoring status, focusing on the work to be done, and raising problems and issues. The meetings adhere to the following principles:

- The meetings are held at the same time and place every day.
- The meetings last less than 30 minutes (the target should be 15 minutes or less).
- All core team members attend the meetings.
- Product and project managers attend as peer participants (not to gather status).
- Other managers usually do not attend these meetings, and if they do, they are observers, not participants.
- A team member or the project manager facilitates the meetings.
- The meetings are used to raise issues and obstacles but not to pursue solutions.

- Each participant is encouraged to address three questions:
  - What did you do yesterday?
  - What are you planning to do today?
  - What impediments are in the way?

To the extent possible, the daily meetings should be held at the same time and place. Attendance may vary from day to day, but that is preferable to the hassle of constantly trying to reschedule. Meetings can be held in a break room, in the corner of a work area, in a conference room—teams are very creative about finding meeting space. (Some teams are fortunate enough to have dedicated space, and in fact, dedicated space makes a positive contribution to agile projects.) Most team members find these short meetings to be efficient and effective. They eliminate the need for other meetings and help the right people to team up to resolve issues.

Time duration is critical to meeting success. When daily meetings begin to slide past 20 to 30 minutes, people gradually stop coming. Even worse, lengthening timeframes are a sure indication that the wrong things are being discussed. For example, these meetings should not be used to solve problems, only to identify them. Usually, when problems are identified, the team members involved in the solution get together briefly after the integration meeting.

The project manager's participation is another delicate factor in successful integration meetings. The objective of these meetings is coordination, not status review. When managers begin asking questions like "Why didn't that task get finished as planned?" team members feel pressure, sometimes subtle, sometimes not so subtle, to conform to the plan rather than discuss coordination issues. The astute PM rephrases the question to uncover impediments to progress and find out what team members need from him to get back on track. Task performance pressure in these integration meetings should come from peers, not from managers.

The meeting facilitator's role, which can be rotated from day to day, is to smooth the progress of the meeting itself. The facilitator might nudge the team, "That's a great point, but let's take the further discussion offline from this meeting."

Responses to the question "What impediments are in the way of your work?" become action items for the team leader or project manager. Impediments may be organizational—"We can't get a response from the marketing department"—or they may be resource related—"We're having trouble getting an electronic circuit board we need"—or have some other cause. It's the PM's job to remove the impediment as quickly as possible.

Daily team integration meetings are a tool for self-organization; they assist the team members in coordinating their own work and solving their own problems. As such, the project manager's role should be as unobtrusive as possible. He should use other forums for gathering status, coaching, or working with the team on performance issues.

As with any other practice, the characteristics of the daily meeting (meeting time, frequency, and attendees) will need to evolve for different situations. One such adaptation might be for the core delivery team members to meet daily, while members from support functions join in weekly.

Other adaptations can be made for projects with multiple subteams or feature teams. Integration meetings can be used to coordinate across these feature teams, with appropriate adjustments. For example, in a project with four feature teams, two members of each team might attend a thrice-weekly inter-team integration meeting. During times of greater coordination needs—say, at the beginning of a project when overall design issues are being discussed—inter-team meetings might be daily, while later on they might be weekly.

Finally, the team should constantly ask questions (especially at milestone reviews) like: "Are these daily team integration meetings adding value to the project?" and "How could we improve them?" The objective of these sessions is coordination, not having daily meetings or answering the three questions (accomplished, planned, impediments) for their own sake. Those activities merely facilitate achieving the objective.

Practice: Participatory Decision Making

Objective

The objective of participatory decision making is to provide the project community with specific practices to frame, make, and analyze the myriad decisions that arise during a project.

Discussion

The lack of adequate decision-making processes in organizations is evident in a couple of quotes from clients I've worked with in the past few years.

"That one decision-gradient diagram [Figure 7.4] was the most important piece of the two-day consulting session," said a product development VP client recently.

"It's difficult to speed up development when management takes weeks to make key decisions," lamented an Irish development manager whose company executives are in Silicon Valley.

"Our project managers are like a herd of deer standing on the highway with a tractor-trailer truck bearing down on them," said one project team member. "They can't figure out which way to jump, but if they don't decide soon, we're going to get run over."

As I trek around the world of product development and project management, I'm continually amazed at how little organizations think about their decision-making processes. Many of them put time and energy into processes like time recording and virtually ignore decision making. However, in a fast-paced agile project, decision making—like other activities—must be done quickly and effectively. Slow decision making, revisiting decisions again and again, over-analyzing decisions, and poor participation in the decision-making process will doom a project, as poor decisions cascade into a flood of additional decisions.

However, decision making can improve, and it can be participatory, as the GE jet engine plant in Durham, North Carolina, proves. "At GE/Durham, every decision is either an A decision, or a B decision, or a C decision," writes Charles Fishman (1999) in an article in *Fast Company*. "An A decision is one that the plant manager makes herself, without consulting anyone. B decisions are also made by the plant manager, but with input from the people affected. C decisions—which make up the most common type—are made by consensus, by the people directly involved, with plenty of discussion." Using this system, the plant manager only makes 10 to 12 "A" decisions in a year and spends significant time explaining those to the staff.

The article goes on to address the very crucial issue that arises in discussing self-organizing teams:

What is the role of a plant manager in a place that manages itself? If the plant needs a manager like Sims to make just 10 decisions a year, what does she do with the bulk of her time?

She does the kinds of things that most managers talk about a lot but that they actually spend very little time on. At the operational level, her job is to keep everyone's attention focused on the goals of the plant: Make perfect engines, quickly, cheaply, safely. Strategically, the plant manager's job is to make sure that the plant as a whole is making smart decisions about talent, about time, and about opportunities for growth (Fishman 1999).

These management roles are analogous to the coaching and team development practices I discussed earlier in this chapter. Oh, and the GE/Durham plant is a model of effectiveness and efficiency. One of the critical skills workers have to learn there is how to function as part of a high-performance team.

Even authors Carl Larson and Frank LaFasto (1989), who at least recognize the importance of decision making, don't delve into how to actually improve the process. They do, however, observe, "The third set of leadership principles, and we believe the most important, clearly focus attention on the creation of a supportive decision-making climate." They also point out that achieving a goal requires change, that change requires decisions be made, and that making decisions involves risk. Without a safe environment in which team members can take risks, effective decision making will be stymied.

At its core, collaboration is about decision making. We can talk, share ideas, and debate issues, but in the final analysis decisions must be made—about design, about features, about tradeoffs, about a host of issues. Collaboration isn't talking, it's delivering, and delivering means making decisions. A participatory decision-making process can be useful for larger groups or for two individuals—the process and the issues are the same. Furthermore, while the steps of the decision-making process may proceed less formally between two individuals than they would in a group, the emphasis on sustainable, win-win decisions based on debate and full participation remains key.

One definitional point is critical: Participatory decision making (everyone participates) is different from consensus decision making (everyone votes in favor). The latter is too slow and isn't appropriate in many project situations where the divergence of ideas and opinions would limit the effectiveness of the decision-making process. The critical element isn't consensus but sustainability: Will the team consistently implement decisions that are made? Participation leads to sustainability more efficiently and effectively than consensus. In consensus decision making everyone votes on the decision, and no decision can be implemented without a unanimous vote. In participatory decision making, team members participate in the decision process, but the project manager may actually make the decisions, or the decision is made by a preponderance of the vote.

No doubt decision making is hard, but it is made harder than necessary by poor practices. While "rational" decision making may be a fantasy, there are practices that can assist project teams in making better, implementable decisions. Three elements compose a decision process: decision framing, decision making, and decision retrospection. Framing establishes "who" gets involved in the process, while decision making establishes "how" the "whos" go about making a decision. Retrospection provides feedback into the decision-making process. As with other APM practices, decision-making practices must be implemented with the Simplify principle in mind; otherwise the team will end up with just another unwieldy set of procedures and forms.

Decision Framing

The intent of the often overused term "empowerment" is to delegate decision-making authority to lower levels of organizations by changing who *makes* decisions. Decision framing focuses on who gets *involved* in the decision process. Managers who make decisions without input from subordinates and peers make poor decisions. Engineers who make decisions without input from managers and peers make poor decisions. Who makes the decision is less important than getting the right people involved in the decision process.

However, framing involves more than "who"; it also means considering the values and principles that participants share. Without these shared values and principles, project teams will have difficulty reaching sustainable decisions. The agile values and principles articulated in earlier chapters, whether adopted verbatim or adapted for a specific organization, are vital to your decision-making process. There is a hierarchy of decision-making criteria—values and principles, product vision, and project tradeoff matrix, as well as detailed criteria such as design parameters (e.g., usability). Teams that fail to agree on principles—explicitly—will have problems making sustainable decisions as projects progress.

The next task in framing decisions involves identifying types of decisions that need to be made. For example, in an agile project, replanning occurs at the end of each iteration or milestone. Replanning often involves making tradeoff decisions—schedule versus cost versus features. Projects should include a defect triage decision framework, which is basically asking and answering the question, "Is this product ready to release?"

For each decision type, typical framing questions are:

- Who is impacted by the decision?
- Who needs to provide input to the decision?
- Who should be involved in the discussions about the decision?
- Who should make the decision (the product manager, the project manager, the project team, the project manager with the team, etc.)?
- What decision criteria should be used?
- How and to whom should the decision results be communicated?
- Who should review the decision?

The answers to these questions will involve several overlapping groups of individuals. For example, there may be a wide group of people impacted by the decision, but only selected individuals from those groups may be contacted for input. Everyone who provides input to a decision may not be involved in the discussions about those decisions. There are many decisions that bore project team members, and thus they don't want to be involved, while they do want to be heard on other decisions. Sorting out the various involvements should be the result of careful thinking by the team members and the project and product managers.

Team members often feel isolated from decision processes, not knowing when, why, or how decisions get made. Making decisions is only part of implementing them. Rapid, effective implementation requires a participatory process that involves the right people, with the relevant information, gathered together at the right time.

Many companies and project managers spend far more time on development processes than decision making, which brings to mind a racecar engine running on increasingly viscous sludge. Both will grind to a halt. Framing is the first step in getting the sludge out of your decision-making process.

Decision Making

In many organizations, decision making is viewed as a win-lose proposition. Participants in the process have a preconceived view of the right answer, and their approach is to argue as loudly as possible until the opposition gives up. Participatory decision making focuses on win-win—or "both/and" rather than "either/or." Win-win decision making focuses on mutual understanding rather than loud posturing. This shouldn't imply a lack of heated discussion but a discussion focused on trying to understand the underlying issues rather than debating preordained positions. Participatory decision making can be contentious but civil, based on mutual trust and respect. It moves teams beyond compromise to reconceiving. Participatory decision making is a process of reconceiving a solution to a problem based on information from all team members. Compromise implies giving up one idea for another (and often results in inferior decisions); reconceiving implies a joining of ideas.

Collaboration is hard. In seemingly interminable meetings, team members often flounder in the "groan zone," author Sam Kaner's (1996) wonderful term for the time period in which meeting participants struggle to understand each other. While many people have heard of the famous team progression process "forming, storming, norming, performing" (or, more aptly at times, forming, storming, thrashing, crashing), Kaner's model consists of the divergent zone, the groan zone, and finally the converging zone.

There are two objectives against which any decision-making process must be judged. First, does the process result in the best choice given the circumstances in which the decision was made? Second, was the decision implemented? As many project managers have found out the hard way, making and implementing decisions are two different things. How many times have you encountered decisions made within the confines of a conference room that fall completely apart when the participants walk out the door? Anyone can make a decision, but effective managers grasp that implementation requires people to understand and support the decision.

A participatory decision-making process has three components: principles, framework, and practices. The fundamental principles have just been alluded to: viewing the process as a win-win process and treating all participants with respect. All collaborative practices are based on trust and respect, or perhaps more precisely, on building trust and respect.[5] Kaner's diverge-groan-converge model provides a framework for building these positive relationship qualities. In the diverge-groan-converge framework, the transition from the divergent zone to the convergent zone explains how team members move from having individual opinions to having a unified position. At first, people's ideas diverge. Even though each person wants to contribute to success and to making a quick decision, each wants to voice his or her own opinion. Everyone has a different perspective or a different experience, which brings needed diversity to the decision process but not much agreement. This groaning period takes time, time for people to speak and hear, time for them to build trust. A little extra time (it's not really extra, but it seems as if it is) taken on decision making in the early stages of a project will significantly reduce time as the project continues.

Convergence occurs as the individual ideas are integrated into a whole solution. Convergence, done correctly, does not necessarily mean that everyone is in complete agreement but that everyone has participated and will support the final decision. The goal is not merely agreement but "sustainable agreement"—a unified position.

The transition period between divergence and convergence, the groan zone, is the time during which team members groan and complain. In the divergent zone, most group members voice their opinions to make sure the group hears their ideas. Much of this time could be considered presentation, during which members are less concerned with understanding each other than with selling their own ideas. Participants begin to groan because they are trying to understand one another, and understanding requires thought. It is relatively easy to take a position and argue for it. It is much more difficult to attempt to understand *why* other participants hold their opinions. Participants want to ask questions, they want to be heard, they want to—participate. The groan zone provides a perfect description of

---

5. The idea of building trust may seem counter to the earlier statement that managers either trust or don't trust. However, a manager can believe in trusting team members but also understand that the level of trust must be earned through actions. People are predisposed to trust or not trust, but they still want proof of that predisposition.

THE EXPLORE PHASE

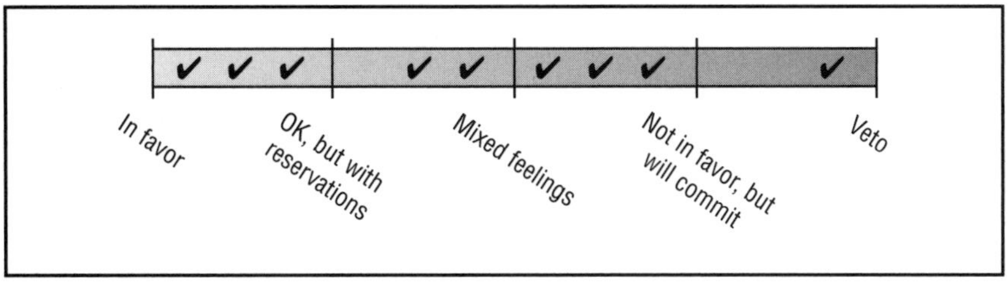

Figure 7.4
Decision Gradient

what happens in most teams; it is a turbulent zone where innovative, creative results are generated.

One of the best tools for testing how the decision process is proceeding, and for arriving at the decision itself, is a decision gradient that replaces the familiar yes-no voting. A decision gradient, as shown in Figure 7.4, gives participants more options: in favor; OK, but with reservations; mixed feelings; not in favor, but will commit to implement; veto. When all participants plot their responses on a line with these gradations, the entire team gets to view its collective opinion. The team can then address issues like trying to understand the person who vetoed the decision or trying to understand why so many people are clustered around "mixed feelings." Voting—or actually, the discussions about why the voting was one way or another—leads to a deeper understanding of the issues and eventually to another vote. Decision gradients make for better discussion and more effective, sustainable decisions.[6]

When some person (manager, technical leader) is designated as the decision maker, a preponderance of agreement among participating team members is helpful but not essential. But when a team as a whole is the decision maker, what actions craft a sustainable decision? In many people's minds, consensus has come to mean "unanimous," and I too was using the unanimous connotation earlier in this section. But consensus has another definition that corresponds to the idea of a preponderance of agreement among participants. Intel is one company known for its attention to decision making. Intel emphasizes decision-making training for employees, and the company focuses on decision framing and decision-making on a regular basis. Intel has an engrained decision-making culture in which the phrase "disagree and commit" is often used. It means that someone might disagree with a decision, but he will commit himself to its implementation.

6. See Kaner (1996) for more information on decision gradients.

This nonunanimous type of consensus is built on the following premises:

- Everyone has had an opportunity to have his or her ideas heard and discussed.
- Consensus does not imply unanimous agreement, but it does mean that people understand the decision rationale.
- No one has been silenced due to fear or intimidation.
- The preponderance of the group votes in favor of the decision (or in favor with some reservations).
- No one vetoes the decision (instead, they disagree and commit).

Decisions thus reached are sustainable in ways that lead to team cohesion and positive outcomes. Arbitrary and capricious decisions, those imposed by force of will or organizational power, have the opposite effect.

An additional benefit to a participatory process such as the one just described is that as mutual understanding of the context (including the decision criteria) increases, the time required to make similar decisions decreases rapidly. For example, a defect triage team that develops a shared understanding of the relevant quality factors involved in reaching decisions will speed up its decisions over time. Conversely, teams that do not take additional time in the beginning to fully understand each other's perspective on some issue (e.g., quality) will constantly argue the same points meeting after meeting, wasting irreplaceable project time.

Different kinds of decisions require different decision criteria. Coin flipping works for what time to go to lunch. The tradeoff matrix steers high-level decisions, just as performance criteria might steer technical decisions. Release decisions might use certain quality criteria. For each kind of decision, one of the discussion topics should be the criteria to be used in making that type of decision. You may even need to go through a decision-making process to arrive at the criteria for making a decision.

Decision Retrospection

End of iteration, milestone, and project retrospectives should include time to review decisions within the context of reviewing the team's performance (which I discuss in the next chapter). However, if project retrospectives are difficult to do in general, then decision retrospectives border on the impossible, because finding whom to blame often seems more important than learning. But how do we get better at decisions unless we understand which ones worked out well and which ones didn't?

We are sometimes our own worst enemies. In the medical profession, for example, airing mistakes is especially difficult because of the threat of medical malpractice suits. Sharing and learning from decisions become severely inhibited; therefore, the same mistakes are repeated by other doctors or other hospitals because little retrospection occurs. A recent television program described an initiative in the northeastern United States in which this veil of secrecy was lifted in a concerted and collaborative effort between doctors and hospitals. Not surprisingly, problems decreased.

Still, few organizations want to examine decisions in any depth, which probably corresponds to the general lack of interest in decision making. Was an error-prone product released? Why? What were the decisions that led up to the release decision? Maybe the decision was actually a "good" one from a market perspective. If so, then the development staff needs to understand the nature of the decision, why it was made, and who was involved in the decision. Maybe the decision was based on market timing information, but the decision makers didn't listen to the developers, and the actual release was a disaster. If the disaster isn't analyzed, if the decision tradeoff of product stability versus market need analysis isn't revisited, then nothing will be learned and similar mistakes will be made in the future. On the other hand, a decision may be perceived as incorrect, but further analysis shows that it was actually the correct one given the circumstances. In this case, lack of analysis might keep us from making the same "correct" decision in the future.

Participatory decision making may spell the difference between success and failure on agile projects. Framing decisions, developing a collaborative decision-making process, and conducting decision retrospectives to learn from both success and failure are components of this practice.

Leadership and Decision Making

A good project manager has to be a visionary, a teacher, a motivator, a facilitator, and other things, but she must also be a decision maker. The same is true of chief engineers for technical issues. So the question becomes, at what point does a manager's decision making damage self-organization? First, when the team loses respect for the leader. But what causes loss of respect? The answer: when the manager begins making unilateral decisions. The more unilateral decisions, the less participation from the team, the less likely the decisions are to be effectively implemented.

Every team and situation are different, so there isn't a quantitative answer to the question of how many unilateral decisions are too many. However, even though presenting absolute numbers risks misinterpretation, I think the following guidelines may help define appropriate "levels" of management decision making that will continue to foster self-organization. For both managers and chief engineers, this rough guide is one unilateral decision every month or two, three to four decisions per month with team involvement, and then delegate the hundreds of other decisions to the team. In practice, few good managers make completely unilateral decisions—they normally talk issues over with at least key members of their team. But occasionally there is a need to get things moving by making a unilateral decision. In that same vein, it is appropriate for project managers and chief engineers to make certain decisions with team participation, but if they are making more than three or four of these decisions per month, even with team involvement, they are probably too absorbed in the details.

Another issue related to management decision making is the leader's job of absorbing ambiguity. In fast-moving product development efforts in which key decisions must be made quickly, consensus (unanimous) decision making fails, but even participatory decision making can get mired in discussion and debate. Many product development issues, both technical and administrative, may be fuzzy and ambiguous. In these cases, once participation has evolved to a certain point, managers have to be willing to make final decisions. "Well, the information available to us isn't crystal clear, but in order to move forward with the project, we'll go in this direction."

Good leaders have earned the credibility to make these decisions. The technical staff respect the leader's judgment (based on previous actions taken), participate in the analysis and debate process, and willingly accept the decision in order to move on. The leader has absorbed the ambiguity of the situation, whereas leaving the decision to consensus would have bogged the project down in interminable debate. Good leaders know when to step in and take charge and when to encourage the team to take charge. They also know when to dig into why team decision making isn't working as it should.

Set- and Delay-Based Decision Making

If we want to build adaptive teams and products, not only do we need a participatory decision-making process, but we also need to look at criteria for decision making that encourage experimentation. Point-based engineering dominates current product development. Point-based engineering views design as a series of decisions in which each decision narrows the options for further decisions, and the product progresses in a steady fashion from a gleam in the marketer's eye to a final product.

Toyota upset this apple cart, at least as it pertains to the automotive industry's design process. Toyota's approach, set-based concurrent engineering (SBCE), provides a new insight into product design. SBCE operates on two fundamental concepts: postpone design decisions as late as possible and maintain "sets" of design solutions throughout the majority of the design process.

"SBCE assumes that reasoning and communicating about sets of ideas leads to more robust, optimized systems and greater overall efficiency than working with one idea at a time, even though the individual steps may look inefficient," write Durward K. Sobek, Allen C. Ward, and Jeffrey K. Liker (1999). Rather than converge on a design "answer," Toyota's engineers maintain sets of designs. For a particular car project, they might maintain six alternative solutions that include prototypes and mock-ups for the exhaust system design.

Unlike point requirements, set-based requirements focus on ranges or minimum constraints. So the body design group would impose a criteria "range" on the exhaust system, keeping the tolerances as broad as possible in the beginning and narrowing them over time as the car approaches manufacturing. As the body design and exhaust system designs evolve, engineers are more likely to balance subsystem optimization with overall vehicle optimization. In a point-based approach, each subsystem team has a tendency to quickly create optimized designs for its particular subsystem that are often at odds with overall system design effectiveness.

Toyota's slow narrowing of options extends even to die making. Rather than specify precise part fit, designers specify wider tolerances. The die makers themselves create the parts, see how they actually fit together, and then send the precise measurements back to the design groups to finalize the detail CAD drawings.

Engineers, whether of automobiles or computers, tend toward point-based solutions—they analyze the problem, review the constraints, and then design "the" solution. But there are always multiple design options, and the larger the product or product family, the more likely that early design decisions will lock the team into suboptimal solutions. Maintaining multiple sets of solutions and delaying final design decisions, even though it may appear to be inefficient, may in fact be faster and more efficient in the long run. As Sobek and his coauthors observe, "Toyota considers a broader range of possible designs and delays certain decisions longer than other automotive companies do, yet has what may be the fastest and most efficient vehicle development cycles in the industry" (Sobek et al. 1999).

Practice: Daily Interaction with the Customer Team

Objective

Daily interaction with the customer team, which includes the product manager, helps ensure that the development efforts stay on track to meet the needs and expectations of the customer.

Discussion

One of the key tenets of APM is close interaction with product managers and customers. When dealing with uncertainty, risk, fluid requirements changes, and technological frontiers, product managers need to be fully involved in identifying features, specifying feature requirements, determining feature priorities, making key tradeoff decisions (cost, schedule, etc.), developing acceptance criteria and tests, and more. Being the "customer" for an agile project is not an insignificant job, but it may not need to be full time. The key to keeping the project moving is very frequent, if not daily, interaction in which the project team receives a constant flow of information and decisions from the product manager.[7] While interaction with customers may be important to other types of projects, it is absolutely essential with high exploration-factor projects.

In both general business and product organizations, individuals often blanch at the prospect of daily interaction with development teams. As I noted earlier, product managers often wear two hats—an external marketing hat and an internal product development one. Unfortunately, the external demands often override the internal ones, and time with the development team suffers. When exploration factors are lower and development teams possess product domain knowledge, the project might not suffer as much from lack of interaction between the customer and development teams, but when exploring uncertainty prevails, this interaction is vital to ultimate success. Feedback is critical to exploration because, without it, experiments veer off into costly and unproductive directions.

Finally, the project manager (and the team in certain circumstances) needs to coordinate not only with customers, but also with stakeholders in order to obtain required resources and ensure support. Dee Hock (1999) has a unique perspective on the responsibilities of a manager. The first is to manage self, which he defines as "One's own integrity, character, ethics, knowledge, wisdom, temperament, words, and acts." The second is to manage the people who have authority over one—managers, supervisors, executives, regulators, and others. The third is to manage peers, "those over whom we have no authority and who have no authority over us—associates, competitors, suppliers, customers."

The response to this list of managerial responsibilities, Hock reports, can often be paraphrased as, "If we do all that, we won't have time to manage subordinates." To which Hock says, "Exactly!" The more teams manage themselves, the less the project manager has to intervene. And the more time the project manager can spend managing upwards and outwards—that is, managing the participants outside the project team—the more effective he is.

---

7. While, strictly speaking, daily interaction may not be necessary or even possible, titling this practice "frequent" interaction leaves too much room for misinterpretation. A more explicit title such as "regular, high-frequency interaction" would be somewhat more specific, but not enough to overcome the verbosity of the phrase. In the long run, I choose to stick with "daily" since it better conveys the sense of this practice.

Stakeholder Coordination

Another project manager responsibility is stakeholder coordination. Project managers must secure resources and ensure ongoing support for the team. A project team may need a component from another team or an external supplier. The accounting department may need periodic information. Executives may need to be briefed on the progress of the project. Project managers who don't identify each stakeholder and initiate a coordination plan to ensure that each one gets the service he or she needs from the team run the risk of getting blindsided by a disgruntled stakeholder. Some stakeholders contribute to the project's success, and others can be serious impediments—but they all have to be managed. While members of the project team can assist, managing up and out is generally the responsibility of the project manager, who must shelter the team from the sometimes crazy politics of stakeholder coordination.[8]

Explore Summary

Exploring is how agile teams execute. Rather than stepping through a prescriptive plan, agile teams execute through a series of planned experiments, a series of feature deliveries, a series of attempts to create a concrete formulation of the product vision within the boundaries of a business model.

Exploring is accomplished by competent, self-disciplined teams led by competent managers who create self-organized environments. Team members work in a semi-autonomous fashion, striving to meet iteration plans that they themselves have had a hand in constructing, managing their own workload, collaborating to generate innovative ideas, and applying specific technical practices aimed at building adaptable products that in turn facilitate the very exploration process that they are employing.

Project managers (and product managers) are direct contributors to the team's exploring process. They encourage rather than motivate; they are demanding, but not arbitrary; they empower the team, but make certain

---

8. For some specific tools for managing stakeholder relationships, see (Thomsett 2002).

decisions themselves; they coach rather than criticize; and they facilitate rather than command. Effective agile project managers work hard to unleash the talent and abilities of their teams by focusing their efforts, molding individuals into jelled teams, developing each individual's capabilities, providing resources to the team, working with customers and stakeholders, and facilitating a participatory decision-making process.

Anyone who still believes that the project manager's role is to buy pizza and get out of the way is ignoring the abundant research on successful projects over the last 15 or more years. Conversely, anyone who believes that project management is mainly about prescriptive tasks, schedules, resource charts, and preordained plans will have a rude awakening trying to apply these ideas to volatile product development projects.

Chapter 8

The Adapt and Close Phases

Progress

"Hi, Maya," Herman said as she picked up the phone. "Ready for another round?"

"Sure, fire away," Maya replied.

"I'm struggling with tracking progress using agile practices. I don't see accountability. When things change during an iteration, you just replan. When developers don't meet their estimates, you change velocity. How can management have any confidence in project status?"

"Mainly because in every iteration we deliver features that are tangible evidence of progress. Whether management likes the results or not, they are confident in our status," said Maya.

"My management just wants to see budget and schedule reports," said Herman.

"But how can they really know your status if they don't talk to you? I sit down with my boss and the product manager, and we discuss issues in depth. I try hard to understand the business drivers, and my boss gets an earful about the technical challenges from my technical folks. We jointly decide on how to adapt going forward, usually with schedule as the highest priority."

"Well, that's what they claim around here, too, but it's really a farce. We never make our dates."

"My management is tough, but they're willing to make tradeoff decisions. They push us, but they understand our situation, and they're not unreasonable. Well, not very."

"It sounds like there's a lot of give and take," Herman said.

"Right," said Maya. "You should hear some of the 'discussions.' It gets hot and heavy—both with management and within my team. But we're honestly trying to get at what's going on, how to make the best decisions. The dev team stays involved in these discussions, so they feel included and are willing to hold themselves accountable for the results."

"That all sounds good, maybe too good. But what happens when the execs cut the schedule? They do it all the time here."

"Last year that happened. My team looked at where we could cut, and we didn't think there were many features that could be pruned and still have a competitive product. Hiring was frozen at the time, so we recommended sticking with the plan or killing the project."

"And?"

"They grumbled some, but after grilling me for an hour, they killed it."

"Wow!" said Herman. "And you're still employed?"

"Sure. It turned out to be the best thing we ever did. If we'd come to market with a poor product, the competition would have killed us," Maya replied. "Oh, which reminds me about managing between the activities."

"What? This your newest insight?"

"It hit me when I was skiing the North Face last weekend at Crested Butte. Looking at trees is one surefire way to hit them. You start worrying about hitting one, and, bang, you do. I keep my eyes focused on where I want to go, the space between them."

"And this relates to project management how?" Herman queried.

"Most project managers are so worried about the silly old maxim that projects get late one day at a time that they micromanage tasks on a daily, or even hourly, basis. Detail tasks are like the trees. The managers lose track of the goal, of the result the team is trying to deliver that iteration. By constantly harassing the team about whether they finished some four-hour task, they run into project trees."

"But what about control?" Herman asked.

"I manage feature completion at the end of the iteration, not daily tasks. Our control mechanism may seem less robust, but it works," said Maya. "The trick is to narrow uncertainty over the life of the project. It completely solves the 90% complete problem 90% of the time."

"We usually have the opposite. The further we get into the project, the more frustrated our management becomes that we haven't hit the original plan, even though in many cases they have caused problems by changing priorities and shuffling people," said Herman. "They always forget that the original plans were often done very quickly—at their request—before we fully understood the requirements."

"So," said Maya, "even though conceptually your traditional process should work fine, in reality it puts all the burden on the project team and almost none on management and the customer."

"Well, I guess you could put it that way," Herman mumbled. "I'm beginning to see how your approach makes it so each party has to step up to their responsibilities. Maybe that's why I'm having a hard time getting people around here to buy into it. Oh well, I'd better get going. My weekly fantasy reports are due."

Note: Although both the Adapt and Close phases are included in this chapter (because the information on Close is brief), it is critical to remember that the Adapt practices are an integral part of every iteration, while Close occurs only once, at the end of the project.

Phase: Adapt

If plans are speculations or hypotheses about the future, then frequent and effective feedback is necessary to test those hypotheses. Agile projects are exploration projects, and as such, success depends upon reality-based feedback. Adaptation depends upon understanding a wide range of information, including an assessment of the project's progress, technical risks, the requirements evolution, and ongoing competitive market analysis. APM has the potential to save money through the early termination of projects, but only if the project team and executives are willing to face reality early. Iterative projects are also prone to oscillation—going back and forth without making progress. Two things counteract this potential risk: a good vision and continual feedback. Every project team needs to constantly evaluate and make appropriate adaptations in the following four areas:

- Product functionality, primarily from the customer team's perspective
- Product quality, primarily from the technical team's perspective

- Team performance
- Project status

Adaptations can take many forms. A team that rushes to deliver features but creates defects—hurrying rather than being quick—needs to adapt its behavior. A creeping design degeneration gives rise to additional "refactoring" activity in the next iteration. Cost overruns are highlighted by the project status review, and appropriate action is taken.

The common project management term for responding to deviations from plan is "corrective action," a phrase that implies that the project team has made an error or underperformed. The "conformance to plan" mentality runs deep in project managers' psyches. The *Project Management Body of Knowledge* defines corrective action as "anything done to bring expected future performance in line with the project plan" (Project Management Institute 2000). The term corrective action is based on the assumption that the plan is correct and the actual performance lacking. Since plans are speculations in the first place, APM abandons the term corrective action in favor of "adaptive action"—reacting to events rather than to a predictive plan. Reacting to events is more difficult than reacting to a plan, because the team has to answer three critical questions:

- Are customers getting value from the project?
- Is the project progressing satisfactorily?
- Is the project team adapting effectively to changes imposed by management, customers, or technology?

"Are customers getting value from the project?" In an agile project, because of changes over the course of an iteration, teams need to continually review the product's value. The customers and product manager make frequent adjustments in the feature priorities based on their interpretation of feature value. Measuring value can be difficult, more difficult than measuring cost or schedule against plan, but without a constant attention to determining value—if only an implicit customer ranking rather than an explicit numerical calculation—guiding an agile project will prove difficult. The product manager needs to assess whether the value generated during an iteration was worth the cost of development.

"Is the project progressing satisfactorily?" This question is also more difficult to answer than whether the project is conforming to plan. Conformance to plan is one aspect of satisfactory progression, but only one. Members of the project team must ask themselves the question, "Given the circumstances during the last iteration, did we make sufficient progress, and what additional information did we learn?" Progress can be measured in a variety of ways depending upon the project. For large projects, especially those involving government contracts, a form of earned value analysis (with value calculated from features completed) may be appropriate. For smaller projects, a simple graph of features completed by iteration should suffice.

"Is the project team adapting effectively to changes imposed by management, customers, or technology?" As requirements evolve, staff changes take place, component delays occur, and a multitude of other things impact a project, the team members need to assess how they are adapting to those changes. Also, if managers and executives want project teams that can be flexible and adapt to change, then they must give teams appropriate credit for that flexibility. When a team deviates from the original plan but effectively responds to a surprise product release from a competitor, that team should be evaluated on the situation and their response, not the outdated plan.

The Adapt phase contains a single practice, which includes several subpractices:

- Product, project, and team review and adaptive action

Some of the practices within this Adapt phase should be scheduled at the end of each iteration (e.g., product evaluations), while others, such as the team performance review, could be scheduled at a milestone. However, if the team is using two-week iterations and two-month milestones, the team review should probably occur every second iteration—waiting two months would be too long. Furthermore, part of the team review should include evaluating the time periods between these various reviews. In APM, nothing should happen by default; the team should always be evaluating the relevance and contribution of every practice.

Practice: Product, Project, and Team Review and Adaptive Action

Objective

The objective of the review and adaptive action practice is to ensure that frequent feedback and high levels of learning occur in multiple project dimensions.

Discussion

There are two main reasons for conducting review and adaptive action sessions at the end of an iteration or milestone. The first reason is obvious—to reflect, learn, and adapt. The second is more subtle—to change pace. Short iterations give a sense of urgency to a project because a lot has to happen in a few weeks. Team members work at a quick pace, not hurrying, but working quickly at a high level of intensity. The end-of-iteration review period should be more relaxed, a brief time (normally a day or so) in which the team reflects on the last iteration and plans ahead for the next. Most teams need this break in intensity periodically to gather their energy for the next iteration. During this reflection period, four types of reviews are useful: product functionality from the customer team's perspective, technical quality from the engineering team's perspective, team performance checkpoints, and a review of overall project status.

Customer Focus Groups

Customer focus group (CFG) sessions demonstrate ongoing versions of the final product to the customer team in order to get periodic feedback on how well the product meets customer requirements. While CFGs are conducted at the end of iterations and milestones, they should be scheduled at the beginning of the project to ensure the right participants are available at the right times.

A CFG is one form of acceptance testing for a product. Individuals from the customer team, together with developers, meet in a facilitated session in which the product features are demonstrated to the customer team. The sessions follow scenarios that demonstrate the product's use by customers. As the "demonstration" proceeds, change requests are generated and recorded.

While customer team representatives work with the engineering team throughout a development iteration, a CFG brings a wider audience into the evaluation process. For example, whereas one or two individual customers from manufacturing might be involved in the day-to-day work with a project team on a manufacturing software application, eight to ten might be involved in a CFG. This wider audience participation helps ensure that features don't get overlooked, the product encompasses more than the viewpoint of a few people, confidence in the product's progress increases over time, and customers begin to become familiar with the product before actual deployment. These review sessions typically take two to four hours, but this timeframe is highly dependent on the type of product and the iteration length. CFG reviews are wonderful vehicles for building customer team–development team partnerships.[1]

In a shoe development process, for example, designers work with ideas, sketches, and then more formal CAD drawings. At several points in the process, the designers take their ideas over to the "lab," where technicians build mock-ups of the shoe. These mock-ups are wearable, usable shoes built in very small quantities. At the end of a milestone, the shoes can be shown to the marketing staff for their feedback or even to a selected group of target customers.

The definition of acceptance testing varies by industry, but in general CFG reviews provide a wider focus than acceptance testing. Acceptance testing concentrates on system behavior related to critical engineering design parameters, while CFGs focus on how the customers use the product. CFG reviews gather feedback on look and feel, general operation of the product, and the use of the product in business, consumer, or operational

---

1. Who participates in CFG sessions depends on whether the product is for internal or external customers. In the case of external customers, product marketing has to determine when, and if, external customers will be brought in to review the product. Considerations that impact these decisions include confidentiality, beta testing strategies, and early sales potential.

scenarios. For example, a specific acceptance test could measure the heat dissipation of an electronic instrument, or a software acceptance test case might ensure a business rule is properly calculated. Running exhaustive engine, electronic, and hydraulic tests to check predetermined values would be part of an airplane's acceptance testing. Actual flight testing—testing the product under conditions of actual use—would be similar to a CFG.

CFG review sessions:

- Should be facilitated
- Should be limited to eight to ten customers (Development teams are present but have limited involvement; they are primarily observers.)
- Review the product itself, not documents
- Focus on discovering and recording desired customer changes, but not on gathering detailed requirements (if, for example, new features are identified)

CFGs are particularly useful in distributed development scenarios in which daily contact between development teams and customers is difficult. When teams have less-than-optimal contact with customers during iterations, end-of-iteration focus groups can keep the team from wandering too far off track.[2]

Customer change requests are recorded for review by the project team *after* the focus group session. It's best to wait until after the CFG to do this because analysis of these requests often leads to technical discussions that aren't relevant to many of the customer participants. Furthermore, the engineering team's initial response to changes tends to be defensive—"That will be difficult (or expensive)"—which customers may interpret as a negative response to their suggestions. This environment discourages further suggestions, and sessions lose their effectiveness. The better approach is for the technical team to evaluate the requests the next day and then discuss options with the product manager. Normally, 80% or more of the requests can be handled with little effort, while the others may require additional study or fall outside the project's scope. Accumulated small changes are handled using the time allocated to the rework and contingency cards described in Chapter 6. Significant changes and new features

---

2. For a detailed examination of customer focus groups, see (Bayer 2001).

are recorded on feature cards that will serve as input to the next iteration planning session.

Technical Reviews

One of the key principles of exploratory, agile projects is to keep the cost of iteration low (both during development and after first deployment) such that the product itself can adapt to changing customer needs. Keeping the cost of iteration low and adaptability high depends on unceasing attention to technical excellence. Poorly designed, poor-quality, defect-prone products are expensive to change and therefore inflexible to changing customer demands. When customers buy a $500,000 biomedical device, they want it to respond to future needs (within limits) quickly and cost effectively. Often, the flexibility of industrial products, such as a biomedical device, depends on the flexibility of its embedded software.

Periodic technical reviews, both informal and regularly scheduled, provide the project team with feedback on technical problems, design issues, and architectural flaws. These reviews should address the key technical practices of simple design, continuous integration, ruthless testing, and refactoring to ensure that they are being effectively implemented. Technical reviews are also a collaborative practice and as such contribute to relationship building within the team. As always, these reviews should be conducted in the spirit of agile development—simple, barely sufficient, minimal documentation, short sessions, lots of interaction.

Technical reviews, informal ones at least, occur continuously during an iterative delivery cycle. However, at periodic intervals—and at least once per milestone—a scheduled technical review should be conducted. It should not take more than a couple of hours, except in special situations.

Technical review sessions:

- Are facilitated
- Are generally limited to two to six individuals who are competent to evaluate the technical material
- Review the product, selected documents, and statistics, such as defect levels (The technical team should take time to reflect on the overall technical quality of the product and make recommendations

about refactoring, additional testing, more frequent integration, or other technical adaptations.)

As with customer change requests, technical change requests can be handled in the time allocated to the rework and contingency cards.[3]

Team Performance Evaluations

A fundamental tenet of APM is that projects are different and people are different (and thus teams are different). Therefore, no team should be shoehorned into the same set of processes and practices as another. Project teams should work within an overall framework and guidelines (such as this APM framework and its associated guiding principles), but they should be able to adapt practices to meet their unique needs. Self-organizing principles dictate that the working framework should grant the team as much flexibility and authority to make decisions as possible. Self-disciplinary principles dictate that once the framework has been agreed upon, team members work within that framework. Assessments of team performance should touch on both of these factors.

While people want a degree of flexibility, they also get very tired of constantly starting with a blank sheet of paper, especially when they know they can use established techniques from similar projects in the same company. For example, changing documentation formats from project to project can be a source of frustration to project team members. Starting with a common framework and adapting it based on project and team needs can eliminate many of these frustrations.

Many project management methodologies recommend doing retrospectives at the end of a project. This may be fine for passing learning on to other teams, but it doesn't help improve performance during a project. Iteration or milestone retrospectives of even an hour or two give teams an opportunity to reflect on what is working and what isn't. In coming up with this assessment, the team will want to examine many aspects of the project, asking questions

---

3. There are several good references on the practice of peer reviews. For example, see (Wiegers 2001).

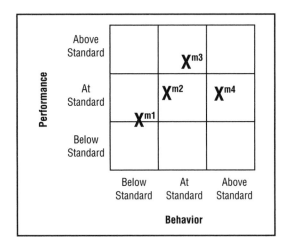

Figure 8.1
Team Self-Assessment Chart (for each milestone, Mn)

like "What went well?" "What didn't go as well?" and "How do we improve next iteration?" The team might also ask Norm Kerth's interesting question, "What don't we understand?"[4]

The information shown in Figure 8.1 can be used as a starting point for evaluating team performance. The team evaluates itself in two dimensions—delivery performance and behavior—on a three-point scale: below standard, at standard, or above standard. On delivery performance, the team members are asking themselves the fundamental question, "Did we do the best job we could do in the last iteration?" Notice that the question isn't related to plans but to the team's assessment of its own performance. Whether teams conform to plan or not depends on both performance and the accuracy of the plan (so one piece of this evaluation might be for the team members to assess how well they planned the iteration). A team could meet the plan and still not be performing at an optimal level. In a well-functioning team, members tend to be open and honest about their performance. The team discussion, not the assessment chart itself, is the important aspect of this exercise.

The second aspect of the evaluation is team behavior, in which the team, again, assesses its own performance. This evaluation involves answering the questions, "How well are we fulfilling our responsibilities?" and "How well

---

4. The best reference book on conducting retrospectives is (Kerth 2001).

is the organization fulfilling its responsibilities?" Answering these two questions could generate a raft of other questions, such as:

- Are all team members participating in discussions?
- Is someone regularly absent from daily meetings?
- Are team members being accountable for their commitments?
- Is the project manager micro-managing?
- Does the team understand how and why key decisions were made during the last iteration?

The team members assess their overall behavior and develop ideas for improvement. For teams that are new to using agile practices, a questionnaire to help them measure their "agility rating" could also be useful.

Finally, the team should evaluate processes and practices that are related to team behavior but not explicitly covered by Figure 8.1. While the team may not want to evaluate the overall development framework at each milestone, it should assess and adapt individual practices to better fit the team. For example, while a team wouldn't decide to eliminate requirements gathering, it might alter the level of ceremony and detail of the requirements documentation. The team might determine that daily integration meetings between feature teams be changed to twice-weekly meetings attended by two members from each feature team. The team might decide that three-week iterations are causing too much overhead. They could switch to four-week iterations and evaluate the impact.

There are a myriad of ways in which teams could adjust their processes and practices. The crucial thing is that they view processes and practices as adjustable and that they not feel the need to continue activities that are not contributing to the goals of the project.

Project Status Reports

Project status reports should have value to the project manager, the product manager, key stakeholders, and the project team itself. The reporting of information should drive activities aimed at enhancing performance. Developing the reports should help the project and product managers reflect on the overall progress of the project—to separate the forest from their daily battle with the trees. The number and frequency of reports and the information in the reports need to match the size, duration, and importance of the project.

Part of the project manager's job involves managing stakeholders, particularly those in upper management, and providing information to them. What stakeholders ask for may be very different from what is needed to manage the project, but the project manager neglects this other information, and periodic interactions with those stakeholders, at her peril. Managing the expectations of various stakeholders can be a delicate balancing act.

Attending status meetings, giving management presentations, gathering accounting information, and a raft of similar activities can drain valuable time from delivering product. At the same time, management and customers are spending money for a product, and they aren't receptive to being told, "Just wait six months until we are finished." Managers have a fiduciary responsibility, and they need periodic information to fulfill that duty. Customers and sponsors need information to make project tradeoff decisions. Status reports must provide information to assist in answering questions such as, "Is the prognosis for the product such that it is no longer economically feasible?" and "Should features be eliminated to ensure we make the product release schedule?"

Most status reporting looks at what was accomplished within the prior reporting period and focuses on the three-legged stool of project management—scope, schedule, and cost. The tradeoff matrix introduced in Chapter 5 contains four attributes to consider in analyzing changes and making decisions—scope, schedule, resources, *and* stability (defect levels, one aspect of technical quality). In evaluating scope, the team needs to examine not only features delivered versus features planned, but also the value of those features delivered. Finally, since uncertainty and risk drive many agile projects, the team should monitor whether risk and uncertainty are being systematically reduced.

While each of the status reports or charts identified below provides useful information to the development team, the customer team, and management, the "parking lot" graphic provides an excellent visual picture of any project's overall progress. In Chapter 6, Figure 6.7 showed a parking lot diagram used for project planning. Similar diagrams, Figures 8.2 and 8.3, are used here as the basis for status reporting. In the figures, the bar just above each scheduled delivery date indicates the percentage of the features that have been completed (partially completed features are excluded). Colors enable a quick analysis of the project's progress, especially as the project continues and the colors change from month to month. A white box indicates that no work has begun on the activity, while a blue box (light shading in figure) indicates work has begun on some of the features. A green box indicates that the features within have been

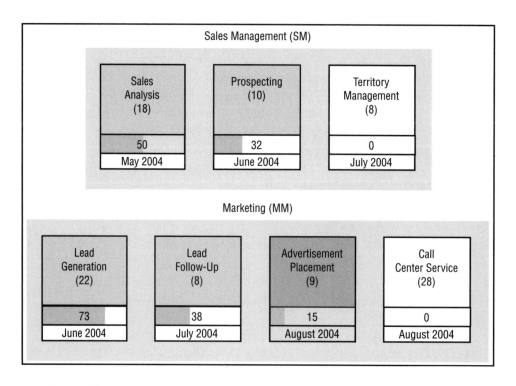

Figure 8.2
Project Parking Lot Report by Business Activity (adapted from Jeff DeLuca's work)

completed, while a red box (heavy shading in figure) indicates that at least one scheduled feature has not been delivered in its planned iteration. Figure 8.2 shows project progress by business activity area, or product component, and Figure 8.3 shows an alternative presentation of the status by month.

Scope and Value Status

In an agile project, scope performance can be measured by measuring features completed versus plan, by iteration, as shown in Figure 8.4. (This chart, and a detailed listing of features and their status, can be used as supplementary detail to the parking lot report.) In general, since features can be added or deleted by the customer team over the life of a project, development teams

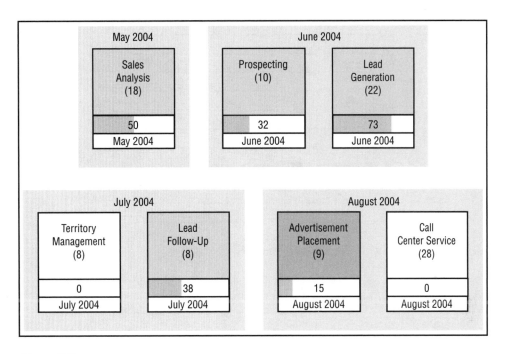

Figure 8.3
Project Parking Lot Report by Month (adapted from Jeff DeLuca's work)

should be evaluated based on the number of features delivered rather than the specific features delivered. If the team delivers 170 of 175 planned features, then its performance is very good, even if 50 of those features are different from those in the original plan.

Scope tells us the raw volume of feature deliverables, but not how valuable they are. Since the objective of agile development is to deliver high-value features early, in some cases to achieve early ROI, then one potentially beneficial report is "features and value delivered," as shown in Figure 8.5. For this report, the customer team needs to apportion the product's value to individual features or to the broader level of a component or business activity. If the development team is burdened with estimating the "cost" of each feature, then the customer team (including the product manager) should be burdened with estimating the "value" of each one. As Tom DeMarco and Tim Lister (2003) say, "Costs and benefits need to be specified with equal

Figure 8.4
Delivery Performance

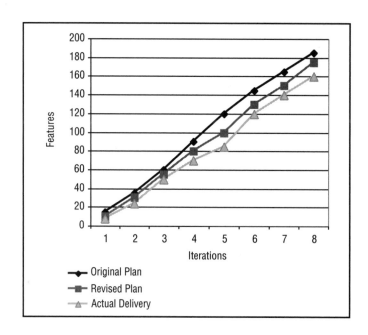

Figure 8.5
Features and Value
Delivered

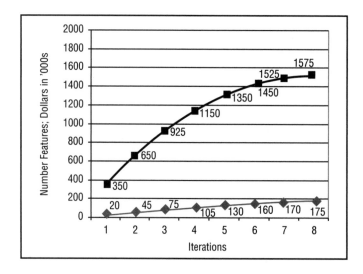

precision." With incremental cost *and* value information for every feature, the stakeholders can make much better tradeoff decisions.

Let's assume that the net present value (NPV) of the revenue stream from the 175-feature product mentioned above is $15 million, and the

THE ADAPT AND CLOSE PHASES

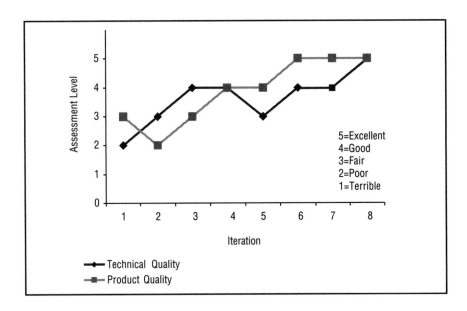

Figure 8.6
Product and
Technical Quality
Assessment

development cost has been estimated at $3 million. The product manager would apportion the $15 million to each of the 20 to 30 components (rather than to all 175 features). Once this analysis and allocation was completed, then a value performance chart like that in Figure 8.5 could accompany the scope performance report. By recognizing value delivered, even using a cursory valuation of features, the project team, customer team, and executives have better information with which to make project decisions.[5]

For a simple value assessment, the customer team can rank order features using an informal value assessment and then indicate its satisfaction with the delivered features from each iteration on a five-point scale, as shown (in combination with a technical quality assessment) in Figure 8.6. Finally, as systematic risk and uncertainty reduction is a strong indicator of increasing value, a technical risk and uncertainty assessment, as shown in Figure 8.7, can be beneficial.

Since delivering customer value and agility may be more important than meeting cost budgets, agility measurements can also be useful. At a feature

---

5. An extension to this idea would be to use feature value in an earned value analysis (EVA). Using feature values can turn the "V" in EVA into a real value measure.

Figure 8.7
Technical Risk
and Uncertainty
Assessment

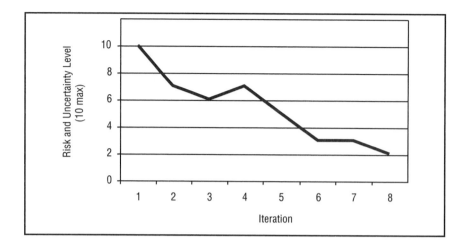

level, the team can track and report on changes each iteration—original features planned, original features deleted or deferred, and new features added. The team can also track the change requests from the customer focus groups and report changes requested, implemented, deleted, or deferred. These reports showing the team's response to customer-requested changes can assist in explaining variances in schedule or costs.

Schedule Status

Schedule reports can take a variety of shapes depending on the organization's standard practices. Figure 8.8 is an example that shows projected end dates (in elapsed weeks) for a project. During the replanning for each iteration, the team estimates, based on progress and feature changes, the projected number of weeks for the entire project. Figure 8.6 shows high, probable, and low schedule estimates. Notice that the range of these estimates is wider at the beginning of the project (greater uncertainty) and narrower at the end (greater certainty). A range that isn't narrowing indicates that uncertainty and risk are not being reduced adequately and the project may be in danger.

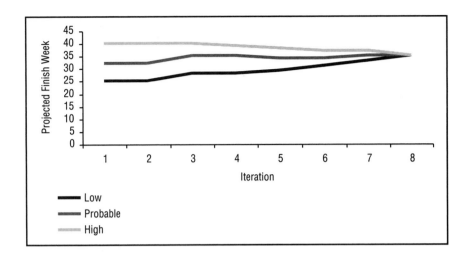

Figure 8.8
Projected Schedule

Cost (Resource) Status

Cost reports can also take a variety of shapes depending on an organization's practices. Although accounting reports are outside the scope of this book, one key number that many managers watch is expected cost to complete, which on an agile project should be calculated at least once per month.

Quality Status

As with other project measurements, there are a wide range of quality metrics, many of which are product dependent. One important aspect of quality is a team's assessment of its work, as shown in Figure 8.4. Given the results of technical reviews, defect reports (e.g., find and fix rates), and the team's sense of the project's "feel" or "smell,"[6] this chart plots the level of technical

---

6. In Extreme Programming, aspects of quality are evaluated by "smell," a term that conveys an intangible, but at the same time a very real, evaluation.

quality—as assessed by the team—each iteration. Another example of a quality measure in software development is the growth of test code compared to executable code—both should be growing proportionally.

Project Team Information

It's not just executives and product managers that need project status information—team members do also. Agile projects are open projects, meaning that project information is widely shared among all team members and with customers and stakeholders. Project teams need to have key information readily available and communally shared. It needs to be visual and prominently posted—either on walls or a whiteboard for collocated teams, or on a common virtual whiteboard for distributed teams. Alistair Cockburn (2002) calls these displays "information radiators": "An information radiator displays information in a place where passersby can see it. With information radiators, the passersby don't need to ask questions; the information simply hits them as they pass."

Visual displays of project information need to concentrate on vision, focus, scope, and issues. Teams often get so caught up in details that the big picture gets lost. Arguments over details can frequently be resolved by reviewing the product vision information or the guiding principles. Risk and issue lists are used to jog team members' consciousness so they are periodically thinking about solutions. A Web site will be needed to display this information for distributed teams.

Adaptive Action

As mentioned earlier, the term "adaptive action" conveys a sense of responding rather than correcting. In answering the three questions on value, progress, and adaptation posed in the beginning of this chapter, there are three further detailed questions to be asked: Where are we? Where did we plan to be? Where should we be? Adaptive actions run the gamut, from minor tweaks to the next iteration's planned features, to adding resources, to shortening the project's schedule (with appropriate feature adjustments). Adaptive adjustments can impact technical activities (e.g., allocating more time for refactoring) or modify delivery processes to make them more effective. Any of the four review types—product, technical, team, project status—can result in adaptive actions.

The two fundamental categories of risk in new product development are technical performance risk (whether we can actually build the product to meet the specifications and performance requirements within the time allotted) and marketing risk (whether customers will buy the product or, for an internal product, use the product to achieve business value). Since the product development process "purchases" information that reduces these risks, the constant attention of the management team should be on activities that systematically deliver value and reduce risk. Adaptive actions should use these two issues as focal points.

Phase: Close

A project close is both a phase and a practice. Organizations have a tendency to spend too much time initiating projects and too little time closing them. During a client engagement, I encountered the "failure to close" problem again. The customers of an IT project considered IT delivery to be less than stellar, partially because they *thought* the project had been underway for years. In reality, the application in question had been installed for several years, but the initial production and ongoing enhancement releases were not differentiated from each other. So from the client's perspective, the "project" just went on and on.

Since resources are always scarce, people are moved on to the next project quickly, often without taking time to close up the last project and get credit for its completion. There are several activities involved in closing a project, most of which don't take much time but do pay off. First and foremost is a celebration. A celebration serves two primary purposes. One, it shows an appreciation for all those who worked hard on the project. Including key clients in the celebration helps declare that this project is over, done, finalized, thus providing a sense of closure. Projects that go on and on without closure (or a series of projects couched as one) are terrible for morale.

Another less-glamorous closing activity is to clean up open items, finalize documentation and production or manufacturing support material (I know, it should have been done by now, but we know what happens in reality), and prepare required end-of-project administrative and financial reports.[7]

A final closing activity is conducting a project retrospective. Teams using APM have done mini-retrospectives each iteration. These minis help the project team learn about its own processes and team dynamics as the project progresses and as such are *intra*-team learning activities. The retrospective at the end is for *inter*-team learning, for one project team to pass along to others in the organization what went well and what went bump in the night. As referenced earlier, the best source on conducting retrospectives is Norm Kerth's (2001) book *Project Retrospectives: A Handbook for Team Reviews.*

Companies often confuse products and projects. Products are ongoing, while projects have a finite lifespan (at least the good ones do!). Differentiating between projects and products—ending projects and getting recognition and closure—is an important but often overlooked aspect of good project management, agile or otherwise.

Adapt and Close Summary

Monitoring and adapting (traditionally referred to as monitoring and control) are part of any good project management approach. While APM teams utilize some common project management practices, their attitudes toward monitoring and adapting are unique. For example, rather than corrective action, agile teams prefer adaptive action. Although corrective actions are necessary from time to time, the predominant attitude of agile project teams is to adapt and move forward rather than to blame and write exception reports.

Frequent iterations that deliver working features allow agile project teams to make frequent adjustments based on verifiable results rather than documentation artifacts. This can create an uncomfortable situation for

---

7. Mike Cohn recommends another activity for software projects that may also be valuable to hardware developers: "One other thing I traditionally do when closing a project is to make sure we archive the development environment. I've seen too many projects where people thought they were covered because they had the code in a configuration management system. But the system was buildable only from inside something like Visual C++, or it required specific versions of software files to build. I always burn CDs of all that stuff at the end."

some managers and customers who don't want to deal constantly with either reality or the need to make tradeoff decisions.

Finally, the Adapt phase provides a short respite from the intensity of short-cycle iterative development. In a serial project, in which a working product may be months or even years in the future, it is very difficult to maintain high levels of work intensity—there is always tomorrow. Agile projects sometimes have the opposite problem—they can be overly intense. The brief review, adapt, and replan activities of the Adapt phase give team members time to catch their breath, and their mental faculties, before rushing off to the next delivery iteration.

Chapter 9

Building Large Adaptive Teams

An Achilles' Heel?

"I've been thinking," Herman said as Maya answered the phone.

"Dangerous business, thinking," Maya laughed.

"Yeah, but first some good news. I'm actually about to finish up this Web project, and it's really gone well. Mostly I've struggled with my management, but they've come around—at least a little."

"Great! These little changes can lead to bigger ones."

"However, about management issues. I've been trying to reconcile this adaptive organization stuff with what I know about how organizations work, and it just doesn't hang together. For the average company, I just don't think depending on self-discipline will work. It's the Achilles' heel of APM," said Herman.

"First of all, who said anything about average? We're striving to be a great company—and I'm striving to be a great employee."

"That's easy for you," Herman said. "You're smart, talented, and skilled. You know the old saying: 'Half of all people are below average.'"

"I've known some individuals who were not the smartest or the most skilled, but they were persistent, courageous, and disciplined. Everyone has a talent for something. Sure, a certain number of people just don't care, but you can't build an organization or a process to control the misfits. You get rid of them and build for the others. Companies are average because that's what they settle for—they don't push themselves or their employees," Maya said.

"But," countered Herman, "won't this adaptive stuff go the way of empowerment—lots of talk, no action?"

"Empowerment failed because it was pushed down rather than pulled up. Organizations sent employees to a workshop and said, 'Now you are empowered.' It didn't work because you can't do either empowerment or self-discipline that way—it takes time, vision, coaching, failing, and trying again. It's hard work, with give and take, success and failure. But it's exciting; at least to me. I want to work in a place where I love coming to work every day. A place where I can contribute to the best of my ability, that values my contributions, where people want to deliver high-quality products, where I feel comfortable being myself and speaking out."

"Doesn't everyone want that?" asked Herman.

"Maybe. But are they willing to contribute or just kibitz?" Maya asked.

"I don't know," laughed Herman. "My head hurts from thinking too much. I also wanted to let you know that having finished up this project, I'm going to catch up on some long-accumulated vacation—nearly two months. So I'll be out of touch. It's been great talking, and I really think these ideas we've discussed have helped."

"Same for me, Herman. I think I'm much better off on my project because of thinking through and talking about agility. Let me know when you get back."

The Scaling Challenge

One myth about agile approaches goes something like this: "APM (or pick any agile methodology) works well for smaller projects, but it doesn't scale to larger ones." To combat the myth, I'd offer a couple of questions: "At what project team size do the core values of creating innovative products and adaptive teams based on self-organization and self-discipline fail to be important?" or "In today's economy, what size company can afford to become static and rigid?" Large project teams and large companies must be agile in order to keep up with competitors. Larger projects scale up by continuing to apply agile principles, creating a larger self-organizing framework, and applying additional practices.

Agility is a mindset, a way of thinking, not a set of practices or processes. The lifecycle framework and practices outlined in this book encourage agile behavior; they reinforce the principles, but they don't define APM. The core values and guiding principles of APM are key to scaling.

In a project management discussion forum, Glen Alleman, VP, Program Management Office at CH2M Hill, described the practices he used on a moderately sized project for the US Department of Energy. Because it was a government contract, a number of specific practices were required. As he described the team's practices, the list appeared to define a heavyweight, not an agile, project management framework. However, the team applied agile principles to the practices they used, trying to keep them as simple as possible given the nature of the agency and contracting requirements. They utilized short iterations and feature-based planning. They used a customized version of earned value analysis. They adjusted based on feedback each iteration. This was an agile project team, even though it was using what might appear on the surface to be nonagile practices. Alleman's team illustrates the point that APM is more about attitude than practices, or more precisely, that agile teams use their guiding principles to shape the processes and practices to the job at hand.

Many of the misconceptions about scaling to larger projects come from managers who focus first on organizational structure (matrix, hierarchy), process (phases, tasks, artifacts), and development practices. They tend to build scaling mechanisms based on hierarchy, control, documents, and ceremony—which slowly but surely cause compliance activities to dominate delivery activities as each hierarchical level justifies its existence. On this drift toward compliance-based management, Dee Hock (1999) comments, "Management expertise has become the creation and control of constants, uniformity, and efficiency, while the need has become the understanding and coordination of variability, complexity, and effectiveness."

Agile teams balance flexibility and structure. So as project size increases, structure—of necessity—increases also. But we don't have to revert to an authoritarian, hierarchical structure. Large organizations can be adaptive, flexible, and exploratory—they just have to expand their structures in concert with agile principles, not abandon them.

There is a plethora of organizational structures, processes, and practices that can be used on larger projects, but they are beyond the scope of this book. What I want to convey in this chapter is how to think about scaling these structures, processes, and practices in an agile way, in a way that increases structure but retains the essence of flexibility and semi-autonomy at the individual and subteam level.

But before launching into a discussion about scaling, there is another issue that arises when companies begin using agile development: Team sizes frequently decrease, obviating the need for more structure. The right small to medium-sized team (25 or fewer people) utilizing an agile framework and practices can often accomplish more than a significantly larger team. So before figuring out how to scale up to a larger project team, consider the possibility of deploying a scaled-down team using agile project management and development to accomplish your goals.

A Scaled Adaptive Framework

Other than the core ideology and principles that remain constant regardless of project team size, the components of larger adaptive teams are:

- A hub organizational structure
- Self-organization extensions
- Team self-discipline
- Additional practices

A project team consists of individuals—quasi-independent agents—who interact within a structure of team and self-disciplined rules of engagement (how people interact with each other). Individuals are given flexibility and a degree of autonomy within this loose structure, and they, in turn, exercise self-discipline to be accountable for results and behave as responsible and thoughtful members of the team. Larger teams, those consisting of multiple subteams, operate the same way—individuals are the agents in teams, while subteams are the agents in a larger project. A "hub" structure replaces the common hierarchical structure, organizational discipline encompasses additional responsibilities, and team discipline reflects rules of engagement among teams just as it does among individuals.

A Hub Organizational Structure

If we are to foster the core values of an adaptive workplace, then the organizational structure of the project team needs to reflect those values—and hierarchical structures fail this test. Hierarchical structures foster many problems, as colleague Bill Ulrich relates:

> *The political agenda was furthered by the hierarchy chart, which had little to do with dynamic, highly functional information management teams. Hierarchical IT infrastructures established an atmosphere where politics flourished and collaboration floundered. Hierarchies also led to an embedded culture that fostered adversity and encouraged the consolidation of individual power bases, as opposed to delivering quality information to the enterprise. As power bases enlarged, struggles ensued and adversity grew. You soon had an environment where 80% of workers' time was dedicated to working around the system, and only 20% was focused on doing their job. Hierarchical management structures are also a classic way to punish those that refuse to play the game and to reward those who know how to manipulate the political machinery* (Ulrich 2003).

A "hub" model for project organizations, as shown in Figure 9.1, reflects aspects of both hierarchical and network structures. Each node represents a team within the larger project organization. Within each node are individual team members. As the figure indicates, there may be several feature teams, a customer team, an architecture team, and even a center of excellence or community of practice team (not shown). Teams may be real, virtual, or a combination. The integration and build team, which has a specific role and meets periodically, could be a virtual team made up of selected part-time members of the other teams. The architecture team might have a combination of full-time and part-time members.

The project management team (which might consist of the project and product managers and leads from subteams) provides leadership and coordination and facilitates project decision making. The hub organizational structure focuses on the collaboration and coordination between autonomous but linked groups. Within a subteam, self-organization and self-discipline are equally important in creating high performance. As the project team size increases to encompass several subteams, there is also a

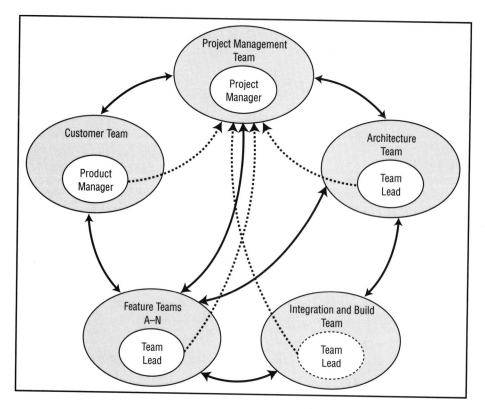

Figure 9.1
Hub Organization Structure

critical combination of self-organization and team self-discipline. Individuals have responsibilities within a team structure, and teams have responsibilities within an overall project structure.

This hub structure isn't a hierarchically controlled one, but neither is it a pure network structure in which all control is delegated to the nodes. A hub might be labeled a "modified network" structure in which a significant amount (but not all) of the power and decision making are distributed to the teams. The development teams at each node work together in a way similar to that of customers and developers, with a bit of formality as defined later in this chapter. The project manager retains final authority, including the power to make unilateral decisions if need be, but her primary style is steering, not controlling.

Self-Organization Extensions

As the number of subteams within a project team increases, the organizational framework needs to be expanded from a team framework within which individuals operate to a project framework within which multiple teams operate. The basics of self-organizing teams from Chapter 3 apply to larger teams, but there are extensions to those ideas that also apply. Creating a self-organizing framework for a larger team entails:

- Getting the right leaders
- Articulating the work breakdown and integration strategies
- Encouraging the interaction and information flow between teams
- Framing project-wide decision making

The organization, through the project manager, is responsible for staffing the project with the right people. At the team level, getting the right people means finding those with appropriate technical and behavioral skills. At the project level, the project manager works to ensure the right leaders are assigned to each team. As with individual team members, the project manager should have the authority to reject any proposed team leader.

The project management team has the responsibility to ensure everyone understands the product vision and his or her subteam's assignment within that overall vision. For larger projects the subteams may even go through a visioning exercise—vision box, elevator test—for their individual piece of the product. An architectural overview, component descriptions, and interface definitions can help each subteam understand both the big picture and its piece of the product.

In addition to understanding its product responsibilities, each subteam also needs to understand its roles with respect to other subteams. For example, feature teams need to understand how they are expected to interact with the architecture team. Larger projects are almost always, in some fashion, distributed projects. Obviously next-door buildings facilitate more frequent face-to-face meetings than a Chicago-Bombay separation, but this does not obviate the fact that larger teams face issues related to distance, culture, and expertise. Defining subteam roles and responsibilities within the hub organization is an initial step in dealing with distribution issues.

As I was working with one client, a very large IT organization, several people lamented the lack of communication—a common complaint. However, another individual saw it differently: "We have too much communication. Just look at my email inbox each morning." He was right. What this organization lacked was not "communication," but a culture of *collaboration*, of jointly working on issues rather than slinging emails and documents at each other. Teams need to figure out new and creative ways to collaborate. For example, teams can use the concept of *traveling pairs* from software development. As I've recommended elsewhere, "Every other iteration, a pair from one feature team could travel to the second site where they then pair with developers from the second team. Traveling pairs transfer knowledge about the team's features at a working level. No matter how good the architectural decomposition of a product, two distributed teams working on the same product need a certain amount of working-level conversation and collaboration" (Highsmith 2002). Exchanging people will be much more effective than exchanging paperwork.

One important inter-team task is managing dependencies, a task frequently relegated to the project manager. All too often dependency management falls into the same trap that serial development does—management by documentation rather than conversation. Within a team, the team members themselves manage dependencies between features. They identify dependencies in planning meetings and note them on feature cards, suggesting alternative scheduling when they anticipate problems. They also identify dependencies during daily team integration meetings. These discussions not only identify the dependency, but also the exact nature of that dependency and how to assign work to allow for it.

The same discussions occur at the inter-team level when feature team members (often team leads and senior engineers) get together to identify dependencies and determine how to handle them. The project manager may know about dependencies, but the team members have the detail information required to figure out how to work with them. Conversations backed up by informal notes can be effective and much quicker, even in fairly large teams, than relying on formal documentation and approval processes.

Although there are practices that create team-to-team interaction (e.g., integration meetings), there is no small set of practices that covers all the situations encountered in larger projects. Each project team is unique, and the project management team will need to experiment with interaction practices just as it does with technical ones.[1] That said, there are several key practices that can help create the right kinds of relationships and interactions among various teams. In this environment the project manager's role should be to facilitate the *interactions* between the teams, not the specific *activities* each team uses to produce deliverables. One practice is the commitment-accountability protocol described later in this chapter. Another such practice is to establish inter-team rules of engagement and accountability. As an example, Extreme Programming proponents have developed a set of rights that govern the interactions between customers and programmers.

Manager and Customer Rights (a sample)
- You have the right to an overall plan, to expect an estimate of what can be accomplished, when, and at what cost.
- You have the right to see progress in a running system, proven to work by passing repeatable tests that you specify.

Programmer Rights (a sample)
- You have the right to produce quality work at all times.
- You have the right to make and update your own estimates (Jeffries et al. 2001).

Another example would be the rules of engagement between architecture and feature teams within a project.

Feature Teams
- Teams shall have input to, involvement in, and the right to vote on any architectural decision that impacts their work.
- Teams shall have the right to assess the impact of any architectural change and adjust estimates and schedules accordingly.
- Teams shall have the right to request that the product and project managers review any architectural decision in which the team's veto is overridden.

---

1. For one such practice, work-state information management, see (Highsmith 2000), Chapter 9.

Architecture Teams

- Teams shall receive prompt information about and feedback on proposed architectural plans.
- Teams shall expect prompt notification of problems that feature teams encounter in implementing architectural decisions.

These rules of engagement, which evolve over time, guide the integration of teams within a project. Rules of engagement place a context around overall collaborative efforts and specific documents. Without rules of engagement, teams will be constantly dragging the project manager into decisions that they should work out among themselves.

Part of team self-discipline is developing these rules of engagement and then working within them. Within a team there are always conflicts whose resolution relies on the leader's coaching skills. Similarly, conflicts arise between teams; any time there is interaction and coordination, conflicts are inevitable. Again, one of the project manager's roles is to coach the teams in resolving conflicts, solidifying how the rules of engagement actually work.

Framing decisions becomes more difficult, and more important, as project organizations grow to multiple teams. Decision making should be distributed. For example, feature teams decide on the details of features assigned to them; the architecture team decides on platform issues; the integration team decides on the integration tools. However, the distribution should also be appropriate. Teams should not make unilateral decisions on items that impact another team without engaging that team in the decision process (a rule of engagement). So, for example, a team could not change an interface design without coordinating it with other teams that use that interface. Framing decisions—deciding which decisions are within the purview of an individual team, which decisions are left to the project manager and leadership team, and which decisions require engaging with other teams—is a critical piece of building large adaptive project teams.

Team Self-Discipline

Just as individuals have responsibilities to the teams that they belong to, teams themselves have to be self-disciplined to work within a larger self-organizing framework. The behaviors required of teams closely parallel those for individuals:

- Be the right team.
- Accept accountability for team results.
- Engage collaboratively with other teams.
- Work within the project self-organizing framework.
- Balance project goals with team goals.

A team that is unwilling to work within the established framework disrupts the work of the larger project in the same way that individuals who are unwilling to work within the team framework do.

Basketball players have a sign—a lightly closed fist tapping against their chest—that signals "my bad." They are taking responsibility for a mistake, admitting the mistake to their teammates and implying a commitment to do better next time. Teams that are accountable strive hard to deliver on commitments to other teams and admit failure when it occurs. But there is an important aspect of accountability—assignment versus sign-on—that determines whether accountability will truly take root. Managers who bemoan a team's (or an individual's) seeming lack of accountability should look first to themselves. Did they assign a deliverable and a date to the team, or did the team sign on and accept the date? Managers often assign impossible tasks and then wonder why the team doesn't accept responsibility. One of the powerful aspects of the commitment-accountability protocol (which I describe in the next section) is that it defines a commitment between two teams that they each enter into freely.

Just as individuals have a responsibility to fully participate in their team's activities, teams have a similar responsibility to participate with other teams within the larger project. For example, when a team estimates how many features it can deliver in an iteration, its members must factor in time to coordinate with other teams. Team members will undoubtedly serve on coordination teams (e.g., the architecture or integration teams). Feature teams will have to interact not only with the customer team, but also with other teams. For instance, a team may utilize a component or information from another feature team, or it may supply a component or information to another feature team. The same trust and respect that form a foundation for individual interaction also apply to team interaction.

Most managers understand the rough guideline that doubling staff size on a project increases throughput by 25% to 50%.[2] Large projects can have appallingly low productivity rates. Why? Coordination, meetings, documentation, approvals, rework due to miscommunications, and more add activity and time to any project. Capers Jones (1991), a consultant and author on software metrics, reports that on large software projects, one-third of the cost could be attributed to paperwork. Unmanaged, the collaborative practices of APM can blow up in a team's face. The larger the project team, the more need there is for collaborative interaction, but also the greater possibility of collaborative paralysis. The project manager in particular must constantly take the pulse of the organization as to the effectiveness of every type of interaction. For example, meetings that served the team well in the early iterations may not be needed as the project progresses. A collaborative structure isn't something to be set up and then ignored; it needs to be constantly monitored and adjusted.

Finally, teams have to align their own goals with those of the project. There will always be too much to do and too little time, and the tendency will be to work on one's team goals rather than on project goals.

The Commitment-Accountability Protocol

As Stephan Haeckel (1999), director of strategic studies at IBM's Advanced Business Institute, has observed, "Organizational responsiveness comes from giving individuals and groups the freedom to behave in ad hoc ways to respond to unforeseen circumstances. For this reason, organizational roles are defined in terms of accountability for commitments to particular outcomes, rather than in terms of activities." If we are going to build a hub organizational structure and manage outcomes rather than activities, then there needs to be a mechanism for teams within the project structure to manage their commitments to each other. Rather than have the project manager keep

---

2. This percentage depends on the size of the initial team (the percentage would be higher for a team that went from 2 to 4 than for one that went from 25 to 50) and the type of work being done.

up with and manage all inter-team dependencies, the teams need to accept that responsibility themselves, just as development teams commit to customer teams on features. However, as project size increases, a slight increase in formality and documentation is necessary to help teams handle these dependencies. A commitment-accountability protocol (CAP), which is based on Haeckel's commitment management protocol, can assist with this task.

The CAP addresses two key issues in managing large project teams: "How do we manage commitments?" and "How do we manage the work itself?" We can think back to the small project model for clues. First, the executive sponsor, with the advice and consent of the project manager and the product manager, agrees to overall project plan boundaries—scope, schedule, and costs. Second, the development team and the customer team make iteration-to-iteration commitments to each other. The product manager can add, modify, or cancel features without going up the management chain for approval, as long as the project stays within its agreed-upon boundaries. The developers and customers agree on features—a commitment for the iteration—and then the customers put the features through acceptance testing at the end of the iteration.

With a few feature cards, requirement descriptions, and informal notes, small teams keep the commitments and the work interactions relatively informal. As project size increases, we need similar mechanisms to allow subteams to work together with minimal management involvement. A practice similar to feature cards will be used to manage the work. This practice, the commitment-accountability protocol, is a brief written agreement between subunits of the organization. Rather than having work assignments flow from the project manager down, the teams themselves decide on how they are going to work together (although the project manager does facilitate and influence the agreements). The objective of the CAP is to enable groups to manage their work for each other with the least amount of management involvement. It also assists in portfolio management by clarifying inter-team dependencies.

A CAP identifies a contract-like relationship between two teams. Rather than have a project manager say, "Do this by this date," the teams contract with each other and document their commitment on a CAP card, as shown in Figure 9.2. (An automated version of the card may be used when additional formality is required.) For example, in the development of an electronic instrument, a CAP card might state that the circuit board team agrees to deliver a prototype board to the instrument design team by a

CAP Card	
Outcome ID:	C42
Outcome Name:	Aquisition System Diagnostics
Supplier Team:	Embedded Software Team
Consumer Team(s):	Electronics Design Team
Description:	Preliminary software to do all the diagnostic testing
	of the data aquisition component
Intermediate Deliverables:	NA
Acceptance Criteria:	All instrument diagnostic tests completed successfully
Estimated Work Effort:	25 hours

Figure 9.2
Commitment-Accountability Protocol Card

certain date. Or the product line architecture team might have an agreement to deliver platform architectural requirements to the instrument design team by a specified date.

The outcome is negotiated between two teams in the same way that a feature card would be negotiated between a development team and the customer team (although a CAP card will usually be for a larger chunk of work than a feature). And just as a feature card acknowledges a relationship between customer and developer and assumes a set of obligations and responsibilities on each party's part, a CAP card acknowledges a relationship and a set of partnership responsibilities between two (or more) project subteams. As in contracts with outside suppliers, the "customer" side in a CAP agreement has the right to accept or reject the work based on documented acceptance criteria.

CAP cards get scheduled into iterations just like feature cards. They state explicitly the cost of team-to-team coordination, and most importantly, they engage the teams with each other in ways that a project manager–drawn dependency arrow on a network diagram cannot. While the project manager should participate (so that he understands what the teams are doing and can provide information they might not have) with the teams in establishing these dependencies and developing the CAP, the fundamental agreement is between teams—and the project manager cannot arbitrarily break such agreements.

Neither can a project manager force a team to accept an agreement. As a team develops commitments with other teams, the members have to keep track of what they can realistically commit to, and scheduling the CAP cards as part of an iteration's workload helps. As is the case with features, when an iteration is full, it's full. At that point, adding additional commitments to other teams requires dropping some other block of work.

Coordination among subteams is critical to large projects, and just as team leaders shouldn't coordinate between individuals in their teams, project managers shouldn't coordinate—at the detail level—among subteams. A practice like a CAP has several advantages:

- It makes coordination work visible so teams can actually see why they are less productive than when they work independently.
- It helps build cooperative relationships between teams.
- It pushes the coordination load to the people who have the detail information.
- It raises the subteams' sense of accountability, since they decide on the commitment.

While some might argue that CAP cards are too structured and time consuming (and they *may* become burdensome if they are created for minor items), in practice they reduce overall coordination time and effort. Not using some form of inter-team commitment-accountability agreement would be analogous to eliminating feature cards. Feature cards create a minimal structure within which team members can work with customers.

CAP cards create a minimal structure within which subteams can interact with each other in this same way.

Is It Working?

Large and small teams alike have similar criteria for success—a working product, model, or simulation. Components must fit together. They must work. They must pass acceptance tests. The longer a team, large or small, goes without delivering an integrated product to a review process, the greater the potential for failure. For large teams, short iterations are used to deliver and integrate components, while milestones are used to deliver and integrate the entire product. Integrated components that work indicate that the team's organizing structure and dynamics are working well. Synchronization problems indicate that organization or process issues need adjustment. Reviews for large teams need to focus on the same topics that those for smaller teams do: the customer's evaluation of the product, a technical evaluation of the product, team performance, and project status. In addition, the success (or failure) of product integration measures how well large project teams are working. Adaptations for larger teams will cover a wider range of issues and problems, but the process is similar to that for smaller projects.

We all know the saying "Don't fix things that aren't broken." For larger teams, we need to give this advice a twist: "Don't always fix things that are broken." While smaller teams are not immune to excessive adaptation, this tendency becomes more prevalent as teams get bigger. Let's say that at the end of a milestone the integration of several modules causes a couple days of extra work. The immediate reaction, particularly by the people who had to clean up the mess, might be to fix the problem by instituting additional coordination meetings. Unfortunately, two things may happen. First, the meetings themselves may take more time than fixing the problem did. Second, there are always different, unanticipated problems that arise. Just as agile teams don't try to anticipate future requirements or design, choosing instead to let them emerge over time, they shouldn't attempt to anticipate every problem and put processes or practices in place to prevent them. It's often cheaper and faster to fix on actual failure than to spend excessive time anticipating failures that may never occur again.

Structure and Tools

By their very nature, larger projects require more structure, and whether we like it or not, some of that structure will involve additional compliance work. The objective isn't to eliminate compliance work but to minimize it and offload it from the project team to the extent possible. However, as this chapter has shown, additional structure doesn't have to mean hierarchy, controls, strict processes, and volumes of formal documentation. Yes, some additional documentation will be required. Yes, some additional up-front planning will be required. Yes, some additional controls will be required (for example, on large government projects, some type of earned value analysis may be mandated). Project managers will need to scrounge in their project management toolboxes—traditional, agile, and otherwise—to assemble the right set of practices for larger projects.

For larger teams, particularly those with far-flung subteams, supporting tools will also be necessary. These tools will fall into three general categories: collaboration, technical information sharing, and project management. Collaboration tools attempt to bring people together as if they were in the same room—an impossible goal, but one that technology gets better at each year. Collaboration tools include email, discussion groups, teleconferences, instant messaging, and that old standby, the telephone. Technical information sharing technology ranges widely—from complex product data management systems for industrial products such as automobiles and electronics to distributed software build and integration systems. Project management tools, including portals that draw together diverse project information, can be effective for large, distributed teams. And as Lynne Nix reminded me, on large projects good administrative personnel are essential for both effective tool usage and supporting the project management team.

Summary

All of the practices and tools just mentioned can be accommodated within the APM framework. The agile principles still apply. The need for self-organizing, self-disciplined organizational structures still applies. Short, feature-based iterative development still applies, as does the need for frequent, comprehensive feedback and adaptive adjustments. Scaling to larger projects requires additional thought, and practices, for both people and product. CAP cards provide a mechanism for scaling the self-organizing practices of single teams to teams of teams. Component-level planning and reporting (using a parking lot graphic) provide a mechanism for scaling feature-based planning to larger projects. There are other tools that project managers will bring to bear on larger projects, while still adhering to the values and principles of Agile Project Management.

Large agile teams will not be as nimble as small ones, but then they probably don't need to be. They just need to fulfill the fundamental purposes of APM—delivering valuable products to customers and creating satisfying work environments.

Chapter 10

Reliable Innovation

The Agile Vision

In the end, the positive answers to two questions form the essence of Agile Project Management: "Are you delivering innovative products to your customers?" and "Are you excited about going to work every day?" Agilists want to build innovative products—products that test the limits of our abilities as individuals and project teams—and create a work environment in which people, as individuals and in teams, can thrive.

The Changing Face of New Product Development

New product development—be it for industrial products, consumer products, or internal business processes—is being driven by two resolute forces: the continuing demand for innovation and the plunging cost of change (low-cost exploration). As the uncertainty about the outcome of a development effort increases, as the complexity of the interactions of design variables daunts cause-and-effect analysis, exploration through experimentation becomes the most effective and reliable mode of discovery. When we can conduct 1,000 experiments a day for $10 apiece, creating elaborate designs that would take a month to complete otherwise makes no sense. On the other hand, conducting 5,000 random experiments makes no sense either. Good experiments require good experimental design.

It is hard to overstate the impact of low-cost exploration on product development or the competitive advantage that will accrue to those companies that can adjust their development and managerial processes appropriately. A significant element of this strategy will involve software and the manipulation of bits rather than atoms, driving a low-cost exploration product development process that should strive to:

- Fill products with "bits"
- Create a bit-oriented product development lifecycle (i.e., model and/or simulate products in software as far into the lifecycle as possible)
- Relentlessly drive down the cost of changing bits (low-cost iteration)
- Develop people and processes capable of the above strategies (agile people and processes)

Embedded software has rapidly become a critical piece of industrial products. Cell phones now boast a million or more lines of code. Automobiles have microprocessors for everything from fuel injection to transmission shifting. Airplanes are fly-by-wire, controlled completely electronically.

Software—developed well, of course—is more flexible than hardware. In fact, drastically shortening the product development lifecycle forces hardware engineers to lock in hardware designs earlier than they would like. Software's flexibility is often used to correct hardware problems or add new features after hardware designs are fixed. So the more "bits" there are in a product, in general, the better. As bits replace atoms, more product features can be developed faster and with greater flexibility.

But we can't drive a bit, or sit on one, or use one to hit a golf ball. At some point, atoms must be assembled into products that we can use. The critical question is, when do we assemble the atoms? There is a furniture manufacturer in West Virginia that completes its entire product design process in software. At the end of the design phase, the software generates instructions to manufacturing robots, and the furniture parts are cut and assembled. The more chemical compound and biological response information there is available in large databases, the further into the drug development process companies can go before lengthy and expensive activities such as animal testing have to begin. Simulations, modeling, and prototyping, for a wide array of products, are all increasingly being done in software prior to any physical assembly. Once physical assembly begins, flexibility suffers.

The point is that the longer teams can manipulate bits rather than atoms, the more effective the product development process can be. So two strategies are critical: increase the number of bits in products and manipulate bits rather than atoms as deep into the development process as possible.

Agile People and Processes Deliver Agile Products

There is, however, a caveat to the above strategies. A company's development and project management processes, and its executive support and performance measurements, must encourage experimentation, exploration, and low-cost iteration. Authors Moshe Rubinstein and Iris Firstenberg (1999) of the University of California write about "minding" organizations, a term that coincides with "adaptive." "The minding organization behaves like a living organism, in which adapting is central to vitality and survival.... Overly rigid and detailed planning must give way to a strategy that combines less planning and more adapting."

Agile, adaptive project management and development processes support exploratory product development. Managers and executives need to understand the kinds of projects in which these processes can best be used and how to encourage employees in their use. As Harvard Business School professor Stefan Thomke (2003) writes, "Experimentation matters because it is through learning equally what works and what doesn't that people develop great new products, services, and entire businesses. But in spite of the lip service that is paid to 'testing' and 'learning from failure,' today's organizations, processes, and management of innovation often impede experimentation." Implementing a low-cost exploration strategy will require a substantial cultural change within the development staff, project manager, and executive ranks of many organizations.

Exploratory processes require adaptive people and adaptive organizations. There are individuals who excel in production environments, those who strive for repeatability and precision through the use of prescriptive processes and performance measures. Every organization requires production processes for a portion of its operations. But every organization also needs exploration processes, those that excel in delivering new products, new services, and new internal business initiatives. Unfortunately, the project cultures and management controls for exploration and production are usually at odds with each other, causing organizational schizophrenia. Great organizations will find a way to deal with both exploration and production processes. Others will languish behind.

So how do organizations deal with two distinct process models that have seemingly incompatible cultures? I think the answer lies in the word "adaptation." Adaptive cultures adjust to the situation, while production cultures have difficulty changing. When the business environment was more stable, production cultures could thrive. However, as the pace of change has accelerated, the mix of exploration versus production activity in organizations has shifted, creating a competitive advantage for those companies with predominantly adaptive cultures.

Culture then identifies a critical piece of the agile vision, which might be expressed with a simple axiom: Don't work in Dilbert's company, and don't be Dilbert. Dilbert's company is the epitome of authoritarianism— the exact opposite of self-organizing. Dilbert complains, but he takes no responsibility for changing his environment. Dilbert and his cohorts lack self-discipline. Agile social architectures have both and thereby deliver innovative products and create great places to work. As Andrew Hill (2001) relates in his book about John Wooden and UCLA basketball, "The Bruins were built on speed, quickness, a tough man-to-man defense, a withering zone press, and a relentless fast break. Now, there may be some kid in America who grows up dreaming of playing slow-down, highly structured, Princeton-style basketball, but I've never met that kid. There was something intoxicating and captivating about the pace and attacking style of the Bruins." I think most product developers want to work on UCLA-style "agile" projects.

A grand vision? A utopian vision? An impractical vision? Possibly. I once received an email response to a message I posted on an online forum in which I argued that traditional project management is often authoritarian and high ceremony. "Jim, your sentence implies that authoritarianism and high ceremony are 'bad' things. Do we really care whether or not something is authoritarian, or should we judge it solely by its ability to deliver value to the customer?" My response was, "I care deeply." Delivering valuable products is important, and it's critical to project management success. No project team can exist for long without delivering value to its customers. But in the long run, how we deliver, how we interact at work, and how we treat each other as human beings are even more important.

Implementing the Vision

Possibly the greatest barrier to becoming agile is dealing with the illusions of causality and certainty. In a production environment in which requirements and technology are relatively stable, we are better able to predict the future—to plan and expect conformance to that plan. As uncertainty in the external world increases, though, managers who have been successful in stable environments attempt to apply the same processes and performance measures to unstable environments. Their certainty—and the belief that if they just push hard enough they can "cause" the right results— is likely to result in failure rather than success.

Causality is easier to believe in than emergence; it's more tangible. Yet nature thrives on emergent results. Evolution itself—adapting to ecosystem changes—is an emergent process fueled by experimentation. Every individual action changes an ecosystem and fosters other changes in response. Just as a theatre play emerges from the interaction of actors, playwright, director, and the audience, a product emerges from the interaction of project team members, the product and project managers, customers, and competitors. But the illusion of certainty continues because in many organizations it's considered poor form to be other than certain. The certainty should be in the vision and the broad goals, not the specific path to reach that vision. When we confuse vision and path, we confuse causality and emergence.

New product development isn't Plan-Do but Envision-Explore. Where there is no uncertainty, no risk, there is no opportunity. Production projects are controlled by predicting schedule, cost, and scope. NPD projects are constrained by schedule and cost in order to deliver on vision. Scope is restrictive, vision expansive, yet vision isn't "anything goes." Poor visioning leads to uncontrolled experimentation in the same way that overly detailed requirements lead to rigid compliance.

It's important to remember that no product, and no organization, can be infinitely agile in all dimensions. Agility always occurs within certain boundaries—platform architectures for products, organizational frameworks for people. It balances structure and flexibility, dependence and autonomy. A restrictive architecture reduces a product's ability to respond to the product vision and market ecosystem, while too little architecture increases the likelihood of increased cost, duplication, and suboptimization.

A restrictive organizational framework reduces a team's ability to respond to changing conditions, while too little framework causes chaos and confusion.

The martial arts are all about balance. Whether defending or attacking, martial artists keep their bodies centered and in balance. Project management artists should also be in balance. Finding that balance is key to agility, and it isn't easy; there isn't a formula. The balance point for every product, for every project team, is different. Finding that balance point requires technical excellence, because it builds both quickness and agility. Skill, talent, and knowledge breed quickness—compelling people to go faster breeds hurrying. Agility can only be achieved through an unwavering focus on technical excellence.

Reliable Innovation

In the end, just like Broadway plays always deliver on opening night, APM delivers on time and to the customer's vision more reliably than any other approach for high exploration-factor projects. Given the high degree of uncertainty on many new product efforts, given the changes in technology, given the ebb and flow of staff, reliable results are still obtainable. Given all the "maybes," agile project management and development still deliver, which is a tribute to the passion, drive, persistence, and ingenuity of project team members.

When executives can articulate a product vision, agile teams deliver. When executives can establish reasonable cost and schedule boundaries, agile teams deliver. When customers and product managers can accept the consequences of their own demands on the product, agile teams deliver. When all participants can deal with the ambiguity of structure and flexibility, when they can focus on results and not activities, agile teams deliver.

Author Ed Yourdon (1999) writes about four kinds of death march projects: kamikaze, suicide, ugly, and mission impossible. Kamikaze projects are doomed from the start, but everyone agrees that the ride might be enjoyable, as in "technically interesting." On suicide projects, everyone involved, from the engineers to the project manager, knows the project will fail and that it will be miserable to work on. Threatened job loss is the only reason to work on such a project. Ugly projects are those in which the project manager is willing to sacrifice others for his own glory. Long hours and a miserable working environment are sure to ensue. Mission impossible projects are doable, barely, with luck and exceptional effort. But mission impossible projects are also usually exciting—they are high-risk, high-reward projects.

If your project falls into one of the first three categories—kamikaze, suicide, or ugly—no project management process in the world—production, exploration, or otherwise—will help. Anyone who guarantees success for a particular process or methodology, under any conditions, for any project, is lying. Any executive who demands success, under any conditions, for any project, strangles her project team's capability. However, if your project falls in the mission impossible category, hire Tom Cruise and use agile project management and development.

APM isn't just a project management process, it is an organizational process. Agile teams won't survive in a hostile, death march environment. In a reasonable organizational environment, however, with executives and managers who understand the reality of marketplace uncertainty, agile teams will deliver more reliably than nonagile ones. They will turn the uncertainty of the marketplace and technology into the certainty of a working product.

Repeatable processes are specification based. They rely on minimal variations in both the process and the specification. Specification-based, strict change-controlled processes founder under uncertainty because when teams using repeatable processes encounter high rates of change, they fail to adapt rapidly enough.

Conversely, reliable processes work with exploration-based projects because both product and process adapt to change. But adapting to change by itself isn't sufficient—over-response to change produces oscillation and chaos. The adaptations must be steered toward some goal—the product vision. Without a clear, well-articulated, continuously communicated vision, adapting to change can become a deadly spiral.

Still, the fundamental nature of new product development cannot be escaped—it always involves uncertainty and risk. As the exploration factor goes up, as product teams push technology to the bleeding edge (and sometimes over it), as market forces change rapidly, no process, nor even the most brilliant team, can ensure success. Yet the right people and an agile, exploratory process offer, by far, the best chance at success. These projects are highly reliable because of the team's ability to adapt to the environment rather than follow a prescribed path.

The Value-Adding Project Manager

This book is about both project management and project managers. Unfortunately, some agilists have been perceived, correctly in some cases, as being anti-management and anti-project management. This is a Dilbert view of the world in which employees are the downtrodden and managers are the trodders. But high-performance agile teams (and organizations) create a balance between managers and individual team members—a balance of self-organization with self-discipline. Agile teams are flexible, but not ad hoc—a difference that escapes cursory examinations. High-performance agile teams are highly self-disciplined; agile team members accept accountability, a development framework, and certain behavioral responsibilities as part of working in an environment that is open and flexible and delegates a high degree of decision making to them as individuals and as a team.

The agile project manager's style is one of leadership-collaboration rather than command-control. Project managers are critical to agile project success, and their role is very demanding. Leading is more difficult, and more rewarding, than commanding. Creating a collaborative work environment is more difficult, and more rewarding, than controlling. Both project and product leaders are the champions of the vision. They articulate it so that everyone understands it, and they nurture it so that no one forgets it. The vision has a customer focus—what delivers value to the customer—and a technical focus—championing the technical excellence that will continue to deliver value in the future. Leaders help the team focus on delivery while minimizing the distractions of compliance work.

Leadership also includes staff selection, staff development, and ongoing encouragement. While others participate in these activities, the leader is accountable for them. Getting the right people on the bus, getting the wrong people off the bus, steering people toward roles that match their talents, developing both technical and behavioral skills, and encouraging people through frequent feedback are all time-consuming and critical activities for the project manager. But that's not all. Project mangers also help create an environment of "no fear" in which collaboration, interaction, participatory decision making, conflict resolution, fierce debate, and collegial respect can flourish. This is the hard part of APM—the people part—or what some deride as the "soft skills" part. The easier part deals with the so-called "hard skills": schedules, budgets, reports, earned value analysis, Gantt charts, and the like. Both are necessary for good project management, but the soft part is really the hard part, and the hard part is really the easy part. Got it?

And that's just the project manager's role within the project team. He then has the task of working with the customer team, executives, and other stakeholders to set and meet their expectations and persuade them to participate as partners with the project team.

Given the uncertainty, ambiguity, speed, anxiety, and constant change of an agile project, the project manager's job zips constantly between mentor and moderator to decision maker and staff developer. It's never dull, and it's rarely part time. Watching hummingbirds fly is good training for the agile project manager.

Conviction

During a tour of France, the German poet Heinrich Heine and his friend visited a cathedral. As they stood in admiration before the magnificent church, the friend asked Heinrich why people couldn't build like this anymore. The poet replied, "Friend, in those days people had convictions. We moderns have opinions. It takes more than opinions to build Gothic cathedrals" (Sweet 1982). And it takes more than opinions to build innovative products and adaptive organizations. We need deep convictions and resolute commitment if we hope to build great products and a better workplace. We need processes and practices grounded in core values and principles.

At the first Agile Development Conference in Salt Lake City in June 2003, the Executive Summit portion concluded with discussion groups being asked to identify the single most important factor to convey to senior executives. One team stated, and the others concurred, that the key factor in becoming agile is realizing that principles are more important than practices—that what we believe drives what we do.

Without concrete practices, principles are sterile; but without principles, practices have no life, no character, no heart. Great products arise from great teams—teams who are principled, who have character, who have heart, who have persistence, and who have courage. Although more than half of this book describes a lifecycle process and specific practices of APM, the other half is ultimately more important—the half that attempts to articulate the values and principles behind the processes and practices. We need modern-day conviction.

There is a great debate in historical circles: Do great men and women make history, or does history make them great? Why were there so many great leaders in the 1930s and 1940s? Churchill, Roosevelt, Montgomery, and Eisenhower all arose as leaders during this era. Did they make history, or did history make them?

We could apply similar reasoning to products: Do great product ideas make great teams, or do great teams make great products? Maybe there is a third alternative—they make each other. World War II, the ten years before it, and the ten years after it were years of tremendous uncertainty and risk. But these times helped people and countries crystallize what was important and what was not. At least for the democracies of the world, what was important was freeing the world from tyranny. That vision, plus superb execution, carried the day.

The conviction at the core of the agile movement is creating a better workplace, free from tyranny, arbitrariness, and authoritarianism. Not free from structure. Not free from responsibility. Not free from project managers and executives making decisions. This conviction flows not only from wanting to create a progressive social architecture in which individuals can thrive, but also from the belief that agile social architectures produce the best, most innovative products. Where self-organization and self-discipline flourish, where processes are designed (and adapted) to support people rather than restrict them, where individual talents and skills are valued—great products emerge.

Bibliography

Adolph, Steve, and Paul Bramble, with Alistair Cockburn and Andy Pols. *Patterns for Effective Use Cases.* Boston: Addison-Wesley, 2003.

Ambler, Scott. *Agile Modeling:Effective Practices for Extreme Programming and the Unified Process.* New York: John Wiley & Sons, 2002.

Austin, Rob. "Surviving Enterprise Systems: Adaptive Strategies for Managing Your Largest IT Investments." Cutter Consortium Business-IT Strategies Advisory Service, *Executive Report* 4, no. 4 (April 2001).

Austin, Rob. "Innovation Interruptus." Cutter Technology Trends and Impacts Advisory Service, *Executive Report*, Vol. 4, No. 2 (February 2003). Cutter Consortium, Arlington, MA.

Austin, Rob, and Lee Devin. *Artful Making: What Managers Need to Know About How Artists Work.* Upper Saddle River, NJ: Financial Times Prentice Hall, 2003.

Bayer, Sam. "Customer-Focused Development: The Art and Science of Conversing with Customers." Cutter Consortium Agile Project Management Advisory Service, *Executive Report* 2, no. 4 (April 2001).

Beck, Kent. *Extreme Programming Explained: Embrace Change.* Boston: Addison-Wesley, 2000.

Boehm, Barry. *Software Engineering Economics.* Englewood Cliffs, NJ: Prentice Hall, 1981.

Boehm, Barry, and Richard Turner. *Balancing Agility and Discipline.* Boston: Addison-Wesley, 2003.

Bonabeau, Eric, and Christopher Meyer. "Swarm Intelligence: A Whole New Way to Think About Business." *Harvard Business Review* (May 2001), 106–14.

Bossidy, Larry, and Ram Charan. *Execution: The Discipline of Getting Things Done.* New York: Crown Business, 2002.

Brown, Shona L., and Kathleen M. Eisenhardt. *Competing on the Edge: Strategy as Structured Chaos.* Boston: Harvard Business School Press, 1998.

Buckingham, Marcus, and Curt Coffman. *First, Break All the Rules.* New York: Simon & Schuster, 1999.

Buckingham, Marcus, and Donald O. Clifton. *Now, Discover Your Strengths.* New York: Free Press, 2001.

Budeir, Robert. "GE Finds Its Inner Edison," *Technology Review* (October 2003), 46–50.

Cockburn, Alistair. *Surviving Object-Oriented Projects.* Boston: Addison-Wesley, 1998.

Cockburn, Alistair. *Writing Effective Use Cases.* Boston: Addison-Wesley, 2001.

Cockburn, Alistair. *Agile Software Development.* Boston: Addison-Wesley, 2002. Quote on p. 230 © 2002 Pearson Education, Inc. Reprinted by permission of Pearson Education, Inc. Publishing as Pearson Addison Wesley.

Collins, James C. and Jerry I. Porras. *Built to Last: Successful Habits of Visionary Companies.* New York: HarperBusiness, 1994.

Collins, Jim. *Good to Great: Why Some Companies Make the Leap...and Others Don't.* New York: HarperBusiness, 2001.

Cooper, Robert G. *Winning at New Products: Accelerating the Process from Idea to Launch.* 3rd ed. Cambridge, MA: Perseus Publishing, 2001. Quote on p. 3 © 1993, 2001 by Perseus Books Group. Reproduced with permission in the format Textbook via Copyright Clearance Center.

DeMarco, Tom. *Slack: Getting Past Burnout, Bustwork, and the Myth of Total Efficiency.* New York: Broadway Books, 2001.

DeMarco, Tom, and Tim Lister. *Peopleware: Productive Projects and Teams.* 2nd ed. New York: Dorset House, 1999.

DeMarco, Tom, and Tim Lister. *Waltzing with Bears: Managing Risk on Software Projects.* New York: Dorset House, 2003.

Dove, Rick. *Response Ability: The Language, Structure, and Culture of the Agile Enterprise.* New York: John Wiley & Sons, 2001.

DSDM Consortium, with Jennifer Stapleton (ed.). *DSDM: Business Focused Development.* Boston: Addison-Wesley, 2003.

Duward, K., and Li Sobek. "Toyoa's Principles of Set-Based Concurrent Engineering." *Sloan Management Review* (Winter 1999): 67–83.

Eisenhardt, Kathleen M., and Donald N. Sull. "Strategy as Simple Rules." *Harvard Business Review* (January 2001): 106–116.

Fishman, Charles. "Engines of Democracy." *Fast Company*, Issue 28 (October 1999): 174.

Fowler, Martin. *Refactoring: Improving the Design of Existing Code.* Reading, MA: Addison-Wesley, 1999.

Fowler, Martin, and Jim Highsmith. "The Agile Manifesto." *Software Development 9*, No. 8 (August 2001): 28–32.

Frick, Don M., and Larry C. Spears, *On Becoming a Servant Leader: The Private Writings of Robert K. Greenleaf.* San Francisco: Jossey-Bass Publishers, 1996.

Gall, John. *Systemantics: How Systems Work and Especially How They Fail.* New York: Times Books, ©1977.

Gardner, Elizabeth. "Ultimate Analysis." *Bio-IT World* 2, No. 11 (November 2003): 39–44.

Goldman, Steven, Roger Nagel, and Kenneth Preiss. *Agile Competitors and Virtual Organizations: Strategies for Enriching the Customer.* New York: Van Nostrand Reinhold, 1995.

Goleman, Daniel, Richard Boyatzis, and Annie McKee. "Primal Leadership: The Hidden Driver of Great Performance." *Harvard Business Review* (December 2001).

Goranson, H. T. *The Agile Virtual Enterprise: Cases, Metrics, Tools,* Westport, CT: Quorum Books, 1999.

Haeckel, Stephan H. *Adaptive Enterprise: Creating and Leading Sense-and-Respond Organizations.* Boston: Harvard Business School Press, 1999.

Highsmith, James A., III. *Adaptive Software Development: A Collaborative Approach to Managing Complex Systems.* New York: Dorset House Publishing, 2000.

Highsmith, Jim. *Agile Software Development Ecosystems.* Boston: Addison-Wesley, 2002.

Hill, Andrew, with John Wooden. *Be Quick—But Don't Hurry: Finding Success in the Teachings of a Lifetime.* New York: Simon & Schuster, 2001. Quotes on pp. 74, 108, 256 © 2001 by Andrew Hill. Reprinted by permission of Simon & Schuster Adult Publishing Group.

Hock, Dee. *Birth of the Chaordic Age.* San Francisco: Berrett-Koehler Publishers, Inc. 1999. Quotes on pp. 59, 207, 237 reprinted with permission of the publisher. All rights reserved. www.bkconnection.com.

Hodgson, Phillip, and Randall White. *Relax, It's Only Uncertainty: Lead the Way When the Way Is Changing.* London: Financial Times Prentice Hall, 2001.

Hohmann, Luke. *Beyond Software Architecture: Creating and Sustaining Winning Solutions.* Boston: Addison-Wesley, 2003.

Howell, Greg, and Lauri Koskela. "Reforming Project Management: The Role of Planning, Execution, and Controlling." In David Chua and Glenn Ballard (eds.), *Proceedings of the 9th International Group for Lean Construction Conference*, 185–198. Singapore: National University of Singapore, 2001.

Iansiti, Marco. *Technology Integration: Making Critical Choices in a Dynamic World.* Boston: Harvard Business School Press, 1998.

Jeffries, Ron, Ann Anderson, and Chet Hendrickson. *Extreme Programming Installed.* Boston: Addison-Wesley, 2001.

Jones, Capers. *Applied Software Measurement: Assuring Productivity and Quality.* New York: McGraw-Hill, 1991.

Jones, Capers. *Assessment and Control of Software Risks.* Englewood Cliffs: Yourdon Press, 1994.

Joyner, Tim. *Magellan.* Camden, ME: International Marine, 1992.

Kaner, Sam, with Lenny Lind, Catherine Toldi, Sarah Fisk, and Duane Berger. *Facilitator's Guide to Participatory Decision-Making.* Philadelphia: New Society Publishers, 1996.

Katzenbach, Jon R., and Douglas K. Smith. *The Wisdom of Teams: Creating the High-Performance Organization.* Boston: Harvard Business School Press, 1993.

Kelley, Tom. *The Art of Innovation*, New York: Currency Books, 2001.

Kennedy, Michael N. *Product Development for the Lean Enterprise: Why Toyota's System is Four Times More Productive and How You Can Implement It.* Richmond, VA: The Oaklea Press, 2003.

Kerth, Norman L. *Project Retrospectives: A Handbook for Team Reviews.* New York: Dorset House, 2001.

Larman, Craig. *Agile and Iterative Development: A Manager's Guide.* Boston: Addison-Wesley, 2004.

Larson, Carl E., and Frank M. J. LaFasto, *Teamwork: What Must Go Right/ What Can Go Wrong.* Newbury Park: Sage Publications, 1989.

Lencioni, Patrick. *The Five Dysfunctions of a Team.* San Francisco: Jossey-Bass, 2002.

Mathiassen, Lars, Jan Pries-Heje, and Ojelanki Ngwenyama. *Improving Software Organizations: From Principles to Practice.* Boston: Addison-Wesley, 2002.

Meyer, Christopher, and Stan Davis. *It's Alive: The Coming Convergence of Information, Biology, and Business.* New York: Crown Business, 2003.

Moore, Geoffrey A. *Crossing the Chasm: Marketing and Selling High-Tech Products to Mainstream Customers.* New York: HarperBusiness, 1991. Quote on pp. 94–95 © 1991 by Geoffrey A. Moore. Reprinted with permission of HarperCollins Publishers, Inc.

Moore, Geoffrey A. *Inside the Tornado: Marketing Strategies from Silicon Valley's Cutting Edge.* New York: HarperBusiness, 1995.

Pascale, Richard T., Mark Millemann, and Linda Gioja. *Surfing the Edge of Chaos: The Laws of Nature and the New Laws of Business.* New York: Crown Business, 2000.

Patterson, Kerry, Joseph Grenny, Ron McMillan, and Al Switzler. *Crucial Conversations: Tools for Talking When Stakes Are High.* New York: McGraw-Hill, 2002.

Petroski, Henry. *Evolution of Useful Things.* Reprint ed. New York: Vintage Books, 1994.

Petzinger, Thomas, Jr. *The New Pioneers: The Men and Women Who Are Transforming the Workplace and Marketplace.* New York: Simon & Schuster, 1999.

Poppendieck, Mary, and Tom Poppendieck. *Lean Software Development: An Agile Toolkit.* Boston: Addison-Wesley, 2003.

Project Management Institute. *A Guide to the Project Management Body of Knowledge.* 2000 ed. New Square, PA: Project Management Institute, 2000.

Reinertsen, Donald G. *Managing the Design Factory: A Product Developer's Toolkit.* New York: Free Press, 1997. Quote on p. 39 © 1997 by Donald G. Reinertsen. Reprinted with permission of The Free Press, a division of Simon & Schuster Adult Publishing Group. All rights reserved.

Rubinstein, Moshe F., and Iris Firstenberg. *The Minding Organization: Bring the Future to the Present and Turn Creative Ideas into Business Solutions.* New York: John Wiley & Sons, 1999. Quote on p. 255 used by permission of John Wiley & Sons, Inc.

Rueping, Andreas. *Agile Documentation: A Pattern Guide to Producing Light-weight Documents for Software Projects.* New York: John Wiley & Sons, 2003.

Schrage, Michael. *No More Teams: Mastering the Dynamics of Creative Collaboration.* New York: Currency Doubleday, 1989.

Schrage, Michael. *Serious Play: How the World's Best Companies Simulate to Innovate.* Boston: Harvard Business School Press, 2000.

Schwaber, Ken, and Mike Beedle. *Agile Software Development with Scrum.* Upper Saddle River, NJ: Prentice Hall, 2002.

Smith, Preston G., and Guy M. Merritt. *Proactive Risk Management: Controlling Uncertainty in Product Development.* New York: Productivity Press, 2002.

Sobek, Durward K., II, Allen C. Ward, and Jeffrey K. Liker. "Toyota's Principles of Set-Based Concurrent Engineering." *MIT Sloan Management Review* (Winter 1999). Quotes on pp. 205, 206 © 1999 by Massachusetts Institute of Technology. Reprinted by permission of the publisher. All rights reserved.

Sweet, Leonard I. "Not All Cats Are Gray: Beyond Liberalism's Uncertain Faith." *The Christian Century*, June 23–30, 1982, p. 721.

Thomke, Stefan H. *Experimentation Matters: Unlocking the Potential of New Technologies for Innovation.* Boston: Harvard Business School Press, 2003.

Thomsett, Rob. *Radical Project Management.* Upper Saddle River, NJ: Prentice Hall, 2002.

Ulrich, William. "The New IT Organization." Cutter Consortium Business-IT Strategies Advisory Service, *Executive Report 3*, No. 7 (July 2003).

Verzuh, Eric. *The Fast Forward MBA in Project Management.* New York: John Wiley & Sons, 1999.

Waldrop, M. Mitchell. *Complexity: The Emerging Science at the Edge of Order and Chaos.* New York: Simon & Schuster, 1992.

Wheelwright, Steven C., and Kim B. Clark. *Revolutionizing Product Development: Quantum Leaps in Speed, Efficiency, and Quality.* New York: The Free Press, 1992.

Wiegers, Karl E. *Peer Reviews in Software.* Redmond, WA: Microsoft Press, 2001.

Williams, Laurie, and Robert Kessler. *Pair Programming Illuminated.* Boston: Addison-Wesley, 2003.

Womack, James P., Daniel T. Jones, and Daniel Roos. *The Machine that Changed the World: The Story of Lean Production.* New York: Harper-Perennial, 1990.

Womack, James P., and Daniel T. Jones. *Lean Thinking: Banish Waste and Create Wealth in Your Corporation.* New York: Simon & Schuster, 1996.

Wujec, Tom, and Sandra Muscat. *Return on Imagination: Realizing the Power of Ideas,* London: Financial Times Prentice Hall, 2002.

Index

Adapt phase of APM model, 19, 81,
  83–84, 232–233
  "adaptive action," 230–231
    vs. "corrective action," 214
  product/project/team review and
      adaptive action practice, 215–216
    customer focus group (CFG)
      sessions, 216–219
    team performance evaluations,
      220–222, 221f
    technical reviews, 219–220
  reacting to events questions, 214
    customer value from project, 214
    effective adaptations to changes, 215
    satisfactory progress, 215
  speculate/adapt vs. plan/build, 80
Adaptive product development case
  examples
  Alias Sketchbook Pro, 2
  BMW, 3
  Toyota, 3
Adaptive product development style, 1, 3,
  14, 21, 173
  adaptable teams, 7
Adaptive team building principle, 64–65
  self-discipline, 71–72
  self-organizing teams, 64–65
    accountablility, 70
    interaction support, 66–68
    participatory decision making,
      68–70
    product vision articulation, 66
    right people acquisition, 65–66
    steering vs. controlling, 70–71
Agile methods
  flexibility and stability balance, 17–18
  lowering cost of change (adaptation), 7
    costs of iteration, 11, 22
  quality focus, 5, 44–45

Agile movement, 14
  conviction, 261–262
  and egalitarian meritocracy core
    value, 9
  lean manufacturing origins, 34
  lean product development ideas,
    34–35
  vision, 256–258
Agile practices, 85–86, 90
  and attitude, 237
  practice selection and tailoring,
    121–124
  see also Elevator test statement;
    Iterative feature plan; Project data
    sheet; Vision box
Agile process framework (APM model),
  18–19, 79–80
  business objectives, 80
  execution-biased model, 32
  model structure, 80–81, 81f
    see also Adapt phase of APM
      model; Close phase of APM
      model; Envision phase of APM
      model; Explore phase of APM
      model; Speculate phase of
      APM model
  project size, 85
  project size/scaling issues, 236–238
    see also Scaled adaptive framework
Agile Project Management (APM), 16, 23,
  253, 259
  adapting (importance of), 7
  applicability, 23
  business objectives, 6
  delivery focus, 32
  estimating, 155–157
  generative vs. prescriptive practices,
    22–23
  rhythm, 191

Agile Project Management (APM),
continued
see also Agile process framework
(APM model); Core agile values;
Guiding principles of APM
Agility, 16–18
Alias Systems (Toronto), 62
Alias Sketchbook Pro iterative
development, 2
Studio Tools, 96–97, 96f
Alleman, Glen, APM attitude example,
237
Anticipatory product development style,
1, 173
elements of, 3
APM framework/model *see* Agile process
framework (APM model)
Austin, Rob, 6, 11

Bell & Howell, 97
Biotechnology, and integration of
information, 5
BMW, simulations, 3
Boeing, product evolution through
technical excellence example, 44
Business practice implementations, 3–4
Business process reengineering (BPR), 14
as added overhead, 35

Capital One, 73
CAS approaches *see* Complex adaptive
systems (CAS) theory
Champion technical excellence
principle, 44
and product evolution, 44
Change management, 173–175
"Chaordic," 19–20
Charan, Ram, 31
Close phase of APM model, 18, 81, 84,
231–232
celebration, 231
clean-up, 231–232
project retrospective, 232
CMM, as added overhead, 33, 35
Coaching and team development
coaching customers, 189–191
developing individuals' capabilities,
188–189

focusing team on results delivery,
182–183
managing resources/roadblocks, 189
molding individuals into team,
184–188
orchestrating team rhythm, 191
Cohn, Mike, "buffered plan" concept,
152
Collaboration, 68
vs. communication, 120, 242
and decision making, 196
see also Project community
Commitment-accountability protocol
(CAP), 246–247
advantages, 249–250
contract-like relationships, 247–249
CAP card example, 248f
key issues, 247
Complex adaptive systems (CAS) theory,
168–169
and APM, 20–21, 23
and creativity, 17, 21
and emergent results, 21
Compliance activities, 32–34
compliance loop, 37, 37f
and critical path/people, 38
external vs. internal, 37
impact on development time, 38
necessary compliance, 36–38
and value, 38
Contracts, 10
vs. customer collaboration, 13
Cooper, Robert, 3, 162
Core agile values, 8–10
customer collaboration, 13
individuals and interactions, 13–14
responding to change, 10–11
working products vs. documentation,
11–12
see also Guiding principles of APM
Creativity issues
Complexity theory, view of, 17, 21
Customer, 13, 29, 111
coaching, 189–191
and expectations, 29–30
feedback in iterative development, 42
focus group (CFG) sessions, 216–219
and value, 15, 36, 47

Explore phase of APM model, *continued*
  see also Project community in Explore
    phase
Extreme Programming
  daily stand-up meetings, 192
  rights between customers and
    programmers, 243
  "smell" (quality measure), 229
  story cards, 135
  technical practices, 168

FBS (feature breakdown structure), 98f,
    99–100, 99f, 131, 132f
  feature cards, 135–138, 136f
    information items, 136–137
    performance requirements cards,
      138–140, 139f
    product feature list, 132–134
Feature, 134
Feature-based delivery, 40
Feature-based development, 130
  iterative feature plan, 90, 91f
Feature-Driven Development (FDD),
    useful practices for medium/large
    projects, 150–152
Fitzgerald, Donna, software project risks
    list, 162
Flow thinking, 36
Focus, 7

Gall, John, systems axioms, 33–34
General Electric
  focus on innovation, 11
  participatory decision making
    (Durham, NC), 195
"Groan zone," 199, 200–201
Guiding principles of APM, 27–28, 28f,
    75
  customer value through innovative
    products category, 27
    see also Customer/products case
      example; Deliver customer
      value principle; Iterative/
      feature-based delivery
      employment principle;
      Technical excellence
      championship principle

leadership/collaboration management
    style category, 27, 56–59
  see also Adaptive team building
    principle; Exploration
    encouragement principle;
    Simplify principle
Guiding principles case examples, 22
  see also Customers/products case
    example; Leadership/collabora-
    tion management case example

Hierarchical structures, limitations, 239
Hock, Dee, 19, 59, 207
Hub organizational structure, 239, 240f
  as "modified network," 240
Human Genome Project, 5

IDEO, innovation strategy, 63
Immelt, Jeffrey, focus on innovation,
    11–12
Incremental development, 40
Index cards, practicalities of, 148
"Information radiators," 230
Innovation
  case example of refusal to
    improvise, 11
  continuous, 6
  and delivering customer value, 30–31
  and iteration, 39
  new corporate focus case examples,
    11–12
  studies of, 20
  see also Reliable innovation
Intel, decision-making focus, 201
Interaction
  "crucial conversations," 185–186
  vs. documentation, 12
  and innovation, 185
Interaction with customer team, 206–207
  vs. CFG (customer focus group)
    sessions, 217–218
  objective, 206
ISO
  as added overhead, 33, 35
  case example, 39
Iteration 0 *see* Release/milestone/
    iteration plan

Iterations, 40
  and acceptance-tested features, 142
  cost impact of technical
    excellence, 46
  creating *deployable* pieces of product,
    155
  and focus, 159
  and innovations, 39
  iterative lifecycle development, 22
Iterative feature plan, 90, 91f
Iterative/feature-based delivery
    employment principle, 39–40
  better product creation, 40–42
    customer feedback, 42
    models/simulations/prototypes, 41
    self-correcting, 42
  earlier benefits, 42–43
  progressive risk reduction, 43–44

"Jelled team," 184
  technical vs. personal conflicts, 185
Johnson, Jim, 157
Jones, Capers, 105

Kaner's decisionmaking model, 199
Kelley, Tom, "Hot Teams" environment,
    63
Knowledge management practices,
    123–124

Leadership, 57, 260–261
  and clear vision of objectives, 89
  coaching role, 68, 170
    see also Coaching and team
      development
  and decision making, 69, 203–204
  "emotional intelligence" level (mood),
    186–187
  good vs. bad goals, 60
  "servant leadership," 189
  steering vs. controlling, 70–71, 183
Leadership/collaboration management
    case example
  change control/scope discussion,
    127–128
  exposure to APM principles and
    practices, 77–79

management style, 49–51
  performance measurement discussion,
    165–166
  progress reporting discussion,
    211–213
  staff issues, 235–236
  staffing issues discussion, 87–88
Leadership/collaboration management
    goal, 56–59
  CAS metaphor, 166–167
  dependable process, 51
  predictable process, 51
  reliable process, 51
    vs. repeatable, 52–54
Lean thinking, 34–36
  tenets, 35–36
Lifecycle development approaches
  iterative, 22
  serial, 39, 46
  waterfall, 39
Low-cost change, 170

Management illusions, 57–58
*Manifesto for Agile Software
  Development,* 9
MDS Sciex, frequent integration
    approach example, 176
Merritt, Guy, 4
Microsoft
  NET technology, 107
  Tablet PC operating system, 2
Milestones, 142–143
Motorola
  innovation initiative, 11
  Iridium project, 15–16

NASA, documentation burden example,
    72
Nix, Lynne, 123
Nordstrom's, simple rules case example,
    73
NPD (new product development)
  challenges, 4
  future directions, 5
  need for delivery and planning,
    31–32
  and time, 3

The Agile Software Development Series

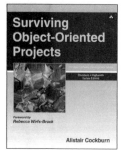

Surviving Object-Oriented Projects

0201498340

Writing Effective Use Cases

0201702258

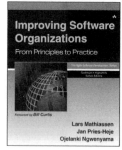

Improving Software Organizations
From Principles to Practice

0201758202

Agile Software Development

0201699699

Agile Software Development Ecosystems

0201760436

Patterns for Effective Use Cases

0201721848

Configuration Management Principles and Practice

0321117662

DSDM
Business Focused Development
Second Edition

0321112245

Lean Software Development
An Agile Toolkit

0321150783

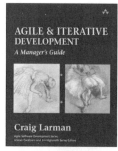

AGILE & ITERATIVE DEVELOPMENT
A Manager's Guide

0131111558

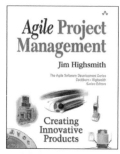

Agile Project Management

0321219775